Charles Williams

An Exploration of His Life and Work

Charles Williams in the 1930's

Charles Williams

An Exploration of His Life and Work

ALICE MARY HADFIELD

New York   Oxford
OXFORD UNIVERSITY PRESS
1983

Copyright © 1983   Alice Mary Hadfield

Library of Congress Cataloging in Publication Data

Hadfield, Alice Mary.
Charles Williams : an exploration of his life and work.

Bibliography: p.
Includes index.
1. Williams, Charles, 1886–1945.   2. Authors, English
—20th century—Biography.   I. Title.
PR6045.I5Z74   1983   828'.91209 [B]   83-8206
ISBN 0-19-503311-6

Printing (last digit):   9 8 7 6 5 4 3 2 1

Printed in the United States of America

Preface

Not everyone writes two books about the same man. In 1959 I published *An Introduction to Charles Williams*. I met him while working in my first jobs at the Oxford University Press, as editor of the *Oxford Dictionary of Quotations*, then being compiled, and later also as the Librarian. The Oxford University Press was then housed in the former Amen House by St. Paul's Cathedral in the City of London. I worked with him, went to his evening lectures, heard him talk about his ideas and his books, and exchanged letters with him during the war. I am glad to say that I was among his friends until the end of his life.

Since that earlier book was written, I have had access to very much new material, notably to some two thousand of his letters. They range from those of the youthful poet to Alice Meynell in 1911 to those written a few days before he died in 1945. Notably they include several hundred written over some ten years to his second love, Phyllis Jones, and the long series sent during the war from Oxford to his wife in London. I have also seen and collected copies of much unpublished work both in poetry and prose, and talked often and deeply with many of his friends.

So another book seemed needed, to grow from the old one long out of print. I have, however, incorporated a few dozen sentences or paragraphs from the old work—mainly those written from personal experiences of Charles Williams which were then close, and are now over twenty years further away.

Charles Williams: An Exploration of His Life and Work is just that. I have not tried to place him as a poet, critic, novelist, biographer, playwright, historian or theologian in the world of his own time, or to assess his importance for ours. That is for others to do better able than I.

His little office room, beautiful Amen House, and that vivid figure are all gone. But his mind, his humour, his speaking to peoples' condition, remain. After an Oxford University lecture on Milton by Charles in January 1940, C. S. Lewis wrote that probably nothing so important had been heard there since some of the great mediaeval or Reformation lectures. 'I have at last', he wrote, 'if only for once, seen a university doing what it was founded to do: teaching wisdom'. If I have succeeded in presenting the man and his wisdom, I am well satisfied.

South Cerney, England　　　　　　　　　　　　　　　　　　　　A.M.H.
July 1983

Acknowledgments

Because my study of Williams's life and work began with my *Introduction to Charles Williams,* published in 1959, a book upon which I have drawn for background material, I must begin by repeating the first three paragraphs of my acknowledgments then.

For early recollections, besides those of Mrs. Charles Williams and of Miss Edith Williams, I want to thank George Robinson for his invaluable details of life with Charles at school and college age; and Miss Alice and Miss Phyllis Pike, who remembered Charles as Sunday School teacher and young man; the late E. K. Bennett, President of Gonville and Caius College, Cambridge, who attended lectures with Charles at the Working Men's College in youth; the Principal of University College, London, for the courtesy and help in answering questions of his secretarial staff; the Headmaster of St. Albans School, who gave his time to take Miss Williams and me round the school and look up records of fifty years ago; and Mr. and Mrs. Swain, the present occupiers of 36 Victoria Street, who very kindly allowed Miss Williams and me to poke about their house and garden.

For help over Charles's life in the Oxford University Press, I want to thank Mr. Fred Page, his oldest friend there, and Mr. Ralph Binfield his personal assistant. The correction and amplification which these two have afforded me cannot be thanked by measure, for it has been incalculable; Miss Peacock and Mr. Gerard Hopkins, Mr. R. C.

Goffin, Mr. K. Sisam, Mr. V. H. Collins, and Mr. A. C. Ward have all patiently answered letters and questions, and I am most grateful to them. Lynton Lamb has helped me in many ways.

For the loan of letters and material I want to thank Lady Raleigh, Mr. Robin Milford, Miss Margaret Douglas, Mrs. Thelma Shuttleworth, and Miss Anne Spalding. For recollections and conversations on Charles's work I must thank Professor Wilson Knight, Mr. T. S. Eliot, Father Gervase Mathew, Captain Field, Mrs. Anne Ridler, and Miss Phyllis Potter.

Many of those named then have given me renewed help, among them Mrs. Anne Ridler, Mrs. Thelma Shuttleworth and Mr. Ralph Binfield.

For the present book I have been able to work in the Marion E. Wade collection of Williams material formed by Wheaton College, Illinois, and especially to read the long series of letters written by C. W. to his wife during World War II. Professor Clyde Kilby and his staff could not have been kinder or more helpful. I have also had access to material in the Bodleian Library at Oxford, and my especial thanks are due to Mr. D. S. Porter of the library staff.

I have been given unrestricted access by the former Phyllis Jones to the very large collection of letters, mostly undated, written to her over ten years and more, and have also been able to enjoy many talks with her and to ask innumerable questions. The quotations the book contains from these letters indicate the extent of my debt. In fifty-odd years of life and travel she kept them, to the day when she handed me a big green plastic bag and said 'Use them, then put them in the Bodleian for me.' This I did, under arrangement made by her. Without these letters we should have known only a limited development of his work; with them we have the expression of his human heart in maturity.

Other letters have been kindly made available to me by the late Sir Wilfrid Meynell, Mr. J. Pellow, Mr. J. Brabazon (Dorothy Sayers), Mrs. Anne Ridler, Mrs. Joan Wallis, Bodleian Library, Victor Gollancz Ltd., Faber & Faber Ltd. and Mrs. V. Eliot, Oxford University Press and Clarendon Press, Miss Lois Lang-Sims, Mr. Alexander Dru, Humanities Research Center, University of Texas at Austin (Alice Meynell), Miss Ursula Grundy and Mrs. Anne Scott.

Very many others have helped me by recollections, in talk, or by making material available. I would especially like to mention Dr. Walter Hooper, Dr. Stephen Matthews, Miss Brenda Rushton, Mr. George Sayer, Miss Ruth Spalding, Dr. Adrian Thomas, Mr. John Topliss and Mr. Richard Wallis.

Mrs. Anne Ridler, Mrs. Anne Scott, Mrs. Thelma Shuttleworth, Mrs. Joan Wallis and Dr. Brian Horne were good enough to read the manuscript. Their comments have been of great value to me; but responsibility for the final text is mine alone.

I would also like to thank the Oxford University Press, Messrs. Faber & Faber and the Charles Williams Society (c/o Williams & Glyns Bank, Holts Branch, Whitehall, London, SW1, England) for permission to quote from work published by them, and the first named also for permission to reproduce the drawing on p. 150, which was made by Lynton Lamb and used for the endpaper of the original edition of *Taliessin Through Logres*. I am also most grateful to Sir John Brown, late Publisher of the Oxford University Press, the librarian, and members of the staff both in London and Oxford, for much detailed help in making files accessible and answering questions.

I am grateful to the following who have kindly provided illustrations: the former Phyllis Jones for Williams as a young man; Miss Anne Spalding for Williams in wartime; the Marion E. Wade Collection, Wheaton College, Illinois, for Williams and Yeats; Michael Williams for Florence Conway; the former Phyllis Jones for her portrait; Mrs. Elizabeth Knight, Oxford University Press, Oxford, for Amen House, the Library, and Sir Humphrey Milford; and the late Lynton Lamb, the Oxford University Press, and the Charles Williams Society for the endpapers of *Taliessin*.

I owe a special debt of gratitude to Mr. Humphrey Carpenter, for it was he who suggested to the New York branch of the Oxford University Press that I should be asked to write this book. His admirable works, *Tolkien, The Inklings* and *W. H. Auden* have much helped me, and I am grateful to him and his publishers, George Allen & Unwin Ltd., for permission to quote from them.

Mr. Stephen Wilburn of O.U.P., in New York, and Mr. Peter Sutcliffe in Oxford, have been both encouraging and constructively critical—it has been a pleasure to work with the kind of book editor that Charles Williams himself was. Mr. Bruce Hunter of David Higham Associates has helped and encouraged me in two capacities, as my own agent and also as that of Michael Williams, owner of the Williams's copyrights.

Finally, I thank my husband Charles Hadfield, who himself knew and worked with Charles Williams, for his indispensable encouragement, help, and lavish sacrifice of his own working time; and my secretaries, first Dawn Bijl, and more recently Jean Cowdall, for coping with my handwriting and my redrafts.

Contents

List of Illustrations

Charles Williams

An Exploration of His Life and Work

1

The Sea-Wood of Making

Charles Williams was a much longed for, much loved son. His father, Walter, and mother, Mary, had had to endure a long engagement[1] because Walter's wages were needed to help his own father, Charles, a chronometer maker. When Walter and Mary finally married, they rented three rooms at 3 Spencer Road (now called Caedmon Road),[2] Holloway, North London, where in due course their son was born. Walter was a surviving twin whose birth had been at the price of his sweet-natured mother's life and of his father's happiness. Walter's grandmother, with whom he had lived, had often told him of it, and he had seen the troubles of his father in a wretched second marriage to a woman who already had a daughter. After making much trouble and unpleasantness, she eventually disappeared. After his own marriage Walter tried for years to trace this second wife, but failed. Now he could thank God, knowing that so long as he kept his job and his eyesight, his son, another Charles, would never know a broken home or a lonely childhood. A son would be a support in time. More, Walter would be able to talk to him about poetry and history, teach him all he had learned from twenty years' reading. And so he did.

Charles was born on 20 September 1886, under the sign of Virgo, pure singularity. A sister, Edith, followed in 1889. The earliest murmur in the child Charles's consciousness 'while he smiled at the sky'[3] was the traffic of London and the sound of the Great Northern steam trains on the nearby viaduct over Hornsey Road.

Walter held a job as foreign correspondence clerk in French and German in a firm of importers. In the second slump in ten years, importing became more and more precarious, and he clung to his job, fearful for his eyesight, which was poor and deterioriating. He was himself thoughtful and intelligent, and wrote short stories, little plays and poems under an uncle's name, 'Stansby'. Some of these earned money by being published in *The Temperance Record* and *Household Words*,[4] an achievement of which his beloved wife Mary was very proud.

She was the eldest daughter of James Wall, a cabinet maker, another skilled man like Walter's father. Mary had a brother, Charles, and sister, Alice, both of whom were interested in literature and history and proved good friends of the Williams family. Charles Wall later wrote several books on abbeys, castles and antiquities, publishing them himself as Talbot & Co.[5] The Walls lived in Walthamstow[6] on the river Lea, a few miles north-east of Holloway.

Walter had been baptised and confirmed at the time of his marriage in 1884.[7] He and Mary took their son to be baptised as Charles Walter Stansby* at the Anglican church of St. Anne's, Finsbury Park, on 7 November.

Life opened for Charles in loving care, attention and security:

> Time and space, duration and extension, to a child
> are in the father's voice, the mother's face.[8]

In the evening the coal would glow and fall with tiny sounds in the iron grate, his mother sat sewing beside it, occasionally stirring the saucepan, saying little, bending over the child with his toys. Both listened for the father's step and his voice in the doorway, of

> . . . one whom evening from his labour frees,
> Brings peace and joy and news of love to be.[9]

The three sat by the fire, Charles on his father's knee. They held his hands and said evening prayers quietly over his head, and put him into his cot in

---

*Charles Williams was of English descent on both his father's and his mother's side. His sister Edith searched out their history through the letters and graves of several generations. Both the Williams and Wall families lived mainly in Hertfordshire, with some periods in Somerset. They were south country Wessex people. In Victorian times some moved nearer to London. None were East Londoners, or Cockneys. There is a family grave in the City of London cemetery at Manor Park; in it are buried Charles's father and mother, his father's father, his mother's mother, and the aunt who brought up Walter. His use of the name of the Welsh poet Taliessin derived from his Arthurian studies.

their bedroom. The morning was busy until Walter gave Charles a hug and Mary a kiss and went off to work. Then she dusted and cleaned, watching 'the smallest act of her smallest child',[10] until she carried him downstairs to his basket-pram and opened the door on to the world—little Spencer Road. As he grew bigger, and waited for his father's return, he would watch the lamplighter in the winter evenings lighting the street gas lamps with his long pole, pushing back the dark.

Sunday was the best day of the week. His father was at home, weekday toys and books were rejoicingly put away, and there was church. Walter and Mary were deeply religious, and Charles had a child's full share. The family went to church together, sometimes twice on a Sunday, Charles and Edith running and skipping along the quiet streets and the rough open grass space by the railway goods depot. St. Anne's Church[11] was modern, built in 1871 with the big scope of Victorian vision. Uninterrupted by a screen, the view swept up the long nave, shallow chancel steps and broad rounded chancel arch to three tall clear-glass lights in the east window. The building had an elementary Byzantine design and colour: a plain formal pattern of red, black and cream decoration and red, black and buff tiled floor. Fourteen clerestory windows on each side lit a dark wooden barrel-vaulted roof. The spread of the church, the vista of arches and dark roof, the regular colour patterns, must have been another world to a child accustomed to little rooms and small streets. The lofty building expanded their familiar home life into another, while the music and singing, the regular yet changing marvel of the psalms and collects, filled their minds with strength, wonder and refreshment.

Here, Sunday after Sunday, from the age of three to eight, outward and inner experiences were forming Charles's impressions of religion. 'He used to march into church as if he owned the place', his mother said, smiling, and he would join in the singing as any small child does, often to its parents' embarrassment. But Walter and Mary were not embarrassed. They took religion as simply and seriously as Charles did. Their common experience upheld them and built an unshakeable strength in the child's mind.

Charles was quick to pick up letters and words, and he could read easily at five years old. Walter recited poetry, taught him, read aloud to him. While Edith was still too young, Walter and Mary found the money for him to go to a private infants' school nearby, St. Mary Magdalene. The brightness of their early married years was clouding, for Walter's sight and his firm's stability were both deteriorating. For a time, relatives would take the children for a fortnight's summer holiday at Lowestoft, or St. Albans, or Brighton where their parents' cousins, Lena and Charley Stone, lived with their six sons. The Williams children were sent to Brighton by train in charge of the guard: Edith remembered how grand they felt. Young Charles loved the Aquarium, and the slot machines on the West Pier. The children rode on Volk's Electric Railway in a little coach with no sides but a striped awning and looped curtains. Indeed they spent all their pocket money on rides. But Edith said of Charles that he never had any desire for travel or holidays; for him home was sweet, and home was, for the time being, London and the streets and shops of Holloway.

The threatened crisis broke on the family in 1894, when Walter's firm closed and an eye specialist pronounced that to save what was left of his sight he must live out of London's coal-smoke, in country air. Small boy though he was, Charles felt the shock:

> My childhood knew too well the fate
> That hangs o'er servants, and the strait
> Wherethrough the large unneeded go.[12]

By now it had probably become clear to Mary that she was better at controlling the family finances than her husband, and that decisions about the future would depend on her. Charles Wall, her brother, was ready to advise. It was agreed that the family should move out of London, and that he would lend money towards opening a shop. Edith writes in her 'Memories' that her parents 'had previously visited St. Albans* and been attracted by it, so when they found an empty shop opposite to a disused burial ground—which was laid out as a garden—it must have seemed the complete answer'. Formerly a greengrocery, No. 15 (now 36) Victoria Street offered them not only a shop with two windows, but a house with its own front door and garden to themselves.

The move was made in March 1894. Uncle Charles Wall helped with the arrangements, the borrowing of money and buying of stock. The shop was called 'The Art Depot'; one window displayed artist's materials and the other stationery. Their neighbours were Mr. Morrison the tobacconist at No. 17 and Mr. Keightley the tailor at No. 13. The house seemed enormous to the family after three rooms, and the garden was a new wonder. Edith remembered it and the life there with deep affection. Mary quickly decided to let two rooms, unfurnished, to add to their income. The question of young Charles's education was conveniently settled by the existence of

---

*St. Albans was an old, small town twenty miles north-west of London in Hertfordshire on the little river Ver, from which its original Roman settlement of Verulamium had been named. Here the first English Christian martyr was executed, a Roman soldier named Alban. A great mediaeval abbey stands with his name. Many Roman building foundations mark the river line, and archaeologists and artists were frequent visitors there in the 1890s.

the Abbey School in Spicer Street, which took bright boys from the age of eight. Edith had lessons at home under her father's supervision in the room behind the shop. Lessons were strict, but as he had to serve in the shop when the doorbell rang, Edith often escaped into the garden. 'I can never remember being punished for this, especially as I had an ally in the land-lord, Henry Lewis, a very cheerful, good-natured man, who frequently came in to chat with Father and when I was missing would say: "Let her alone: it will do her more good than lessons".'[13] Charles would play with her with a bat and ball but refused to have a 'child's garden'. On winter nights their mother would throw a bucketful of water down on the path to make a slide for the children next morning. When Edith was eight and Charles had won a scholarship to the Grammar School (now called St. Albans School), she was sent to a little private school run by a Miss Crouch at the back of a house in College Street; there she spent all her school days. Miss Crouch must have been a devoted teacher of the Victorian time, for Edith developed into a woman of deep ability and spiritual insight, as well as one with a good business head.

Trade was uncertain and money tight. As Edith wrote, soon there were 'creditors clamouring for payment.' Charles Wall, who had by now with-drawn from the business, seems to have overstocked it. But with the excep-tion of young Charles, here in familiar Victoria Street they all stayed nearly to the end. Walter, Mary and Edith felt that the services in St. Albans Abbey (the cathedral), and the beauty of the building, made a rich centre for their lives.

Charles's school was in the old Monastery gateway, immediately next to the Abbey and scarcely altered in structure since mediaeval times. Charles clattered up and down a stone spiral stair with his lesson books, and sat in high dark classrooms with timbered roofs, carved stone pillars and narrow windows. There were huge fire-places with worn coats of arms over them, and out of every window the boys saw the grandeur of St. Albans Abbey and heard the bells ring out the hours.

Charles was a robust, curly-haired boy, with blue eyes, a good forehead, and much determination. He took school life in his stride, being neither brilliant nor dull, and made one or two close friends, one of whom, George Robinson, later recalled the years spent together at school and college. They both won yearly prizes for classwork, both liked the same kinds of books, which at eleven were Dumas, Anthony Hope, Max Pemberton, Jules Verne and Hawthorne. Since Charles's father 'would always pursue any fresh point until he knew the answer', Edith wrote, 'this meant that there were books on all kinds of subjects to which Charles had free access, but whereas Father's interest extended to any subject, Charles was con-

cerned mainly with history and literature'.[14] Charles read Dickens, introduced to him by his father, George Robinson read Scott; but Charles said
that Scott did not play fair,[15] as under cover of a good yarn he surrepti-
tiously fed into it lumps of historical instruction. A letter of his to Dorothy
Sayers some forty years later makes the same point: he objected to writers
of religious plays feeding lumps of religion into them, instead of writing
good drama which concerned religion.[16] Edith writes, 'We had charades,
amateur theatricals, parlour games at Christmas time, and at any time
quite a lot of reciting in unison, Father, Charles and I. Our amateur theatricals at home were mostly small plays written by Father. Occasionally
we launched into something more ambitious e.g. 'As You Like It'.[17]

Life was historical-romantic or it was nothing; knights, bishops, monks,
lords, chivalry and vows filled Charles's mind. An annual historical pageant was produced at the school but Charles's theatrical appetites needed
much more than that. George Robinson says that he maintained 'a sort of
running drama concerning one Prince Rudolph (Ruritania, of course, in
the background) Princess Rosalind and a Baron de Bracey (!) a comic
character in the Falstaff vein. I was usually Rudolph, Charles' sister Edith
the Princess and Charles was Baron de Bracey, in which character he
showed a ripe sense of humour and power of dramatic portrayal'.

A few years later the scene changed. A manuscript survives[18] headed
'Ministry at the End of 1902' (when Charles was sixteen and a half), a
rambling drama, which has hints of things to come. The British Empire
and the Diamond Jubilee of the Queen Empress in 1897, with the proces-
sions of contingents from Canada, Australia, New Zealand, South Africa,
India and islands strung round the still peaceful world, had expanded the
minds of the young. In Charles's imagination the personal ruler Prince
Rudolph is now His Imperial Highness, son of Maximilian IX. After
romance, rivalry and fighting, Prince Rudolph does homage for his kingdom (to a power now called Otto) which is seen as part of a bigger world.
In imagination he has moved from a comic role to themes of royalty and
empire.

How fortunate he was to have a secluded childhood, with no fashions of
thought to follow that he did not fully understand. Rupert Brooke, Middleton Murry, Eliot, Flecker, Pound, Sassoon, the Sitwells, Sackville-
West—all were growing through the same life-stage at the same time in
1902. Later, Charles looked back lovingly to father and mother, never to
childhood and youth; he never saw perfection in a miniature of the kitchen,
the fire, the lamp and table, nor a lost ecstasy in a spring morning in the
old town with the bells of the Abbey calling. Throughout the formative
first eighteen years he was part of the world about him, absorbed in learn-

ing and living it. He scribbled continuously, but the historical-romantic veil through which he had seen life was thinning here and there, and he was feeling for other knowledge. His phenomenal memory now became noticeable. Edith recalls that he had a vigorous sense of rhythm, rhyme and word music, but not of melody. The psalms in church were therefore a peculiar delight, and he revelled in the bellowing bulls, the great water pipes and the knapped bow, the stiff neck and the high stomach.

Though he was not interested in games, his father and he loved walking. When the shop was shut on Thursday afternoons and in the evenings, the family went for walks together. On holidays he and Walter used to walk for miles through the Hertfordshire lanes and villages—twenty miles was not unusual. At that time a country lane knew little motor traffic. On the white untarred surface a horse's trot could be heard from round a curve, and walkers could stop when they wished to pick blackberries, roses, mint, or to argue a point. Perhaps these two were too deep in talk to notice much about nature, especially since Walter could not well see it; but its influence, and odd accurate details, remain in many of Charles's poems and novels. Walking in lanes or streets remained a habit and pleasure for life.

The walks must have been the time for talk on poetry, as Victoria Road, where his mother presided, was the sphere of business, money concern, and worry. We can read in the name poem of his book *Divorce* that Charles showed his poems to Walter, and imagine how closely they discussed them. Walter became in those short spells of free time the only tutor that Charles recollected, and clearly his father's mind had range, variety and balance of learning, and judgement in using it.

> Each to his teachers,—nor of mine,
> Though long and lofty be the line,
>   Shall any, sir, be set
> More high in this poor heart than you
> Who taught me all the good I knew
>   Ere Love and I were met:
>
> Great good and small,—the terms of fate,
> The nature of the gods, the strait
>   Path of the climbing mind,
> The freedom of the commonwealth,
> The laws of soul's and body's health,
>   The commerce of mankind.
>
> The charges launched on Christendom
> You showed me, ere the years had come

> When I endured the strain,
> Yet warned me, unfair tales to balk,
> What slanders still the pious talk
>   Of Voltaire and Tom Paine.
>
> What early verse of mine you chid,
> Rebuked the use of *doth* and *did,*
>   Measuring the rhythm's beat;
> Or read with me how Caesar passed,
> On the March Ides, to hold his last
>   Senate at Pompey's feet!

The poem shows too the boy's awareness of his father's anguish at losing the ability to read, write, live independently—a slow personal, incurable anguish.

> What words of grace, not understood
> Until the years had proved them good,
>   Your wisdom set in me,—
> Until the asps of blindness lay
> Upon your brows and sucked away
>   Joy, sweetness, memory
>
>   .   .   .
>
> Now, now in you the great divorce
> Begins . . .

An awareness, too, of a great debt:

> O if in holier hours I meet
> Your happier head in Sarras'* street,
>   When our blind years are done,
> What song remains shall run to pay
> Its duty, sir, from me that day,
>   Your pupil and your son.

The great Victorian century was ending, and unbelievably one had to date letters 1900. In 1901 on 27 March, Charles was confirmed in St. Albans Abbey by Bishop Wogan Festing. Lawrence, later Dean of St. Albans, prepared him for confirmation and remarked that the boy had too many brains for him, he could not get to the bottom of him. While young

---

*The heavenly city of the old Grail-Arthurian romances.

Edith at eleven and a half was adopting total atheism, Charles was not interested. She was never aware of any reaction in him against religion. In his last book, the biography of William Flecker of Dean Close, Charles wrote words about Flecker that were appropriate also to himself: 'He had grown up in a tradition against which . . . he had never revolted. Like the great doctors of Alexandria, he grew at once in the graces of this world and the grace of another; he breathed heaven in with the common air. He had to make no violent retrogression in order to find Christ; he had not to agonise as Augustine and others of the "twice-born" did. It was a fortunate and blessed fate'.[19]

Charles now entered the sacramental life, as the young men of Arthurian history entered the Castle of the Grail. They failed, one after another, to ask 'What serves the Grail?' or 'What purpose does the Grail serve?' because they were overcome by mystery, their own reactions, or inattention. Already to Charles, history and today, other worlds and himself, were all of one life, and he was concerned about its meaning. What was eating and drinking the bread and wine for? Why was it started? How did it work? How did it preserve your body, or your soul? This exploring mind worked in him all his life and the theme of the Eucharist was the subject of the book he was planning to write after *The Figure of Arthur*,[20] left unfinished by his last illness in 1945.

In January 1903 came London again and College. He and George Robinson won intermediate scholarships to University College in Gower Street, London. It must have been a joy to Walter and a light in his darkness. Mary was willing to find the fares and the fees not covered by the scholarship, and to forego what contribution Charles might have made to the family income had he taken a job. He lived at home and with George commuted by train to St. Pancras station and back every day. We know nothing of Charles in the college period, except that he studied mathematics as well as literature, history and languages. He seems to have had no restless desires to throw over studying and seek the world of literary men, writers, editors, artists. Paris cafés did not lure him as, for instance, they did his contemporary John Middleton Murry. Instead, he learned a good deal of Latin and French, with much of their literature. Probably the whole time was spent filling up with knowledge and ideas from the resources of a good library. The great Housman was then Professor of Latin at University College. His *Shropshire Lad* had been published seven years earlier in 1896 but made no mark on Charles. Poetry, however, was swelling in him, though not in George Robinson. Slowly they moved apart.

In time, home life began to seem intolerable. Edith wrote later that with their father frustrated by blindness and their mother overworked trying to feed and clothe the family, do the housework and shopping, and increasingly help with the hardly profitable shop, there was bound to be tension and some disagreement. 'This may have been partly responsible for the nervous explosions which Charles developed during his adolescence', she wrote, 'which in turn, may have accounted for the shakiness of hand which lasted for the rest of his life'.[21] Certainly slight neuralgia bothered him when tired, then and throughout his life. Earlier than this, Charles and Edith had both had measles, Charles severely, so that his eyesight was affected and later on he had to wear glasses. But his sight was to stand up to continuous reading and writing, and it was also good out of doors.

Life at home became an increasing strain, but though he might flare out he did not think of leaving. He would not abandon his father. But money to keep him at college ran out after Charles had been there two years, and his parents had to withdraw him. He was of course not qualified for any kind of paid work, could not type, and was unpractical. (Edith did the repair jobs at home.) He took the Civil Service clerical examination but failed to pass high enough to qualify for a job. The good Wall family again came to the rescue. Aunt Alice found an advertisement for a small job at the Methodist Bookroom in London and sent it to Charles, who started work there in 1904. Edith's 'Memories' say, 'The work was mostly packing, but at the same time he attended classes at the Working Men's College, where he met Fred Page, who introduced him to the Oxford University Press',[22] Here also was E. K. Bennett, who exchanged verses with him,[22] and later became president of Gonville and Caius College, Cambridge.

There too, Charles met Harold Eyers and Ernest Nottingham, who formed for him a pattern of the heavenly society of friendship, discovery and humour. We know little of either, except that they were equal to the stretch of Charles's search for ideas and information. His later books of verse, *Poems of Conformity* and *Divorce,* show the warmth of that friendship. During his daily train journeys he went on with his insatiable reading, or wrote poetry. In the evenings there might be classes, or he would go walking with his father, or one or other of his friends. Indeed, one night when he abandoned, or missed, the last train home from St. Pancras, the three friends walked, talking through the night, the twenty miles to St. Albans.

He was writing much poetry now, and growing up. Towards the end of his life, in 'The Calling of Taliessin', he said of the young poet pulled out of the water as a baby by Elphin,

> In Elphin's house he grew and practised verse;
> striving in his young body with the double living

of the breath in the lung and the sung breath in the brain,
the growing and the knowing and the union of both in the showing,
the triune union in each line of verse,
but lacking the formulae and the grand backing of the Empire.[23]

Freed by having a job, he opened out. He taught in the Abbey Sunday School, joined one debating society in Holborn (London), and another, 'The Theological Smokers', in St. Albans. The Smokers' meetings discussed weighty matters such as the Royal Commission on Ecclesiastical Discipline, or theological and social problems of the day. They met in members' houses, Edith remembered sometimes providing coffee and cakes. Charles wrote poetry continuously. Light, serious, humorous, it bubbled out of him—as if it were a mode of living. He was insatiable for communication, whether by reading, talking or listening to others. The poets of this time were chiefly Alice Meynell, Abercrombie, Bridges, Chesterton, Hardy, Kipling, Yeats, Gibson, de la Mare, W. H. Davies, Masefield, Drinkwater, Gosse and Harold Munro, but it is impossible to say who, other than Alice Meynell and Bridges, seriously influenced him.

Charles's meeting with Fred Page led to the turning point in his outer life. Fred worked at the Oxford University Press, on the editorial side. The Press was housed then at Amen Corner, in Ave Maria Lane off Ludgate Hill, close to St. Paul's Cathedral. Henry Frowde was Publisher and head of the London side of the firm. Fred Page had been given the long slow job of checking the proofs of a seventeen-volume edition of Thackeray, and needed an assistant. He suggested Charles, who joined the Oxford University Press on 9 June 1908, and never left it.

2

To King Arthur's Court

He was rising twenty-three, tall, with a good figure; not handsome, but with an excellently shaped head and forehead, thick wavy brown hair, blue eyes, slim beautiful hands, a quick easy walk. He wore a pince-nez and later gold rimmed spectacles. He was no social revolutionary or aesthete rebel, but he shared the unease and fears of most young people—'I, a stranger and afraid, in a world I never made'—faced with the need to find a way through the new ideas, books and people that pressed round him. He was in the Paper, Printing, and Proof-reading Department of the Press, where he sat in various small offices proof-reading under Fred Page, a strict master. For lunch hours the Thames was a five-minute stroll away, or there were the forecourt and steps of St. Paul's Cathedral, bounded by the roaring traffic of St. Paul's Churchyard, a main centre of the City of London at the top of Ludgate Hill above the river, crowded with young workers. Every City function, ceremonial and celebratory, passed through the Churchyard. After work he caught the crowded tube or train to an evening class or back to St. Albans. He was lively, though shy, with a quick humour and intelligence, and a surprisingly wide knowledge of daily events and news. Outwardly, there was in him far more of Benedick than of Romeo.

Inwardly two ways opened: he became convinced of the validity and unused depths for verse of the Arthurian and Grail myths, and he discovered romantic love. A book of notes and cuttings called his Commonplace

14

Book[1] shows all sorts of facts or sidelights which, for him, formed links
with the stories of Arthur, King of Britain, and the chalice, called the Holy
Grail, used by Jesus Christ at his last supper with his followers (see Chapter 9).[2] Twenty years later, looking back to the beginning of his awareness
and to his decision to work at the myths, Williams writes of a blindfold
track, and terrors of the mind:

> I cast my heart in the way;
> all the Mercy I called
> to give courage to my tongue.[3]

Like any poet, he felt guidings, and growth in himself. From his poetry he
heard 'a signal word' in his search:

> The hooves of King Arthur's horse
> rounded me in the night.
> I heard the running of flame
> faster than fast through Logres
> I Taliessin came into the camp by the hazels.[4]

As Taliessin came into the service of King Arthur to build up the new
kingdom of Logres, so Williams entered the service of the publisher of the
Oxford University Press in the great world of London. At the same time
he was

> all shining fishlike scales of poetry
> and shooting this way or the other through
> an ocean of dark longing. . . .[5]

But the longing did not lead him into exploratory sex affairs. In the
same year, 1908, he fell in love, while helping at a parish children's
Christmas party,

> ' . . . in a noisy room
> With a carven roof above.'

> What did you say to your love, young man,
> With all your mother wit?
> ' "How hot it is!" or "How do you do?"
> And there was an end of it!'[6]

The girl was Florence Conway, a young teacher whose father was manager of Hallam's ironmongery shop in St. Albans. The youngest of five

lively good-looking daughters, she was dark and handsome, full of life, dramatic in feeling and in act, and naturally outstanding in amateur theatricals and pageants. Her mind was perceptive and clear and she carried herself with an impressive air. Her family was socially above the Williamses in 1908; James Conway's business was active and he had a house of his own instead of living above the shop. This made for an altogether different life, and, in a small world, a different class of living. As Charles was teaching in the Abbey Sunday School, he may have seen Florence before the Christmas party, but he was clear that this meeting was a signal. Florence's memorable comment on the meeting was that for the first five minutes of the evening she thought she had never met a young man who talked so little, and for the rest of the evening that she had never met a young man who talked so much.[7]

Outwardly, nothing happened. Privately, Charles had sufficient time to write eighty-four sonnets in a sequence called *The Silver Stair*. Florence said he thrust them into her hands one January night of snow and bitter weather, which may have been after that same Christmas. He told her that the theme of the sequence was Renunciation, and would she give him her opinion of it. She wrote long after, 'I thought "Oh dear! Is he going to enter a monastery?"' As she read, 'Comprehension dawned and I cried aloud "Why, I believe they are about me!"' The acquaintance continued.[8]

She was a brave girl if she replied in any depth, for the sonnets are as dense as the milky air on the first planet of Dante's experience of Paradise, through which he could make out white brows, eyes, smiles and sweet voices. In this little book are the first gleams of the poet's vision, of his experience of love and of the nature of poetry. He already had imagination, will and desire, and wide knowledge of the literature and language of love. Now he was overthrown by the flash of love, appalled, but with a sense of new power in himself. The flash was only a blur of glory, but he must search for its meaning. He knew the Bible story of love in God as the man from Nazareth, the wonder, the failure, rejection, mockery, slow dying, and renewed life. But although knowledge of both fear and glory grew with him all his life, from now on he would never separate himself from love.

In the prefatory quotation from W. B. Yeats in the published book of these sonnets,

It is love that I am seeking for,
But of a beautiful, unheard-of kind
That is not in the world.

he is in line with all young poets. But his introductory sonnet II asks who yet has written of the secret path of love through creation, through matter, a pebble, light and shadow on leaves, clay, flesh, and man.

> This shall be told and borne upon whose breath,
> Since in a cloud His own voice ceased from time?

His following eighty-two sonnets are an answer.

The poetry is all images, ritual and aspiration, but within there is power. Desire seeks love and not possession of mind or body. Here Charles's virgin development gave him freedom and understanding. The little book is the opening of a lifelong study of romantic theology—the nature of the relationship between love in the flesh and the Creator of both. There is affirmation in plenty. Florence would delight in the sonnet on the morning after he fell in love:

> memory stirs
> Of laughing eyes and voices, and of hers
> Who parted from us at the turn of the way[9]

and of the many lines on looking for her by chance in the street:

> in so small town,
> So long have lighted not upon her ways?
> But now each street is a path venturous,
> Each cross of roads a passage perilous
> With loveliness which is this city's praise.[10]

Indeed, all his life he supported the affirmation of love in such simple facts and moments, in himself or others.

The poetry is intimately concerned with the body, as the second introductory sonnet declared it must be:

> His fleet
> Passage in light and shadow of leaves, O soul,
> Hast thou escaped; wilt thou deny thy clay
> If thereupon He stablish His control
> In mortal eyes that snare it, mortal feet
> That tread the windings of salvation's way?

And in LXVII the sextet reads:

> All lives of lovers are His song of love,
>   Now low and soft and holy as a kiss,
>   Now high and clear and holy as a star.
> Slave in Man's house, yet builder-up thereof,
> The silver and the golden stairs are His,
>   The altar His—yea, His the lupanar.*

His renunciation is to be of a different kind of desire: renunciation not of human relationship but of particular qualities: self-will, personal power over one's choices, desires, aims or achievements without concern for the beloved. The octet of sonnet XXXVIII is a declaration:

> I love her. O! what other word could keep
>   In many tongues one clear immutable sound,
>   Having so many meanings? It is bound,
> First, to religion, signifying: "The steep
> Whence I see God," translated into sleep
>   It is: "Glad waking," into thought: "Fixed ground;
>   A measuring-rod," and for the body: "Found."
> These know I, with one more, which is: "To weep."

The young man was shaken by the greatness of the vision, the necessity of its authority over him, the joy and pain that it would bring. Later, he very seldom spoke of these sonnets. But in his more developed work many phrases and insights spring to the mind, recalling their first glimpses in *The Silver Stair*.[11]

The style is serious and concerned with its subject, the matter of poetry, rather than with itself. There is no Hopkins, almost no Yeats, a little Bridges, but, as his best critics Alice Meynell and Sir Walter Raleigh, Professor of Poetry at Oxford, saw, a singular originality and freshness. I do not know why he gave the sequence its title, and no one whom I have consulted can find a reason. Perhaps it looks to an image in literature or painting. Sonnet LXVII, referring to 'all lives of lovers', which may mean 'from youth to age', has the line just quoted: 'The silver and the golden stairs are His'. Two thoughts may be linked in the title, *The Silver Stair*: one is of 'silver' for youth and 'gold' for maturity as in the 'silver cord' and 'golden bowl' of Ecclesiastes;[12] the other, 'silver' meaning 'virgin', for sonnet LXXXII reads:

> the image that Time's followers bear
> Into the world's house: under it the stair
> Gleams to the feet of virgin loves.

*Latin for a brothel.

Failing new evidence, I think that the book's title relates directly to sonnet LXVII. The two stairs are his names for the holy and the human ways of access to Man's house, and he calls his sonnet sequence after the human.

He had no plans to get the sequence published. But Fred Page, through his editorial contact, had made the acquaintance of Alice Meynell, then a distinguished poet and also a woman of religion and love. Fred wrote to her, and she consented to read them. She must have approved, for she invited Charles to come and see her. The first letter in his series to the Meynells is dated 25 June 1911, and in it he accepts the invitation. 'Your name has, if one may say so, carried so much weight for so long, that it seems hardly credible, even now, that you are interested in it' (i.e. the sonnet-sequence).[13] She was impressed by the poems, and urged the young poet to publish.

He talked with her about the titles of sonnets and the varying merit of some of them. His letters show him shy, amazed but not timid, indeed a persistent young poet. When she found that he was too poor to hope for publication,[14] Alice and her husband Wilfrid paid for it and advised the publisher, Herbert & Daniel. So it was the Meynells who got Charles first into print, in November 1912. He was overwhelmed by the physical sight of his first book ('the book will be much more in appearance than I ever dreamed of'.[15])

He already had enough new poems to be thinking about another volume. One or two came out in magazines, perhaps with the Meynells' help. He could, and did, hold himself a poet, the holiest name in his dreams of possibility. He wrote to Alice of his longing to be 'another tattered rhymester in the ring', but he doubted the validity of modern lyrics. 'It has been of late discovered so often!—that "the daisy has a ring of red" '. He wanted not only a variation of the theme, but 'something with a bigger or more definite idea behind it'.[16] The young poet was reaching out to explore the nature of poetry, and something even greater.

He had been noticed in Amen Corner. Humphrey Milford, then Assistant Secretary and in 1913 Publisher, sent *The Silver Stair* to the Professor of Poetry at Oxford University, Sir Walter Raleigh, a man of individuality and original views. Milford's discernment was immediately approved. On 22 November 1912, Raleigh wrote, 'There is no doubt about it; real poetry'. It read, he said, as if the author had not suspected there was such a thing as love, and has written about it 'almost before any touch of familiarity had fallen on it'.[17] Charles sent copies to Hilaire Belloc, G. K. Chesterton and Lascelles Abercrombie. Belloc acknowledged politely, Chesterton not at all, and there is no record of a reply from Abercrombie, though later Charles knew him in his role as editor.

There is no mention, even from Edith, of Charles and Florence getting engaged or planning marriage. Parties on both sides discouraged it—Edith said that the Conways thought him no match for Florence, and his own family needed much of his wages. Delay, in fact, gave him three or four more years of development in a stable world before the Great War broke out in 1914. These years were spent in working all day, including of course Saturday mornings, with intelligent and lively people. He read and wrote during lunch hours and on trains, attended evening classes, helped his parents at home, adored Florence, and walked, talked and joked with Harold Eyers and Ernest Nottingham.

On summer evenings and Sundays after church, the young men would walk along the river banks of Ver or Colne, through hill paths and bushy lanes, often while the moon rose on them talking, arguing, enquiring. How he remembered!

> Of you, in Surrey, yet ere blood
> Parted forever mood from mood,
>   The tryst was kept with two:
> O that last way, as war shut down,
> From Dorking pines to Guildford town,
>   Of night and dawn and you![18]

Others sometimes joined them. Fred Page told of an evening when several friends challenged Charles to write a sonnet on the spot in a set number of minutes. The watch and chain were laid out, and he did it.

His mind developed in depth and perception as he struggled with the great questions: patriotism or pacifism, faith or unbelief, love or conflict, choice or chance, freewill or predestination. Something of each, it seemed to him, inhered in its opposite, and he saw that there could be a constructive scepticism. But there were times when opposites failed to inhere, and gaps remained of solitary terror and knowledge of darkness. These remained in the centre of him and his love and his poetry, as he found them also at the centre of man and of religion. In the poem 'Richmond Park' in *Poems of Conformity*, he says of walking over Richmond Park with two friends:

> My soul was 'ware, all suddenly,
>   It trod a dangerous cleft.

All familiar life was gone; the men on each side of him were alien, voices unknown, perhaps setting an ambush:

> I dropped to separating depths,
> And drifted there alone.

Later on he spoke a little of these horrors, which are indeed common to most people—suspicion of cancer, fear of madness, of the drowning of talent by one's own generation, of impending anarchy, social or political. He thought too of consciousness after death fading into eternal unchangingness. Keats's poem 'La Belle Dame Sans Merci' was frightful to him because of its merciless woman who sideways leans and sings a fairy song, deluding her listener with a world of another order, without pain, discipline or effort. In his teens and twenties he seems to have kept the dark pit in himself boarded off from other people. The boards began to break soon after his marriage.

He had grown up much aware of political structure. He saw the *res publica*, the matter of public life, the political community, presented in the experience of love and the family, in Victorian poetry, in eighteenth century thought in France and England, in mediaeval feeling, as a balance between equality and hierarchy. Though youthfully a very temporary republican, he slowly created for himself over the years a synthesis in which all men and women were equal and yet different within their hierarchies of excellence and distinction, in which above political equality everyone's distinctness was embodied in the single person of the monarch, as everyone's personal equality and distinctness was held in Christ. He retained his sense of monarchy, hereditary in that it must have a blood link with the long history of England, visible to high and low, free from fashion, choice or vote, apex of an administration free, equal and yet hierarchical in public distinction. His poem 'Celestial Cities'[19] combines his passionate feeling for being a citizen of London with his sense of public authority held under the young Lord Mayor, man in London, Christ in Sarras.

> When our translated cities
>   Are joyous and divine,
> And through the streets of London
>   The streets of Sarras shine. . . .
>
>   .   .   .
>
> When we shall hear—how gladly!—
>   The general shout declare

That up Cheapside his pageant*
Conveys the young Lord Mayor,
When all applause salutes him,
Man chosen among men,
By proof of former friendship
Known to each citizen.

Meantime, Edith was grown up and had taken an office training course. She must always have known that she would never to able to leave her blind father and burdened mother who could not have saved anything for old age. Non-contributing old age pensions had begun in 1909, but only for married people of seventy and with incomes less than ten shillings a week. Walter and Mary would not qualify. So Edith decided to earn money at home. With a friend, Marion House, she set up a secretarial office (called 'college' in her obituary notice) at 36 Victoria Street and took in typing. It succeeded and brought her contacts with local writers and businesses. By means of it she gave psychological and financial security to her parents, and thereby some release to Charles. Walter died in January 1929, aged seventy-nine or eighty, after years of near blindness which did not prevent him from talking literature with his neighbours, and attending the Abbey services. Their mother, Mary, was to outlive Charles.

Active in the congregational life of the Abbey, Edith was also developing a devotional life at a deep and hidden level, which was to enrich her whole long life. She wrote poetry, probably very privately, though one poem, 'Jesus so lowly' was included in the 1931 edition of *Songs of Praise* with music by Martin Shaw.

As for Charles, in spite of grumbles by its employees about money, the Oxford University Press meant security (in my working experience of the firm in the thirties I never heard of anyone getting sacked), and a widening range of work in the Press's growing production of English literature, including contemporary writing. The most important figure in the whole organization was its head, the Publisher, Humphrey Milford. He became the keystone of Charles's working life. He was an ideal patron—serious, intelligent, with a sense of humour, handsome, aloof, highly-cultured, perceptive of truth. He created a huge international business upon Frowde's foundations and administered it successfully.

Charles had risen in the Press; he had learned to be brief and clear, and under Fred Page was now doing editorial work. He was proud of his posi-

*The reference is to the annual procession through the streets or down the river of London of the Lord Mayor's Show, which celebrates the election of the new Lord Mayor of London and exhibits him to the people.

tion, and at the end of a formal, detailed letter to Wilfrid Meynell on the choice of poems by Francis Thompson, he put in a ring 'Can't poets write business letters?' New bright young men were joining the staff, and although still lowly in the firm, Charles's intelligence, conversation and humour broke down all formality or barriers. Everybody talked to him and he added new people to his experience. He continued to correspond with the Meynells and to send them his verse, while they talked of another publication.

In August 1914 the War broke out, and men began to drain away. Harold Eyers and Ernest Nottingham joined up, but Charles was passed unfit for active service. He dug trenches in Hyde Park, London, and did civilian war work at St. Albans. His fruitful personal life was broken, and in February 1915, he wrote to Alice Meynell, 'I have wanted so much and so long to write a poem: but one can't, somehow'[20]. A foreboding prohibited it, one which came true in May 1915, when Harold Eyers was killed. A year of darkness and silence followed.

He wrote two short poems, one called 'Emigravit', of four lines:

> Mortal, of mortals hardly Earth
> Knew love or laughter more of worth;
> Immortal, join the immortals, find
> Laughter nor love thou left'st behind.

And 'May 20th, 1915', containing the verse:

> In a beggared lane we go,
>   Palsied of the better hand;
> Purposes none else can show
>   Are for ever hidden land.[21]

In 1916 he wrote in reply to Alice, who had asked after him: 'I feel rather that young men in England ought not to have health or affairs, unless they are using them more distinctly for national ends than I can do'.[22]

Though one could say he never 'recovered', he slowly accepted that he was committed to life. Indeed there were interesting things going on, apart from war. He kept up his 'Commonplace Book' with notes on the Arthurian theme, and discussed with Alice Meynell the pronunciation of the 'a' in Arthurian names such as 'Galahad' in Tennyson's verse. He went on in the same letter to her: 'You see from this that I am still moved by the thought of an Arthurian—or rather a "Grail" poem. If *you* say that Tennyson is final, I will promise to drop the idea at once. But perhaps. . . .'[23]

This was the year of the tercentenary of Shakespeare's death, and the O.U.P. was busy producing the long-planned *Shakespeare's England* with 43 contributors, and *A Book of Homage to Shakespeare* with 166 contributors in thirty languages. A publication which brought new friends to Charles was also on the stocks, *The Oxford Book of Mystical Verse* (published 1917), edited by Daniel Nicholson and the Reverend Henry Lee. They must have discussed the contents with Charles, for they became lifelong friends, even confidants of his.[24] In 1916 Charles wrote to Alice Meynell: 'I sent a copy of my book to Mr. A. E. Waite (do you by any chance know his name?) who is a student of secret tradition in various forms—it was his book on the Grail literature that provoked me!—and he answered very kindly, asking me to go and see him, and saying pleasant things generally.—So I owe you a greater debt still'.[25] Six of Waite's poems were to be included in *Mystical Verse,* and his letter is probably the origin of Charles's first contact with him in 1915.[26]

Fred Page was called up into the Army Pay Corps in February, and by October was near Ypres. Charles was indignant at the lack of historical grasp by Primrose League* members when he saw them that year rejoicing over the Russian advance in the Caucasus. Was Disraeli likely to be so glad that 'The Russians have taken Trebizond'?

Charles was enjoying life at Amen Corner, working enormously hard, making friends and conversation with every grade of staff, anyone he met on the stairs. Stairs were a site for conversation. Departmental managers, typists, correspondence and invoice clerks, and junior editors all found themselves having odd but cheerful conversations on the stair on social, theological, literary matters—'What do you think of this'?—'Did you see this in the *Mail*'?

His position was secure enough for him to marry. The war was dragging on and might last for years more. He was thirty, and Florence nearly as old. She must have wearied in the past nine years of the suspended state which Charles's poetic and passionate love had done nothing to settle. He, it seems, was dismayed by problems of flats and rents, probably also by the decline, in poverty and physical failing, of his parents' marriage. He loved, but he feared; he did not know what he feared, except that he understood so much, but knew so little, and in marriage would be responsible

---

*The Primrose League was founded 1883 to spread Conservative principles; it took the primrose as being the favourite flower of Disraeli, Lord Beaconsfield, leading Conservative politician from 1842 to 1880, and Prime Minister. He regarded Russia as a dangerous power.

for the contentment of his lady. One sees it in a reply to an enquiry from Alice Meynell about his prospective marriage: 'We did wonder about next year, but the whole financial position of my own people is so very unpleasant, and trade is so thin, that I sometimes think—Do you ever condescend to read Anthony Hope? "Marriages are made in heaven" said I. Mrs. Hilary beamed assent. "I thought of waiting till I got there," I added'.[27] But he mentions that he had quoted Alice's lines on 'ignorant arms that fold/ a poet to a foolish breast'[28] to his 'friend' that evening. In fact he was seeing Florence regularly and often. A poem probably written at about this time shows a deep development in personal relations and knowledge.

> So will her mind, in fellowship
>   Of art, see, hear, rebuke, admire,
> Whose heart, in touch of breast and lip,
>   Flames upward in love's flying fire.[29]

Florence was probably the more resolute and enterprising of the two, and at last it was decided that the wedding should take place at Easter, 1917, and that north London should be their home, away from their families and former life. Florence's family probably still thought poorly of the match.

Charles wrote to the Meynells a little dolefully of flat-hunting, and cheerfully about a sudden proposition by the O.U.P.[30] He had sent the manuscript of a second book, *Poems of Conformity,* to Elkin Mathews who turned it down. In a temper, Charles threw it aside and marched out of the office at five-thirty. Fred Page rescued it, taking it to Milford's office with a note that the poems might deserve a better fate. Again Milford sent them to Sir Walter Raleigh and again they succeeded. In spite of their great dissimilarity to contemporary war poetry, Milford decided to publish them himself. Charles asked Alice Meynell's help in the final choice of poems to be included, and by July 1917 the book had been published by the Oxford University Press, a month after Ernest Nottingham had been killed in France.

Florence found a flat at 18 Parkhill Road, London NW3 and they were married on 12 April 1917, on a Thursday afternoon when the shop was shut. No one of Florence's family was bridesmaid, but only Edith, Charles's sister, and no close friend was best man, but instead Pickles, a fellow member of the Press. The wedding was in St. Albans Abbey in the solemn lovely choir where he had worshipped at so many Eucharists and Evensongs. The Rev. E. R. Evans, an old acquaintance from Sunday School teaching days, married them. After the wedding the little group went back, not to the Conways' home but to 15 Victoria Street, and had a gathering behind the shop. Seemingly the Conways thought so little of the match that Florence, indignant, turned wholly towards the Williamses. Unconscious distinctions lie hidden in such marriages and contribute some of the many difficulties that are overcome in good and fruitful relationships. Certainly there was reconciliation later.

A couple of verses in Charles's poem 'Black-Letter Days' perhaps express his feeling about the wedding, whether written before or after it:

> Yea, all that racked us since in one consent
> Our young virginities together went,
> With Agnes, maid and saint, toward Love's self bent,
>
> Adventuring all we doubted on a day
> He should on us, as once on Alban, lay,
> Who should our selfhoods mystically slay.[31]

The first evenings in the flat, and the first nights, cannot have been easy for either. After waiting so long, diffidences, fears and tensions must have built up. Florence was the more open character, and no doubt helped the sexual encounter, but one imagines Charles, self-described virgin at thirty, as ardent and well-informed in theory, while petrified in practice.

The day after the wedding he wrote a note to thank Wilfrid Meynell for their wedding present, and added the thanks of 'my wife (of how short a formality, but how long a love!)'.[32] He had now to relate his vision of love to the experiences and scale of married life in its planned and unplanned moments, to find the vision in the real woman, and to learn and love her nature increasingly by clarification of the vision.

We have the outline of this huge enterprise and where it was to lead him in three books of verse and one short work: *Outlines of Romantic Theology, Poems of Conformity* (1917), *Divorce* (1920) and *Windows of Night* (1925) contain all the clues. The definition of his seminal lay theology is contained in *Outlines of Romantic Theology,* written during 1923 and 1924, a book on the implications for personal love and marriage of the word Immanuel, 'God with us'. So, in *Poems of Conformity,* far from showing us how difficult marriage is, how different from courting or being in love, he shows the pattern of his learning, the effort to conform with the life glimpsed in *The Silver Stair.* The subjects are old in poetry; sex (sonnets I–XII, 'Orthodoxy', 'Churches', 'A Song of Implications'); love ('A Song of Opposites', 'Marriage', 'Commentaries I–IV', 'Gratia Plena', 'Black-Letter Days', 'In the Land of Juda'); marriage ('The Christian Year', 'Commentaries V', 'Ascension', 'Christmas'); dread ('The Continuing Doctrine', 'The Epiphany', 'Pentecost', 'Hope'). All these poems concern experiences as well as ideas. Other subjects include war, friendship, and the earliest printed poems on Sarras, city of the Grail; ('The Assumption', 'Quicunque Vult' and 'Inland Travel'.) A hint that Charles and Florence had earlier agreed mutually to postpone their marriage may be in 'Epilogue':

> Ourselves by separate consent
> On separate pilgrimages went,
>   To find ourself at last!

But there is more in *Conformity*. The poems, he said to Alice Meynell, sang in their own small way as hers had done, 'manifestation of the truth of dogma in ordinary piteous men'[33]—not *to* ordinary piteous men. This is the significant difference that he was to pursue in all his central work. Something other was happening within the actions of man in the world, through man and in itself. The taking of the life of Christ into man through the simple eating of bread and drinking of wine articulately witnessed to the process, but it lived everywhere and in all experiences, though too often unobserved. This 'something other' was active also in poetry, in the double way of the words he wrote and the words of great men working in him. However deep he went, there the process was, and it must be studied and then grown into. He had to go forward. His own actions and the words written in his poetry, must pursue that knowledge of the 'something other'. It was for him to seek it, learn about it, and understand as much of it as his mind could encompass.

In a letter to Alice Meynell accompanying a copy of *Conformity* and thanking her for bringing *The Silver Stair* into being, he says of the poems in the two books: 'I cannot recollect any verse in English that does just exactly what they do. Don't think that I do not know that Patmore, for example, is to me 'as the table-land of Tibet to the peak of Teneriffe' (wasn't it?); only he never did care to write *Commentaries,* say, or *Gratia Plena*'.[34] Both are in *Poems of Conformity*. 'Commentaries' shows the events of the earthly life of Christ as lived continuously in the lives of men and women, and as Love, born, accepted, despised as useless, hated, killed and perhaps reborn—early thoughts of his romantic theology. 'Commentaries—I' takes the city of Zion in the Psalms as the person of Florence, where to Charles love was born; 'II' the twins, Florence the mother of Charles's love, with the Virgin Mother of ' . . . fair love/ Knowledge and fear and holy hope!' 'Commentaries—V', quoting the Athanasian Creed, claims experience of Love in the body:

> O who can doubt the perfect Whole
> In his eternal trysting,—
> Love, of the reasonable soul
> And human flesh subsisting!

'Gratia Plena', full of grace, is part of the greeting of the Archangel Gabriel to the Virgin Mary. Gabriel hears her choice of acceptance, 'Behold the handmaid of the Lord', in her own provincial dialect, provincial as Florence's Hertfordshire accent. The heavens will to obey the girl's decision, 'to fulfil their pact with man'. The body teaches love. Florence springs 'to them and me'.

> What angel can with thee compare,
> Since, for that swift heart's recompense,
> Himself the God established there?
> Yet clasp and cling, O more than me.
> *Ecce ancilla Domini!* *

Poems of Conformity shows much sense of power—not in considering feelings, but in living them. The whole of his spiritual and intellectual power is drawn into the personal experience. All mighty concepts of love are related here and now in this kiss, this service to the beloved. He knows that the body and feelings of romantic love must be learned from, seriously and fully, not merely indulged. He must take not only what he wants to take but the whole doctrine, the leaven which raises the bread. There are glimpses of a renovation of sex, marriage and the relationship of both persons.

The last poem but one, 'Invocation', is a prayer for his own poetry. Born as he was under the sign of Virgo, which was also Galahad's sign, he wrote an invocation to the Virgin that she guard him from both haste and sloth:

> Till thou, at the full of time,
> Breathe in rhythm, thought, and rhyme,
> And art my song's justice, clad
> In the sign of Galahad!
>
> Keep me high in courage; nor
> Lose me, Michael conqueror,
> From thy legions' marching, who
> Were men's poor souls bound unto,

---

*Behold, the handmaid of the Lord.

> Since began our Grail-quest toward
> The Incarnation of the Lord!

Poems of Conformity had few reviews. However, an American, Theodore M. Maynard, accused Charles of 'Satanism' in the *North American Review*. Charles wrote to Alice Meynell in July 1918 that this controversy had concluded pleasantly and that Maynard had asked Charles to review his new book of poems.[35]

Charles's contacts with A. E. Waite had led to their meeting and thus to an invitation for Charles to join his Order of the Golden Dawn. This society had been originally formed in Paris by S. L. Macgregor Mathers, also a Mason and a Rosicrucian. W. B. Yeats was much involved with this. It had not flourished, and had been re-formed and moved to London by Waite. Evelyn Underhill also was a member.

On 6 September 1917 Waite wrote to Charles arranging for his reception into the neophyte (lowest) grade of the Society at the autumnal equinox (17 September), and reminding him to visit the outfitter 'Spencer & Co. promptly, as the habit takes a little time'.[36] Accordingly Charles joined the Order under the oath of secrecy, which he scrupulously kept. His active membership was probably no more than four or five years. It may be that after his son was born in 1922 he had difficulty in finding a free evening besides his regular lectures and the time he needed for writing. Or he may simply have had enough.

He was already well read in early theological and mystical literature, Grail and Rosicrucian works among them, and would have been acquainted with some ideas and symbols which Waite used in ceremonies and rituals. Charles later was to use the Order's image of the Sephirotic tree with its branches of opposed or balancing qualities leading through created beings and the frame of man up to Ain Soph, the unknowable God, Limitless Light. He spoke of its intellectual and aesthetic uses, though not as an object of faith. He uses 'O emanation of Ain Soph!' in a letter,[37] and the Sephirotic tree is recalled in his poem 'Taliessin at Lancelot's Mass' before the Epiclesis began,

> We sang in Our office the cycle of names
> of their great attributed virtues.[38]

Charles certainly knew the desire of the opposite of love and good. He experienced it as part of the desire for knowledge, of his feeling of himself, as some poems in *Divorce* express, and also in his realization that opposites must be known and understood, and then there must be choice. There was something of the Manichaean in him, but to torment, not to rule him.

In the end, what did Waite's Golden Dawn[39] mean to him? Surely his outlook and philosophy were not generated, or indeed much affected, by it. He was thirty-one when he joined and his mind was already well-based, developed and directed. His three following works, *Divorce, Windows of Night,* and *Outlines of Romantic Theology,* scatter the shadows of such a suggestion. Referring long afterwards to the making of a magical circle against the dangers of the Dark, he wrote that he still felt the darkness, though it is 'known to be merely untrue'.[40]

What he had read and learned, whether from the Golden Dawn or elsewhere, was, however, later to be valuable to him as a novelist. Yet towards the end of his life, in the last chapter of his last novel *All Hallows' Eve,* his final presentation of magical formula and act, where the self is the origin and the end of adoration, is a clear statement of rejection. The magical process followed throughout the book is finally brought to its climax. The Clerk, Simon, aiming and working for future domination of the world, had made and sent out to other countries two images of himself to do expertly all that was needed to prepare his power. They, insofar as they were anything, were Simon himself. 'All the years, in the most secret corner of his heart, he had sustained them so. His thoughts had shaped their brains, his words their voices. He had spoken in himself and in them. What he now said to them, he must say to himself'. But now he had finished with them, he wished to destroy them. The two figures approached him. 'He moved his hand to trace against them in the air a significant and compelling figure of magic, and he felt the earth shake under him and the burden of the air weigh on him to crush him as he did so. To unmake them he must unmake himself'. There was only one possibility—'to unite them again with himself, and make them again he'. He moved towards them, and they towards him. 'He began to murmur spells, of which the beating rhythm mingles with those which sustain flesh, but he felt again a creeping in his own flesh, and desisted'. Suddenly the shapes were close to him. 'He unexpectedly thought "This is death", and knew himself weaken at the thought. He managed to pronounce a word of command. They stopped, but then also he too stopped. He obeyed himself'. They all stood, two not able to speak, and one not daring to speak. 'There went out from all three a blast of antipathy. He hated them, and since they held his hate they hated him. . . . All he could do against them was only done to himself. . . . He stared, as he sank and as that in which he was held moved in its own fashion. . . . The City, so, was visible to him'.[41]

Simon had chosen only himself in all the universe, the central infidelity, and now he had only that and his hate. It is Charles's clear understanding of magic. Origin and End must be something other than self acknowledged and accepted.

Whether or not he formally resigned and gave back the habit, he kept some ceremonial items in a drawer of his desk, perhaps including one sometimes illustrated in connection with the Order, a scarf or small banner. When he cleared his desk on moving to Oxford in 1939, he gave them, or some of them, to a friend, who destroyed them.

His meeting with Yeats must have been enormously exciting, though not necessarily influential. By 1917 Yeats was fifty-two, a famous figure in Irish literary and dramatic circles, and his lyrical poems were of the best being written in England or Ireland. In 1914 he had published *Responsibilities*, a book of his heart-searing disappointment at what was to have been an Irish heroic and literary renascence, and of the separation of Maud, his love, from him and (in her politics) from the common good of life.[42] How often the two poets met after a gathering of the Order, we cannot know, but they certainly met. A photograph exists of Yeats and Charles standing together, smiling, dressed much alike, with homburg hats and the ordinary town clothes of the time.[43] He writes in the Yeats chapter in *Poetry at Present* that he had 'seen Mr Yeats at the old Coronet Theatre in Notting Hill,[44] and joined in the tumultuous shouts that greeted him'.

Williams was an explorer, a man for discovery. 'God is a circle whose centre is everywhere and circumference nowhere'.[45] He believed it. But he knew he must look to all times and at all facts for evidence of the centre. 'Clear imagination and yet perhaps very little imagery in it' he thought possible for such a poet as he.[46] So much literature, criticism and teaching stopped at the near frontier of experience and expression—'the daisy hath a ring of red'. Why did Tennyson stop at merely describing the Grail? Why did the Great War poets tear themselves with outrage at war and death, both as natural to man as marriage and life? Why in the Grail histories was 'the question not asked' fatal to the knight's progress if not because attention to the meaning, nature and purpose of the Grail was vital to it? Why did students of the Grail literature concern themselves with comparisons, textual and literary treatment, but not with meaning, understanding and its relevance to our own life?

He continued to write verse and finished his third volume, *Divorce*, published also by Humphrey Milford in 1920 and dedicated 'To my Father and my other teachers'. Like the earlier *Poems of Conformity* (1917), it did not sell well. (Writing to John Pellow in 1923, Charles gives the sales as 198 for *Conformity* and 126 for *Divorce*.[47])

A change has come over Charles's poetry in three years. He has made discoveries and faced the terrors underlying them. Most serious to him is the realization that within his deepest happiness there is a contest between the wanting and willing of love and the wanting and willing of himself. A sense of his own abilities strains in him, the compelling non-personal call of poetry, a drive to reach intellectual conclusions and a fear of what those conclusions could be. He needed a worthy partner in talk—once his father had been that—in thought, and perhaps, deeply hidden, he needed a full contest in love.

The first poem, lovingly recording his relationship with, and debt to, his father, has already been quoted. There are poems about the war, in which come an early feeling for co-inherence*, for living one's life from another person through love, and so more distantly from all others, and for bearing some of the pain of the dead. He has not lost his friends' (Eyers and Nottingham) 'continual company'; he felt their bodies return, marching in sudden strangers' footsteps, while

> To walls and window-curtains cling
> Your voices at each breakfasting,
> As the cups pass from hand to hand,
> Crying for drink in No Man's Land.[48]

There is more of a touch of haunting than of true co-inherence here, but the idea, developed in his novel *Descent into Hell,* is rising through his

---

*Three principles, *co-inherence, exchange* and *substitution,* underlie Williams's poetic, romantic and theological thought. Their development can be traced throughout his work. They are valid, he considered, whether or not the people concerned hold themselves to be Christians.

Co-inherence. Christ gave his life for us, and his risen life is in each one if we will to accept it. Simply as men and women, without being self-conscious or portentous, we can share in this life within the divine co-inherence of the Trinity, and in so doing live as members one of another. In our degrees of power, intelligence, love or suffering, we are not divided from God or each other, for Christ's nature is not divided.

Exchange. The whole natural and social life of the world works as a process of living by and with each other, for good or bad. We cannot be born without physical exchange, nor can we live without it. But we can each day choose or grudge it, in personal contacts, in neighbourhood, and in our society under the law. To practise this approach to co-inherence we can find strength in the risen power of Christ linking all men.

Substitution. Another way of approach to co-inherence is by compact to bear another's burden. One can take by love the worry of another, or hold a terror, as one member of Christ's life helping, through that life, another member in trouble.

Williams saw these three principles as operating not only between the living in space and time, but also between the living and the dead—or the unborn.

mind. The never-healed loss of shared perceptions, lucent hours, is bleak in him; he prays

> Your heavenly conversation turn
> Some while in aid of me,
> That I may now, in these dark ways,
> Glimpse of your city see. . . .[49]

A group of poems meditating on forgiveness is particularly strong: 'To Michal: on Forgiveness', 'On the German Emperor' and 'At the Gates'.

His name for his wife has changed now to Michal, the name of King Saul's daughter who laughed at David when he danced before the Ark of God as it was carried into Jerusalem.[50] Florence's laughter at Charles's exuberance in declamation of poetry must have been painful, and yet reconciled, or it would not have produced from such a grievous Bible story a life-long name, which she herself used. Long after, in 1940, he wrote: 'my wife came to be called Michal—after King David's wife—O a century ago; because I said she had the same attitude, and we both thought the name prettier than her own'.[51]

Did his marriage bring a hope, a touch of real strength? 'To Michal: After a Vigil' shows that it is doing so; 'First Love', 'To Michal meditating a new Costume', 'To Michal: On Brushing her Hair', 'Her dark Eyes sparkle', 'For a Cathedral Door', 'Christmas', shows a tenderness towards her sense of guilt in quarrelling, when they love so well:

> Chafe not, madonna, that the foe could cheat
>   This moment from thy heart outworn and slack.
>   In the main battle's brunt thou didst not lack:
> Think what huge field of conquest or defeat
> This hour was closed;

He certainly was no 'broken backed snake', in the language of D. H. Lawrence. He had found sex in marriage an experience which in being repeated carried a continuously re-created sense of order and meaning, as in Eliot's 'still point of the turning world'.[52]

But his concern was more for progress into love. The longer poems in *Divorce* have a flavour of Chesterton and are weak, but the short poems dig strongly into himself and Michal and daily life. There has always been darkness, and now it is more finely observed. In the high town of Eternity all times and all towns have a place as modes of our interior city. Can he and Florence regain

> The county where our lives were truest, lane
> Of Hertfordshire, cottage of Somerset,
> Or—more familiar—Hampstead's road and ridge?[53]

What if worsening will and tempers lead them

> Into the huts and tenements man's mind
> Here by Zambezi builds or Thames,—the sum
> And dwelling of our foul lives and unkind,
> In the last haunts of Pandemonium![54]

The strength of his vision of love shows up his own performance badly. He sees that Michal loves Love more than he does, and after death she may go with Love away from him, and he will find himself bound by his choice of poetry and the power 'To stamp eternity upon an hour. . . .' If this had indeed been his choice it will be his fate, and he will not be able to 'recognize/ Your fragrant head, your glad eternal face?'[55] Remorse for 'selfish and hid treachery' dogs him, without self-deception or excuse. Yet enjoyment and love shine alongside them and the great change is not yet. He feels its long shadow in 'Three Friends', a poor poem but containing

> Woe on the day when blindness passed from me,
> When cruel gods touched and bade me see,
>
> . . .
>
> Now can I behold the things I must do.[56]

At the end of his life, in 1945, in a letter acknowledging a quotation to be from *Divorce,* he wrote that 'a lot of the verse in *Conformity* and *Divorce* is not very good, or it doesn't seem so now, but at least it is a proof that I developed my own view of romantic love by myself, and not through reading Dante'.[57] Certainly there are poor poems in *Divorce;* but still he can in some poems say directly what he means without using thought forms and diction, however expressive, from other centuries. 'Celestial Cities', 'Her dark Eyes sparkle', 'Loving and Loved', are far more free. Though 'At the "Ye that do Truly"'* is old-fashioned in style, it breaks new ground in religious thought expressed in poetry—in a quiet unemphatic way which is probably a mark of inner experience. 'The Fourth

---

*Included in the *New Oxford Book of Christian Verse* ed. D. Davie (OUP, 1982).

Dimension' is a remarkable imagination of how the flames of Pentecost and the process of the Ascension happened. How true it is to Charles's later mind, that he did not care to call happenings 'miracles', but saw in them the eternal efficient cause. There is a glance at Teilhard de Chardin in 'The Fourth Dimension', but only as one mind may greet another.

The *res publica,* or the city, or the common man in relationship, balances all personal concentrations. 'Politics', 'Hot Cross Buns', 'On the German Emperor', 'In an Ecclesiastical Procession', 'On Walt Whitman's "Song of Myself"', and 'Incidents', in detail or in general, concern common life.

He consciously makes a few experiments in contemporary styles, and calls them such. There is a cheerful poem to his feet, which he addresses as bearers of the mystery of the body,

> That heavenly equilibrium, that discreet
> Balance of passion whereof song is fain:
> Blessing and honour to you, O my feet![58]

Five more 'Commentaries' show contemporary application of verses or phrases in the Bible or Book of Common Prayer, that he had thought well of in his previous book and mentioned to Alice Meynell. And there is the bold 'Office Hymn for the feast of St Thomas Didymus, Apostle and Sceptic'. Belief? Certainty? Confidence? Charles claimed nothing of them. He was no mystic, though Edith had something of that greatness. He said man could not know, but must choose what he would believe. How dearly he loved Job!

> Lord God, the mystics gather
>   To Thy familiar tones,
> The sons who know their Father
>   Assume their judgement thrones.
> With terrible assessors
>   Thy seat is thronged about:
> We too are Thy confessors,
>   Lord, hear us too who doubt!
>
>   .   .   .
>
> Yet no wise dare we falter
>   In one word,—hear us so!
> We stand before Thine altar,
>   Denying that we know.
>
>   .   .   .

> Confess thou, ere thou sever
> Us from thy household true,
> Lord God, confess we never,
> Knowing not, swore we knew.[59]

This climax still brings me the shudder down the spine that comes with a completeness in verse. *Divorce* ends Charles's use of biblical or liturgical language in his poetry. It had passed with its thought into his bloodstream.

3

The Building of Camelot

Divorce brought him a new friend, John Pellow. In 1920 John, son of a Methodist minister, was a young civil servant. Lively, cheerful and intelligent, with theological and poetic interests, he was widely read and well informed. He reviewed *Divorce* in the *New Highway*, and in July 1920 as a stranger Charles wrote to him, thanking him 'for your very kind and quite unexpected review of *Divorce*'. The letter went on to say that Pellow 'can also be thanked for his own poems, rarely though these are seen'.[1] This led to a friendship valuable to both. John was capable of commenting on Charles's work using its own standards. He had a mind and humour that Charles could respect and enjoy. Happily married, he and his wife lived in Harrow, near enough to visit. John has been an intelligent, valuable source of masculine knowledge about Charles, and also has kept the only known letters dating from Charles's early married period.

By now Charles was a responsible editor in the Press and beginning to hold his own in the London literary world. In a letter to Alice Meynell of February 1921, he discusses a volume of her essays which he is editing for the O.U.P. In it she says that Aubrey de Vere was the last writer of mad songs. Charles suggests Thompson's 'Tom o' Bedlam'. She rebukes Wordsworth for his 'cruel fiction'. 'Justly', Charles writes, 'but was Patmore's less cruel when he pretended that animals loved to be sacrificed in woman's honour?'[2] Later in the summer he asked the august lady for another volume, making suggestions for subjects, and sending her proofs.

John Pellow sent his manuscript poems to the Oxford University Press by way of Charles, who acknowledged them and agreed with John about the need for favourable criticism.[3] He is himself ambitious, eager for appreciation, and frank about it in mostly undated letters of 1921 to Pellow. 'I blush even to myself when I think of it. If some futile babbler . . . speaks admiringly, one thinks: "Well, of course, he's no judgement, but still I think he may be right here by a fluke!" Mysterious self-love! Mysterious and maddening knowledge of one's idiocy all the time!'[4] In another letter, he has just brought out an anthology, with a man who 'controls the educational department here, whereas I control nothing and no-one, not even myself, ... Not a book to be vain about; scissors and paste and much toil. He had the idea, I did the toil . . . Mrs Hemans and Conan Doyle and O. W. Holmes in and Shakespeare to round all up & Blake to give it an air and Kipling to give it a flag. . . . The book would have been much worse if it hadn't been for me. Mrs Hemans and Shakespeare without the Blake'.[5] In the same letter is his poem to Michal singing the *Gloria* which, slightly altered, is printed in his next book of verse, *Windows of Night*.[6] For the first time he uses the initials 'C. W.' at the end of this long letter to Pellow.

Only to Pellow does he write about his family background. In November an aunt fell ill and 'till Christmas we spent our weekends at her rooms: not, you understand, being useful, but visiting the sick in Evangelical fashion. I drew the line at reading the Bible (which anyhow she didn't want— not being what one would call *really* religious, although feeling that CHURCH, not *the* Church, nor a church, but just CHURCH, plays an important although vague and not essential part, in life), but I bought medicine & talked gossip & patted a dog & scratched a parrot. When I might have bought pleasure & talked verse & patted your preferences & scratched your prejudices. And since Christmas we have been hampered one way & another & have yet certain duteous visits to pay, as to my Grandmother. . . . I hope the Church gave itself indigestion on Christmas Day, & the World all along. . . . And I hope you will write a great many poems as beautiful as the one in the *Mercury* this month'.[7]

There is some evidence of how the marriage was going from *Divorce*, and from the letters to John Pellow. It comes up from these pages vivid, veined with disputes, convinced, and with the convincement deeply studied. The Pellow letters give the only glimpse of the effect of family claims on Charles, not as provider of money but as husband, son and grandson and nephew, and now father.

In 1922 Charles's son was born, and christened Michael Stansby.

Charles wrote to John a moderately ridiculous and self-conscious letter about the birth of his son.[8] Two pages of cheerful phantasy on the See of Canterbury and the idea that St. John the Divine came to England, open it. 'I expect to have a closer connection with Canterbury in the future'. He suggests a dedication in his next book to the Archbishop of Canterbury: 'even Rome hasn't the sacred heart of Glastonbury or the divine legends of the Graal. However, all this is a parenthesis ... a genuflection, an offering, a petition, a meditation, but not a facing facts, a letter, an information, a statement, a profit-&-loss account, a nothing more or less than, a worldly business, a real thing. We have the real thing here;—to be more accurate we have the worldly appearance of the real thing here. In the Divine & only true World of Eternity there exists (we find) a spirit who now thrusts himself into Time. I hope he likes it; his lamentations suggest a doubt. He arrived on the first Sunday after Trinity (he might have come on Pentecost, Trinity, or Corpus Christi, and his choice of feast convinces me he will be a moderate churchman & probably an Archbishop when he grows up: hence my premonition of closer relations with Canterbury.)

'I have (laus Deo) no conscious change of emotion: a child is a guest of a somewhat insistent temperament, rather difficult to get rid of, almost pushing; a poor relation of a fairly pleasant kind. His little voice pulls at my ears; my heartstrings are unplucked. . . . Still, I add to his library. I bought for a penny a volume of Tertullian. I don't suppose I shall read him, but Michael (Michael Stansby Williams, Gentleman) may one day. . . . Do you like Blunden? I do: though I haven't read this last volume'. He was surely pleased to have a friend to whom he could write like this, and who would know exactly how much seriousness to find.

Pellow's poems, *Parentalia,* had been rejected by the O.U.P. In December Charles wrote that Humphrey Milford was brooding on them again and had said to him, 'Why, Mr. Williams, did we reject Mr. Pellow?' Publishing costs had gone down a little, so Charles asked John to send the poems in again. In the same letter he sighs about the baby: 'how intelligent Our Lord was! "I come not to bring peace but a sword!"' The baby slays "all the happy little innocent busynesses of one's life" and one can never write verse. 'A hundred unfinished poems lie about the flat'.[9]

He finished a play and sent it to John on 10 May 1924 saying 'nobody loves it (except me)', asking for his opinion on the theology rather than the verse. He tried to turn the manuscript from a two-act into a one-act piece and messed it up. Is this, perhaps, the lost *Chapel of the Thorn?*[10] He is getting interested now in the baby, and in December told John that Michael, aged two, was building a road of bricks. 'We then walk down it and sing "I walked along the Roman road as Caesar walked before"'. Perhaps he was conscious also of his reputation for talking, for he wrote to John, 'There is no doubt a time to be silent; but only when the other man is talking. If the other man isn't talking, why be silent? Is God ever silent? You are an Arian if you say so: was there ever a time when the Logos was not?' The painful cancelling of engagements with the Pellows because of Michal's headaches or the baby's ailments is now beginning to exacerbate Charles.

He added to his difficulties, but perhaps jumped at a change from domesticity, by accepting an invitation from the London County Council to give a course of evening lectures at the Holloway Literary Institute. There was great keenness among many people to continue their education and develop their minds. Evening classes, which anyone could attend on payment of a small fee, were run by local authorities and covered a wide range of subjects—not only technical instruction, but literature, art and (an old word) 'enlightenment'. They were not meant for people seeking professional qualifications. Audiences ranged from youngsters who had left school at fourteen or soon afterwards, through office and factory workers to the elderly, part of whose motive was to save coal or gas heating in their own rooms. Because people wanted to learn, attendance was good.

With these lectures a new way opened in Williams's life and continued until the outbreak of war in 1939. Over a range of literary institutes (as they were then called) in London's suburbs and the City, he developed his literary and religious studies, and enjoyed testing ideas in discussion. This led him to write his critical books, and later to the height of lecturing in the School of English of Oxford University.

He spoke from the briefest notes, often beginning before he had reached the desk, fast, excitingly, throwing out original ideas like sparks in seeming asides, opening unexpected fresh glimpses upon old thoughts. At intense moments an old lady's dog would bark, and no one was surprised. Yet he ended his lecture exactly on time and with every item on the evening's syllabus covered. After each lecture and discussion he would walk back to the nearest tube station with anyone who wanted to go on listening or discussing, or even to the station beyond that. A group of London Territorial volunteer soldiers came to one series of his lectures: one evening their drill night clashed with his hour, so he met them afterwards, had a drink, and summarised what he had said.

Lecturing brought him many friends, who used to sign up for one series of his talks after another. Some remained friends all his life, as he did to them: Raymond Hunt, tireless recorder, was one; John Topliss and his future wife, came to their first lecture in 1926, and, on John's leave from the army, lunched with Charles in Oxford in 1944. These friends, most of whom were more like the kind of people with whom he had been brought up than those he met at the Press, he valued all his life.

Marriage was pressing claims on him, his time, his devotion and his integrity. He searched his heart, as is shown in poems in *Divorce,* among them 'After Marriage'. He was not the only one. When the old St. Albans friend Miss Pike visited him and Florence, during talk of familiar times in St. Albans, Florence said 'Married life isn't in the least what we thought it would be like'. Miss Pike remembered Charles saying quickly, 'We should have been married years and years ago'. Power lay in marriage, he had found, not only to endure and keep going, to give and take, but to open a new life, more potent, more delightful, ever renewing, ever enlarging both man and woman. He recalled *The Silver Stair.* The vision of a life lived from a new centre was there. In living the life in practice he had found a union which he felt included the ways both of affirmation and of rejection. In the intercourse hours of sexual love, the two of them were acting the affirmation and asserting the rejection that this was the whole of love.[12] But, outside sex, had he slipped from that centre, ever so little, in feeling his other concerns to be more important than his marriage?

The Church, brought into existence by incarnate Love-in-God, had been unsure, uneasy, about incarnate love in man and woman and had never made a great statement on it, even in the marriage service. Charles accepted that for this there had been many reasons, but he did not think them sufficient.[13] God had created man and woman and also said that this creation was in his own image. A personal and sexual union might be a union of the single human potentiality in a restoration of the single image of God; the personal relationship an image of the mystical body which through the Incarnation is a holy fellowship, as daily and acceptable as Jesus working in the carpenter's shop. Charles talked to the few on whom he could rely (certainly Nicholson, Lee, Fred Page and probably Pellow) and sat down after his day's work to write his first prose book about his findings: *Outlines of Romantic Theology.*

The thought is clear. Mysteries and clouds were to Charles matters for examination, for accurate understanding up to the point where he would say, 'further than this is unknown to us'. Such an approach is welcome in metaphysical writing. It also keeps it short. The principle of Romantic Theology he saw in 'any two lovers who knew that their love was Christ, and that their marriage was His life, and pursued Him in holy fellowship together'. Each marriage can partake in His (Love's) conception, birth, private childhood, young adult development, temptations, career work, miracles, failures, pain, death and resurrection to yet a new life. 'Remote beyond our present apprehension, except dimly, lies even the beginning of that Way, though it may have been followed (without perhaps the intellectual formulation) in many obscure households'.[14]

Remember 'Gratia Plena',[15] remember the 'doctrine in ordinary piteous men'. God is involved in our chosen love, blessed, awkward, painful, unwanted sometimes, but always offering power and joy through our bodies, minds, and relationship. That relationship does not exalt itself into assumption of deity, but learns the incarnation of Jesus in itself. Jesus is seen as God but also as man, for he prays to the Father although he is included in the Trinity. Prayer is to a greater love than our own. Devoted and happy lovers do not achieve their state by effort. 'Their business is not to be, but to know that they are, His symbols, and that their marriage is His life'—my, your, marriage is living the Gospel story of the human life of Jesus, though not necessarily in exact temporal sequence.[16] At our Bethlehem our bodies are the shepherds, our highest imagination the Magi, both finding the birth of love.

And from that crude, half-magical experience, the strangeness goes on, if we will serve it, in our most intimate and hidden knowledge. The work of redemption which Christ carried out in his earthly life is fulfilled in this mystical life of love: the silent growth of young love in the common ways of Nazareth; His public commitment in baptism is our marriage, immediately followed by the temptation, not of lovers but of their love.

'The three temptations are really but one, to hasten in some way for his own benefit the process which is himself'.[17] Who would desire free will if by any means this most bitter of any gift could be removed from man in a state of love? But love's slowly attained acceptance is to be a state throbbing with a deliberate choice. Lovers are not expected to convert the stones of depression, boredom, monotony, dislike, into bread, or to escape from the wilderness problem; but they can realize themselves to be, in those states, exactly that, stones in Christ's wilderness. Christ could have converted the stones by a miracle, as he could in the second and third temptations have maintained his royalty and sustained himself against the laws of natural things. But he chose not to do it. He awaits the choice of men, the continued choice of lovers to live the life of love.

The parallels, the identifications are carried through. Must church and state kill this divine love? It very often happens. The mere process of things, of duties and obligations, seems to destroy love—tyrannical desire, treacherous manners, abstruse or indifferent religion, the cares of life or the pull of a competing career or fruitful talent. The warning is clear to the church, lest she fail to recognise the Messias she proclaims; to the state, lest the means become the end, and the purpose of man and woman's life be distorted for some need of convention or order. Passion and a crucifixion must be part of the experience of lovers, who indeed tend to fly from it crying 'If thou be the Son of God, come down from the Cross'—the same temptation that was offered to Him earlier 'to produce a contradiction in His nature, to set His Mercy against His Justice, His Compassion against His Inevitability'.[18] The desolation of His disciples, their desertion of Himself, does not compel Him to recede, in the slow work of redemption or the work of marriage, one step from the laws which are Himself. We learn with a wrench to choose joy and ability instead of sullenness, and self to be part of continuous miracles of healing, plenty, revival from apparent death, between each other. We don't *do* it; we *become* it if we continue to choose love.

Using the Anglican rite of the time, 1924, and the word 'Catholic' as he always did for 'universal' or 'general', Charles goes through the Communion Service with sexual love in focus.[19] It is Christ or Love, who draws the world into Himself in Communion. The Body of Christ is in a hidden way one with the bodies of his saints, all true lovers. At the same time the 'otherness' of the beloved, the plain individual, is also to be known, as the plain bread. Our daily selves are drawn in. The sacrifice of the Crucifixion, and of this Communion, was the unmaking of all life so that it should be remade after the original pattern, a deliberate remaking instead of an inevitable decay.

'If the Christ of the Eucharist and the Love of the marriage-night are indeed not two but one, if the devout and Catholic lover bestows and receives more than either he desires or deserves—the Real Presence of the Most Sacred Body, then certainly marriage has been rightly if darkly honoured by the whole Church. . . . Here also the work of sanctification is carried on, and that mysterious reality—the Body of the Resurrection—may already be shaped and nourished throughout the sacred bodies of lovers'. Consciousness of this has caused the Church to speak as she has done of marriage. Her unconsciousness of it has hampered her in speaking of it.

Charles was aware of the dangers which secretly accompany deep feelings: longings for personal satisfaction not genuinely concerned with the central life of love; substitutions of lesser preoccupations for greater, such as sentimentality, niggling curiosity, indulgent fantasy. Another danger was the temptation of Ananias and Sapphira to keep 'back part of the price',[20] some self-love. Poems in *Divorce* and *Windows of Night* show that he felt this to be one of his own dangers. Most insinuating of all he reckoned to be a form of infidelity, an opposition to love itself, a persistent dislike of one's fellows. It can lead to a separation which becomes an antipathy to all, such as one finds in some old people. This opposition to love he recognised as a feeling of oneself so pervading that it was the beginning of the way to the eternal ice at the bottom of Dante's *Inferno*, the ape of divinity, the opposite everywhere of Christ. It was a danger that he never ignored.[21] The safeguards against all these persistent enemies he declares to be scepticism and devotion, and certainly he maintained both in his own life. Sonnets in *The Silver Stair* are recalled in *Romantic Theology*: LXVIII sees in following love 'strange and familiar things and joy thereof'; LXXVI sees our lives being the life of Christ and also such help as He was given to carry the Cross.

'No belief in the dogmas of Romantic Theology will make give-and-take between two sensitive natures an easy thing, any more than a belief in Dogmatic Theology makes it easier to be courteous to a man who has trodden on one's toe in a railway queue. It is here that the *otherness* of the beloved is to be felt; and as it is one of the difficulties of marriage that the otherness is so acute, so it is one of its graces that it is delightedly accepted. It does not get easier as we are often told. The later life can be harder'. 'The slow approach to the beloved gives place to a slow recoil. Love, which in the earlier stages appeared to intensify her love and her beauty, now thrusts itself between them. The road into eternity is found to be strait and to involve the turning of the attention from that lady who was earlier its sole means of manifestation'.

Sexual intercourse, 'usually referred to as the consummation of marriage' is 'nothing of the sort; at best it is the channel by which a deeper marriage is instituted; the consummation, however it may be in this act signified, foretold and hastened, is usually far away in the Divine Life'.[22] But this act, capable of being a sacrament, makes marriage itself more sacramental than any other occupation. He goes on to other concentrations of love than marriage, such as the commonwealth of friendship, chosen virginity, Nature. He parries the wrath of followers of Mystical Theology, perhaps of his friends Nicholson and Lee. He looks at Dante's *Vita Nuova* and at Malory's story of the Grail Mass in Sarras. He speaks of Sir Percivale and his dead sister, of Sir Lancelot whose devotion, toil and agony were recognized in Sir Galahad's greeting at the achievement of the Grail which Sir Lancelot never saw. 'Salute me to my lord Sir Lancelot my father'. Charles recognizes the nature of substitution between Sir Lancelot and Sir Galahad, but has not yet reached identification by the word. He finds awareness of the identification of romantic love with Christ's earthly life in Donne, but hidden; in Patmore guessed but finally shrunk from; the Song of Solomon's passion is a mortal passion sustained by an immortal principle, not known as love and Christ, as Romantic Theology proposes.

The Church contains the secrets of Christ's passion and resurrection. It was left to that group after the Ascension to allow the identification of his life with the life of love in man to become known.

In *Outlines of Romantic Theology* Charles was teaching himself. He was articulating his glimpses of Love living in human happenings exactly where the glimpses led him. As ever, he declared that he said nothing new, that it was there for all to see. The book is prefaced with the single quotation, 'Have I been so long time with you, and yet hast thou not known me, Philip?'[23] Sexual life was to him, as *Poems of Conformity* and *Divorce* show, part of the life of love in the body interacting with mind and soul. He saw man and woman as entirely equal and different. The double myths of creation, of a single form—'God created man in His own image'—'male and female created He them' interested him but did not break up his thought. To speak of masculine or feminine principles in God's transcendence, or sexual life as an activity separate in itself, is for him substituting the lesser for the greater concentration.

Letters to John Pellow* show that the manuscript was offered to the Oxford University Press and rejected in September 1924. Humphrey Milford wrote a memorable note to Charles on it: 'I fear this is not for us. It may be for all time and I may be like the poor Indian,[24] but I am afraid of it and of you'. Charles quoted this in a letter to Pellow, and continued 'so the unfortunate *Romantic Theology* shall cuddle the equally unfortunate *Chapel of the Thorn* in private seclusion'.[25]

Fred Page sent *Romantic Theology* to the Nonesuch Press, which rejected it in 1925 after either long thought or just silence. It had another chance when Osbert Burdett, a reader for Faber and Gwyer, asked to see it. Charles wrote to Pellow on 2 November 1925, asking him to send the manuscript to Burdett. Charles was by now busy writing his first novel, then called *The Black Bastard* (later *Shadows of Ecstasy*) and had given up hope of *Romantic Theology*. Burdett put him in touch with Faber's and Charles offered them both the novel and *Romantic Theology*. From February to April 1926, the correspondence goes on. Faber did not like the title of either manuscript. Charles wrote to Pellow that he had finished his second novel, *The Corpse* (later *War in Heaven*). This must also have gone to Faber's. In a following letter to Pellow, undated but probably written in May 1926, he metaphorically raised his fists to heaven against Faber's, who had refused *Romantic Theology* and *The Black Bastard*, saying 'the General Strike[26] had adversely affected the firm, but could they

---

*The first use I have found of the nickname 'Serge', which he uses in many later letters to his wife, comes in a letter to John of 21 September 1924.

keep *Romantic Theology* to consider for 1927'. The indignant author must have refused, for his letter to Pellow ends, 'So it and *The Black Bastard* and *The Corpse* can all go away with *The Chapel of the Thorn*. . . . I am in such a temper that I sha'n't go on with this letter, indeed there is nothing more to say. My only life is all smelling of the literary taint and when that becomes more corrupt than usual it smells *very* unpleasant indeed. I shall leave off writing books. Write and soothe me'. One can at any rate agree with Faber's that these early manuscripts show Charles's weakness in choosing saleable book titles.

Perhaps Michal's attention at home was becoming more concentrated on the child than on the husband. Evenings, or Saturday afternoons, of talk with the Pellows were therefore valuable to Charles. They often produced light or semi-serious poems, mental stimulus, immense enjoyment. Michal may have felt differently, a little jealous of her husband's literary preoccupation and enthusiasm, and of the Pellows' background. She may have begun, even unconsciously, to compensate herself for the whole literary pull by the importance of the child. So many arrangements for a visit to or from the Pellows were cancelled for rather flimsy doubts about Michael's health, or worse still, his routine. One's heart sinks to read the lines. 'The young star usually sleeps till 1.00 and Michal doesn't want to wake him for feed in case it makes him peevish for the afternoon. I don't think it would but you never know'.[27] John Pellow later spoke of Michal, saying she was fond of Mrs. Pellow and they all got on well together, 'but Michal seemed to wear a mask all the time'. She was seldom relaxed or natural. He added that George Robinson, Charles's St. Albans friend from schooldays, talked to John of this, and agreed with him, adding that he thought there was nothing behind the mask.

The bad temper hung over Charles. In December 1926 he wrote to John, 'Nothing ever happens to us—at least nothing beyond domesticities. (I suppose the same thing might be said of God? no, it mightn't.) There is a ridiculous amount of work somehow, and all hack work at that. Nothing happens about my more serious efforts. *R. T.* wanders among desiring & private readers. The *B. B.* (through the intervention of Bumpus's in persona J. G. W.*) has gone to Mr Alfred Knopf. I should love to be published by Mr Knopf, if only for the name'.[28] Humphrey Milford, ever a silent, intelligent sympathiser, spoke of a new book of verse.

---

* J. G. Wilson, manager of Bumpus's bookshop in Oxford Street, London. Wilson was a great 'character' in the book trade.

An old story that he wrote the novels to pay for his son's school fees cannot be true, though many people believed it.* In 1925, when he began, Michael was three years old. Michal herself was still earning, teaching at a school in Soho, London, till 1930, and Charles was paid on the same scale as any other editor. He was also lecturing. With one two-year-old child and a small flat, he was in a reasonably secure condition, much like Fred Page who also had one son. He was, however, always conscious of money, as a value which his youth and his parents had lacked. 'I don't think anyone but the mystic can appreciate the beauty and value of money. The wretched woman (in the flat) below us tells Michal she hates it'.[29]

The year 1924 was a year of upheaval for all O.U.P. staff, for the firm moved, staff, files, counting-house and vast book stocks, some 600 yards from Amen Corner to Amen House in Warwick Square† off Warwick Lane, to gain space to expand. The front of the new building, facing into the square, was of beautiful eighteenth-century brick, while behind, giving on to Old Bailey, a connected new building provided offices and warehouse room. On another side of the square was a different, more scrambling kind of publishing firm, Hodder and Stoughton. Other businesses occupied all the rest of the square.

On the ground floor a broad facing staircase led upstairs, notably to the Publisher's beautiful front room with its Adam ceiling. The hall held 'Sergeant', his face badly scarred from the War, and the lift, hydraulic and silent and smooth. To the left was the Show Room, where Bibles, prayer books and fine bindings were displayed; to the right an elegant waiting room led on to a long, wide library with windows at each end, a broad display shelf at the waiting room end to occupy visitors, a good table, and at the back end a desk for the librarian. All the productions of the mighty Oxford University Press from past ages still in print were on the shelves for display or consultation. A small staircase, flat against the wall, led to the first floor and the rest of the building, and a door by the desk gave working access to the hall and main stairs. The Music Department was on the ground floor beyond the Library, with its own entrance from Warwick Square and no access to the Library except by an upper floor. Its

---

*Indeed, after I wrote the story—believing it—in my *Introduction to Charles Williams,* Mrs. Williams wrote me an indignant letter, and she had an individual style in indignation.

†I joined the firm nine years later, and loved the whole site—the crowded square full of vans, lorries, cars edging in and backing out, men shouting, people running with sacks of ordered books, stately visitors, nervous authors, people who had lost their way, and people noting who of the staff was going out with whom.

separate entrance gave the Music Department a rakish feel,[30] investing its world with importance and interest.

There was a small canteen, with access to the cook, who could be cajoled at right moments to produce big crusts with beef dripping for hungry juniors, and a scold. The Publisher of course had his dining room and private cooking. All the editorial or managerial levels ate out at the cafés or pubs packed into this crowded, popular part of the old City—now bombed, burnt and gone, rebuilt into new space and pleasantness—but in Charles's and in how many souls 'so singular in each particular'.[31]

Charles does not mention the move in letters to Pellow. Having shared with Fred Page since 1908, he probably hoped to be given a room to himself, but they were together again. It was a small slit of a room on the second floor well-lined with bookshelves, with linoleum on the floor, a hat and coat stand in one corner, a window on to the yard of the Old Bailey (Central Criminal Court), a desk at each end and a door opening on to a dark passage. Three of Charles's long strides could include the whole length. Across the passage was the big Printing Office, generating noise of typewriters and people. Here Charles Williams stayed till 1939, when Amen House was abandoned and the firm was evacuated to Oxford for the war.

He wanted success and fame. His patron Alice Meynell had died in 1922. He was thirty-six and had published only three poorly-selling small books of verse. His head was full of ideas on poetry, the Grail and King Arthur, love, metaphysics, human life, all of which seemed to him ignored in contemporary writing. He pretended not to care. John Pellow asked for sales figures of his own *Parentalia*. Charles said 'Wait'. 'The counting-house murder us if we ask for figures in the first few weeks of the New Year. (But why ask for figures? Alas! is not one's wife the curiosity of one's own detachment? I never ask for figures. If HSM* *will* encourage young poets, say "Gawd bless you, genleman, for 'elping a pore young fellow what lost 'is legs in the war!"' But he added 'I can't, I simply *can't*, bring myself to reject HSM's offer to do another book: I despise myself, but I like to see myself in print'.[32] He worked over his last four years' poems (several of which had already been published in magazines, as he noted at the beginning of the new book), wrote more, and discussed the pronunciation of 'Palomides' with John, declaring he wanted to use Palōmides to scan in lines beginning, 'In the high town of Ispahan/where palmers walk on peas/ . . . was he born/the prince Palōmides'.[33]

---

*Humphrey Milford, the Publisher.

At some time during this period he wrote the poems he called *The Advent of Galahad*. He never tried to publish them, but forty-five have survived in typescript and may well be the complete series. Young and poetical, coloured with archaisms, the writing of the verse seems as much a joyful preoccupation as the meaning. All but nine of the poems are called 'Songs'—of Lancelot, Dinadan and so on—and have that song quality, which disappears altogether from the mature poetry except for 'Taliessin's Song of the Unicorn'.[34] They probably came straight from reading such a gripping original as Chrétien de Troyes or Marie de France; These sources certainly contributed. 'Taliessin's Song of Lancelot's Mass' grew into the consummation of a life's experience in 'Taliessin at Lancelot's Mass', which concluded his later book of Arthurian poems, *Taliessin Through Logres*.

Windows of Night came out on 8 January 1925.[35] It is a sombre book with macabre colouring. Fears and darkness move across many of its poems. They were rising in *Divorce,* but now a terror of existence, a longing for extinction of consciousness weighs on many of them. Only love and poetry hold open a window of starlight and air. The first poem 'Prelude' (to H. S. M.) gives a more bitter and dark picture of his life when he began work in London than does *Divorce* or *Conformity*. Three 'Night Poems', 'To Michal: On Bringing her Breakfast in Bed', 'To Michal: Sonnets after Marriage', 'In Time of Danger' (childbirth), and three poems 'For a Child' show his strength in love, his sense of 'the full passion of her abounding heart'.[36] Their best child is Love, their elder son, who lifts his brother, young Michael in strong hands; their best moments lying awake in bed when

> this soft betwixt-between
>
> Flows through our limbs; eternity
> Breathes at the lattices; and we,
>
> Lightly together folded, prove
> The immortal friendliness of love . . . [37]

And when Charles knows Michal as 'In a world insignificant thou significant wholly'.[38]

He enjoys the differences between Michal's ways and his own, in 'To Michal: Sonnets after Marriage, VI At the Seaside', she is quick and varied, drawn to the bright sea-edge and its rush of waves, as he is to forests, paths and brooks, 'fixed and helpless' trees, 'Corners and holes of soft indwelling night'. 'A Cup of Water' is burdened with night fears, until

Michal wakes and asks him for a cup of water; he brings it to her and goes back to bed for a renewed onslaught of fears, but

> Slumber was there, and Love, and an end to thinking;
>   Only I saw, remote and far in the night,
> Our mother Christendom pausing from war and drinking
>   A cup of water,—and sleep came down on the sight.

Four sonnets 'On the Sanctissimum' have been recognized for their quality and reprinted in magazines. His quality of treating religion as if it were as continuous and necessary as earning a wage keeps his treatment instant, relevant. Yet it is not the pattern of religion he seeks, but what moves through it or even in some personalities without it.

He writes more freely in the poems on poetry—to Alice Meynell, after her death, in the streets of heaven talking of English poets[39] in 'Sub specie Aeternitatis', of the 'starry and invisible land' of England, discovered by Constable, its deep supernatural language heard by Wordsworth, its common speech as

> Authentic accents of eternity
>   Heard here in Milton's, Blake's, or Shakespeare's line

and her heart 'filled with Humour, Irony, and Song.'

He sees Shakespeare on a Central London line tube station, come from an office, smoking, a cheap thriller under his arm, and skimming the evening paper, with notes for the moonlight scene of *The Merchant of Venice* in his pocket, and his chief wish to be earning more money.[40] On a London bus he sees the English tradition, a hefty, elderly, cheerful man, saying as he leaves the bus: 'Good-night to all you ladies!' On the words Charles hears

> Young and fresh and wild,
> Tossed on the London light;
>   Lovelace, Sackville, and Carew,
>   All were singing, and we too,
> 'Good-night to all you ladies,
>   Good-night!'[41]

How dark are the dark poems—thirteen or more of them—rising from the terrors that opened in the depths of his mind. Fear, sour taste of evil in his mouth, not despairing, defiant, sadistic, discoveringly evil, but dreary, shabby, insistent, futile as his poems show the nature of evil.

Between these and the living poems are a few strange ones, which face a
sense of being picked out for some purpose, not splendid, probably gloomy.
'Easter' thinks of the moment among the disciples of Jesus after the Crucifixion, when the women burst into the upper room crying that Jesus'
body was gone. Was there not one disciple who felt his soul go down under
a still heavier doom,

> Knew himself chosen, by a dreadful lot,
> To grace and strife and immortality,
> And blessed but perpetual martyrdom,
> Uttered one last lost cry, 'Ah, not to me!'
> Even as from air he saw the Arisen come;
> Nor felt within him the black terror cease
> Even as around them fell the greeting, 'Peace'?

And in 'Saint Mary Magdelene' the same terror waits

> Silent, unmanifest,
> Hiding his power,
> During a time and times,
> Waits he his hour.

Imagination waits till a sudden rumour fulfils the moment of truth. 'Saint
Michael' sees a motion within Deity, when Michael and his angels as a
lantern on an Admiral's vessel set moving

> through the ocean of the unknown vast
> The twelve huge ships of the moving Zodiac.

This Zodiac-creation was to move through his love and poetry for the
next twenty years. In 'Domesticity' the last defences of home, books, the
child's cot against inner darkness and fear are gone. Every friendly thing,
the hearth fire, water in the basin, bars of the cot, has also a deathly purpose. His least act is haunted by cruelty, evil and death. Perhaps from this
horror there sprang in him the first movement of the idea that if evil were
consumed by good in the suffering of Christ on the cross, so our least act
might now be united to the good in the earthly life of Christ, and draw its
life not from hate but somehow, joyfully, from Christ. Substitution and co-
inherence, on which Charles was to build his thought, might have had
their strange beginning of awareness here.

The book reflects the last two years, inward growth and outward standstill, as he laments in letters to John Pellow. There are hints of standstill
in love:

> Whose is the guilt if still the frost invade
> The hoped-for Spring, and check the piercing blade
> Of love? what love, when warmth deserts the air?[42]

The style is plain. It has discarded decoration and support from religious or poetic sources, but not found a new life. The most charming piece is 'Walking Song', for young Michael, where a rhythm moves gently through young images round the world and through history to the garden gate in Hampstead and the open door and candles.

> For here the noble lady is who meets us from our wanderings,
>   Here are all the sensible and very needful things,
> Here are blankets, here is milk, here are rest and slumber,
>   And the courteous prince of angels with the fire about his wings.

'To a Publisher', addressed to Humphrey Milford, is last but one in the book. Different in kind, subject and mood from the rest, it is a first expression of another group of theological ideas that were beginning to spring in his mind, those connected with the work done at Amen House and the people who did it.

The book got eleven reviews soon after publication, mostly in literary journals but also in the *Times Literary Supplement* and two national papers. The reviews varied from being annihilating to discovering a good new book. What keenness of literary interest there was fifty years ago, when so many critical journals reviewed a little-known poet so promptly. An interesting note on the book survives, addressed by the O.U.P. to its travellers and representatives: 'Mr. Milford is particularly anxious to make a sensation with this book and to get with it for Williams the sales and the reputation he deserves. Do *please* impress on your customers that it is *not* a book of minor poems but a collection that shall rank high in the scale of contemporary literature. . . . There is no doubt that Williams will one day be recognized as a very fine poet, and *then* those who possess early editions will be lucky!'[43]

Charles Williams as a young man, taken by a St. Albans photographer

Charles Williams in wartime, 1939–1945, writing at 9 South Parks Road, Oxford

Charles Williams with W. B. Yeats

Phyllis Jones

Florence Conway (Williams's wife) in pageant dress

Amen House as Charles Williams knew it; front entrance on the left; next two windows the reception room; following three windows the Library; entrance beyond is the Music Department

Amen House Library interior; librarian's table at the back

Sir Humphrey Milford, Publisher

4

The Library at Amen House

The move in March 1924 of the Oxford University Press from its crowded offices at Amen Corner to the beauty and spaciousness of Amen House caused a release within Charles Williams of a new vision and a new kind of theology. Indeed, it was to Chapter 21 of the *Book of Revelation* of St. John the Divine that he went:

> Then I saw a new heaven and a new earth. . . . I saw the holy city, new Jerusalem, coming down out of heaven from God. . . . It had a great high wall, with twelve gates. . . . And the city had no need of sun or moon to shine upon it; for the glory of God gave it light. . . . By its light shall the nations walk. . . . The wealth and splendour of the nations shall be brought into it; but nothing unclean shall enter, nor anyone whose ways are false or foul. . . .

The long poem, 'To a Publisher' that is last but one in *Windows of Night,* is addressed to Humphrey Milford and begins

> When the divine John out of heaven, great sir,
> Saw the Free City over earth expand . . .

It proceeds to a vision of twelve guilds (St. John's tribes) representing twelve great occupations, 'Twelve principles of being', who round the year hold each a solemn fair before the mayor who is also deity. He names three such, farmers, discoverers and carpenters. He is, however, concerned with a fourth, those who as printers or publishers work to spread the word.

It is the fair day of those who work with words:

> But O what dawn, sir, shall behold our state,
>   Our carnival, our triumph, our good cheer,
> When through the streets from our in-pouring gate,
> Under observant galleries everywhere,
>   We range the City, and at last draw near
> The dais and the high mayoral chair.

In the procession march the workers of the Oxford University Press under its dark blue and gold banner of the three crowns and the motto, *Dominus Illuminatio Mea* (the Lord is my Light), among them both Milford and Williams:

> Company there by company shall pass by,
>   Each with its tossing banner,—and our own,
> Not least in that exalted pageantry,
> Bright with its golden legend, *Dominus*
>   *Illuminatio,* and the triple crown,
> And you, and I perchance; and over us
>
> Shall all the songs who here on earth were books,
>   Whom we, according to our wealth, made free,
> Flutter like cupids, and with gentle looks
> Present us to their lord and principal,
>   Good craftsmen, prudent in our mystery,
> Not slothful here at task, not slow at call.

Words wait shut up, unhappy, miserable, until some poet brings them forth. Yet words need not only poets, but publishers, printers and book distributors:

> of earth's fame still shyly covetous,
> And still with nothing but their love for fee,
> Petitionary came, and found with us
> Shelter and shipping for what voyages
>   To ports of mind beyond the public sea
> They risked their hopes on and their health's increase.

Patrons and printers, what we had we gave,
  Blessing them with devotion and desire
Meetly to serve. . . .

Before the throne of deity all those who are concerned with words live
in the *res publica,* interchanging from topmost to least their hierarchical
degrees. Moreover, those who practise the mystery and art of words are
the interpreters of all, for

without us eleven guilds should be
  But a dumb joy, we are their singing part,
Their publication and epiphany.

More, they are the interpreters of deity:

Let the rest hear his praise and cherish it,
  We are the praise he speaks, we are his voice.

Here in this poem, almost certainly written in the second half of 1924, is
the beginning of a vision that over the next three years was to explode into
a theology of work for the Oxford University Press at Amen House under
Humphrey Milford, within the hierarchy of the firm's staff, in the service
of the word embodied in the book.

Ironically, last in *Windows of Night* is a quiet love-poem to his wife,
'Last Thoughts before Sleep',

But now, my mind is so clear,
  You are so warm and close, so warm I lie,
That now is the time to think great things; with you near,
  I feel such thoughts as I never had go by. . . .
Such deep things. . . .

But in the library of the new Amen House a second revelation was about
to reveal herself. Amen Corner had had no library, but at Amen House a
roomy and beautiful one had been provided for the use of staff and public.
A librarian was therefore needed. The Publisher advertised the post, not
as nowadays stating necessary qualifications. Various people applied. One
was Phyllis Jones, a young woman who lived in Wandsworth, South London, with her parents, sister and brother.[1] Born on 4 July 1901, she had
been to a small private school nearby and in 1918 to King's College for
Women (later Queen Elizabeth College) on Campden Hill, Kensington.
Her course, in Household and Social Science, was later upgraded from

diploma to degree level. She was only seventeen, but restless, intelligent, and feeling the onset of change at the end of the war in 1918. She took a job teaching science at a girls boarding school in Tunbridge Wells under Miss Ferguson as headmistress. She left after two years, in 1923, 'with rest of the junior staff rather in disgrace owing to too flippant behaviour— in spite of getting girls through their School Certificate'. Jobs were scarce then as standards rose for women teachers. She became nursery governess to a family whom she described as 'very grand' and left after two months.

She was unemployed at home with a father retired from business through a severe nervous breakdown, a mother and sister not entirely con- genial, and a brother, Gerald, who was her best outlet. Mr. Jones read Humphrey Milford's advertisement. He went to Amen Corner, saw the Publisher and told him he had a book-mad daughter. Humphrey Milford put three questions to her: 'Do you read French?' 'Yes'. 'Do you read Proust?' 'No'. 'Do you suffer fools gladly?' 'No'. He turned to his secre- tary, Tommy Curtis, and said 'She'll do. Send the rest away'.

So, when the firm moved to Amen House in March 1924, Phyllis Jones joined the Press as librarian. She was short, slim, with intelligent good looks, a well-proportioned face with good bone structure, dark blue eyes with clearly marked eyebrows, a dainty beaky nose, a mouth quick to smile or compress, and very beautiful thick fair hair. Like her face, her hands were fine-boned, well-shaped and expressive. She had 'quality', but no conceit. She was ambitious, but for her own aims rather than the fashion's. In 1924 she wanted to move in a wider, newer world of brains and per- sonality and to do so was not afraid to learn and compete.

Her first recollection of Charles Williams is of hearing him talking with Hubert Foss on the stairs of Amen House—those stairs which, with the stone spiral stairs of St. Albans School, became so significant in his Arthu- rian poetry. Perhaps he had told Michal about the new offices and the Library, for Phyllis remembers Michal bringing little Michael to visit Amen House early on. It was the only time the tall dark woman in Charles's life met the short fair one.

Britain's economic condition was shaky in those post-war years, but people hungered to read good modern books. There was then, of course, no television and little radio. Amen House was a good place in which to work, human, interesting, exciting, full of personalities of all grades, the centre of an expanding and successful worldwide business with an unri- valled publishing reputation. Humphrey Milford had acute perception, sensitivity and daring. His choice of titles and styles, his moves into new publishing fields, kept Amen House busy expanding its output.[2] Notably he opened a Music Department in 1923, which was therefore a part of the firm's life before the move, with an electric character Hubert Foss as manager.

Milford, Williams, Foss, Hopkins; it must have seemed then that 'the world's great age begins anew!'[3] Gerard (Gerry) Hopkins, nephew of the poet Gerard Manley Hopkins, was a big, tall man with bushy eyebrows, large features and an attractive voice. He was in charge of the firm's publicity, and a specialist in modern French literature. Married but childless, he was socially above all but Milford. There was, too, Miss Helen Peacock, head of Production. She was tall, large, with brown hair pinned up on top, gold-rimmed spectacles and a blunt manner. She always wore a blouse and skirt, and was Gerry's counterpart in German literature.

Then, too, there were the juniors, young and not so young, from all departments, Counting House, Publicity, Editorial (like R. D. Binfield, later to be C. W.'s assistant), Production, and Juvenile, who caught the glow, through talk about work on the stairs, in the canteen, in the Dramatic Society.

By 1925 the Library had become a place where senior staff could chat with visitors or authors or, in their absence, talk among themselves. Offices were small and spartan, whereas the Library was the place of mental and physical expansion. Ideas and jokes proliferated on work, whether from music or books. Friendships began, a society grew, delighting and yet efficient. H. S. M., might stroll through, sit a little while in the wing chair and make a point in the talk. As Librarian, Phyllis behind her long table was on the edge of it all, taking in everything, noting people, subjects, ideas. This was the adult world she had desired, very different from school teaching or her home life. She found it excellent.

It was an increasingly busy time for Williams. The files of the Clarendon Press (the base of the firm located in Oxford) show that he continued to choose and edit the poetry anthologies which were then popular with schools as well as the general public in England, and with the firms' overseas branches. Through this work he came to know the staff at Oxford, felt himself stabilizing in the literary and publishing world, and earned extra money. He had also since 1920 been writing occasional articles or reviews for outside publication.

In 'Prelude', the poem dedicated to H. S. M., which opens *Windows of Night*, Charles acknowledged his debt to Milford for security

> Among the starving I was fed,
> Into security was led,
>   And guarded from the wild.

and also for the gift of colleagues

> And what more joys, what friendships new,
> Had happily their source in you!

and for London

> As London, my own city. . . .
>
>   .   .   .
>
> Re-risen for me, stood in the void
> Of my desire, and was enjoyed,
>   For you were part of it.

He faintly foreshadows, too, what is to come:

> On many a mightier shield than mine
> Your quartered arms shall they design
>   Who keep the heraldic scrolls
> Of Art; but though the future paints
> You in the list of their All Saints,
>   You will not scorn All Souls?

Now, in the holiday period of summer 1926 Charles carried forward his feeling for the living of a common life and the doing of a common work under a common head in *An Urbanity,* eight pages of light couplets written by himself as Tityrus to Phyllis as Phillida upon the absence on holiday of five of their colleagues from 'The Court'. Names were chosen for their friends, Caesar of course for Humphrey Milford, and, for the others, names chosen mostly from Virgil's *Eclogues* and often used in English seventeenth-century masques: Dorinda for Helen Peacock, Alexis for Gerry Hopkins, Colin for Fred Page, and Menalcas, 'the sudden comet of the Court' for Norman Collins, who flashed briefly through Amen House before he left for a wider world. The verse pictures these same powers in their holiday settings, happily forgetting those left behind, who were given no names but initials and blanks. It glances at Whitehead on time and place, at Arnold on noble renouncing and resignation, the contemporary peril of getting the sack, and goes on to consider the staff left at work.

> If we had chanced to make mankind,
> Phillida, we should have inclined
> To limit the chief types to seven
> (since music hath its separate heaven)-
> these five and us two, what remains

worth creation's growing-pains?
look round the House, say, what beside,
if you were God, could you abide?
and yet they are, our life they share,
Phillida, they are moving there;
they are not dreams (or so are we).
He made them then? ah mystery!
He made them? yes, that sigh subdue,
He made them—AND HE LOVES THEM TOO.

The stuff was irresistible. It was printed and rapidly passed round
Amen House. The more people enjoyed it the more he delighted to write
it. Besides his day's work, his lectures, private reading, his home life, he
poured out sparkling light verse which needed no more occasion than
someone dropping a pile of books or Phillida leaning over the banisters,
Caesar writing his name, or himself arriving in time. His verse shook off
its turgid or florid encumbrances without losing fire. Darkness was
purged, and the old humour of schoolboy days shone through again, yet
always he was as some watcher of the skies, in communication with live
ideas and final ends.

No one can say when Charles first began to be aware that he had
stepped into a new world, or when his passion first broke through his
secrecy, though surely it took many months. There were few official reasons why Phyllis and he should meet. He could go down to the Library
briefly to check an edition or reference for the work piled on his desk. She
was not able to leave the Library for any length of time, with the telephone
to answer, staff coming in with queries, and accessibility of the books to
strangers coming in from the front door and waiting room. Sergeant on
the door kept an eye on visitors and also on absences of the Librarian.
There was no question of meeting after working hours, because she had
to go home: her father had become an invalid and her mother needed help.
The household was concentrated on care and nursing, and after having
been out all day Phyllis had to do her share in the evenings. At the same
time that Charles's spell was growing over himself and over her, she was
unable to go to his lectures or to be away from Amen House for much
more than a lunch hour.

Late in 1926 Phyllis's father died of tuberculosis. She was therefore
freed in the evenings and began to attend Charles's lectures, though for the
time being she went on living with her mother in Wandsworth. In his
lectures, the startled perception, the expansion of mental grasp, the pon-
dering and delight, could well have precipitated the natural development

between the two. Phyllis knows that it happened in 1926-7. She has identified *The Century*, a group of a hundred poems to her, as written in that time. Part by poetry and part by content they trace a growth of love, knowledge and pain.

> Never again, till time itself be ended,
> shall we by such a year of grace be friended.

The first-known letter to Phyllis was written soon after *An Urbanity*, 1–3 August 1926[4], when she was away, a cheerful friendly letter telling her that Milford delighted in his new poem on Miss Peacock in a bad moment, 'Ad Pavonem Iracundum' (To the Wrathful Peacock). He remarks on marriage, and on *Outlines of Romantic Theology*. 'Why has the Church gathered to itself so many detestable creatures all professing to adore Love—our burning and angry and terrific lord!' He has a mild feeling for a dozen people, has pledged devotion to one; he has affection for two, of whom she is one.

The second letter is dated 27 December 1926,[5] three weeks after a cry to John Pellow that nothing has happened to him and Florence but domesticities. He, she and young Michael were spending Christmas with his parents and Edith at St. Albans, and he wrote to Phyllis. It is not a love-letter. Part of his pleasure in her, he writes, is part of hers in him, that he has never pretended anything, and has shown more of himself to her than to any. He is aware of his central self-concealment, in which silent depths—of neither oblivion nor refusal—lie his religious and psychic development. She has talked to him of her gloom at four days of Christmas with her family, and her guilt at the gloom. On Christmas Day, after Michael has had his Christmas presents, Charles is aware of a 'slight interior boredom' which he suggests is a hint of significance to man and is to be recognized as such. All true life is the discovery of platitudes. The intellect realizes sharply at times what it ought to have known all along. One ought not to use words like 'great' or 'small' about God. The core of Christmas is neither small or great. Hymns, sermons and so on should not announce the greatness of God. The most dangerous time of boredom is directly after devotion. Mental overthrow is most likely then. (So in *Romantic Theology* he mentions that Christ's temptations came directly after his baptism and recognition by the voice from heaven). The notion of 'getting good' from prayer, church, communion, is damaging; one collapses to the opposite and then says 'What is God about?' and decides against the effort. One's return from such experiences should be to a point more interior than the start.

One cannot say when his passion for Phyllis, clearly existing early in 1927, first broke through his secrecy. It is likely that he contained it for months, even that it contained itself until she had begun to withdraw from its scope and its involvements. For in the wings, the cast of another play was gathering. In 1927 Phyllis's mother sold her house. Phyllis and her brother Gerald were now on their own, and took rooms in a boarding house, Lancaster House in Upper Bedford Place off Russell Square, a busy, working, literary centre of London. Here they met a young man, Billie Somervaille, who was studying for his final examinations for company secretary and aiming at employment with an oil company in Java.

Williams's passion, his feeling for Milford, for Amen House and for his colleagues, and the new-found efflorescence of his light verse, combined to produce *The Carol of Amen House*, for which Hubert Foss wrote the music, and then the first of the masques, of which it became a part.

In the *Carol* it all bursts out of him:

> Over this house a star
> Shines in the heavens high . . .
>
> .   .   .
>
> Beauty desired and dreamed,
> Followed in storm and sun,
> Beauty the gods have schemed
> And mortals at last have won.
>
> Beauty arose of old
> And dreamed of a perfect thing,
>
> .   .   .
>
> Where the world shall be made anew,
> For the gods shall breathe its air,
> And Phoebus Apollo there—through
> Shall move on a golden stair.
>
> .   .   .
>
> Shakespeare in utmost night
> Moved on no other quest
> Than waits him who reads aright
> Edition and palimpsest.

O'er the toil that is giv'n to do,
O'er the search and the grinding pain,
Seen by the holy few,
Perfection glimmers again.
O dreamed in an eager youth,
O known between friend and friend,
Seen by the seekers of truth,
Lo, peace and the perfect end!

Some light word sparked off a Masque of Amen House, a light play which would include some of the characters of *An Urbanity*'s along with others. Charles was to write it, Hubert Foss to compose the music. Instead of the love or morality of the traditional masque, this would have as theme the inspirations, aims and tensions of writing and publishing books.

For the first time Charles was engaged upon a work of poetic creation with a woman with whom he had affinity, who looked to him as magister, dominus, and for whom he could create a character to speak his best lines. Gerry Hopkins designed the costumes, which were home-made by the cast, and rehearsals were in Hubert's room, where Phyllis remembers Charles declaring that she was the worst actress he had ever seen.

The Masque of the Manuscript[6] was performed in the Library, with the stage at the Warwick Square end and the audience at the desk end, on 28 April 1927 (in honour of Sir Humphrey Milford's birthday), before an invited audience. It seeks to show doubly the process of publication of a manuscript and the pursuit in all proper work of a perfect end. The scene is the Library, the place of good effort and happiness. Every book on its shelves is the author's attempt to present his glimpse of a perfect End, and to follow its way. Among them move the personalities of the *Masque,* at once greater than the books as working in their vision and lesser as still struggling, not yet having achieved.

So delicately, so deeply, Charles speaks from his experience of religion, love, the Grail myths, and work at Amen House. The Editorial, Production, Sales and Music departments are ministrants in the service of mortal pursuit of immortal, timeless perfection, and the Librarian is portress of the whole and of the detail. The verse is an apposite shifting blend of middle with low, and matching of vowels and consonants with alteration of speed.

The cast comprised the Introducer (Charles Williams), the Master of the Music (Hubert Foss), Phillida (Phyllis Jones), the Manuscript (Nina

Condron*), Dorinda (Helen Peacock), Alexis (Gerard Hopkins), Colin
(Fred Page) and a Singer.

The occasion is Milford's birthday:

Joy—
Wandering one autumn day about our minds,
Met with a chance and high-fantastic thought,
And for some season of pure nonsense sought—
Twelfth Night or Shrovetide or what carnival
Of private honour levels with them all,
Caesar, the praise of fair months made your own
In this imperial and sacred throne.
Since still such thought and fantasy endures,
Missing God's birthday, let it fix on yours.

The theme is joy in the work done at Amen House under Milford's
headship:

But since by you and in this house at least
Joy hath not wholly ended, nor surceased
From labour, nor from anger (if such be),
But makes a glad and perfect memory
Mixed with some worth of every day's employ.

And as Bottom, Snug and Quince made offerings to their Duke,

so we to ours;
As he to theirs, be tender to our powers.
If it amuses, well; if not, forgive,
And bid your children and your liegemen live.
In this fifteenth and happiest year of grace†
Let our Birth Night solemnity have place.

The Library is introduced:

The books upon the shelves
Sing sweetly by themselves

---

*Nina Condron left the Press soon afterwards. I never met her, but Phyllis says she was a delightful
person, a good young member of staff who had joined the Press only for a short time.
†Milford became Publisher, head of the London business of the Oxford University Press, in 1913,
so 1927 was his fifteenth year in office.

and Phillida the librarian follows,

> Lo, fairer than her books
> She rules them by her looks.

Phillida opens the action, speaking as the Delphic symbol buoyed by the sea of knowledge and time in the books of the Library

> As if an African and warrior maid
> Rode through the waters with her people, stayed
> On some huge hippopotamus's back
> Fabled divine.

After the Wandsworth suburb, a girl's school and college, close family life, she has reached marvellous regions, and she is responding and opening.

A Manuscript arrives at Amen House and is shown into the Library. She dances twice round the room before stopping opposite Phillida.

> Is this then the place of achievement, the end of the waiting,
> The portal of freedom, the high city's final ungating?
> Am I come at the last to the house of all holy indwelling,
> Where is peace for desire, and the time for the printing and selling?

Phillida asks her name.

> To fill up a certain *lacuna* my aim,
> I am called *A Short Treatise on Syrian Nouns*
> *As used in the Northern and Sub-Northern Towns*
> *In Five Hundred B.C., with two maps and three charts:*
> *By Walter* Lackpenny, poor Master of Arts.*

Phillida examines the manuscript, in dismay.

> What are these bandages?
>   Corrections.
>   These?
> Additions.
>   These long tails?
>   Appendices.
> Alas, unfortunate!

---

*Walter after Charles's father.

Phillida knows what Production and Publicity will say. Nevertheless, she telephones them and cajoles them to come to the Library. They agree that the Manuscript is hopeless. But in antiphonal verse they fall out between themselves in rivalry of each department's importance, and Phillida is able to delay their decision. They call in Colin, who has to leave Samuel Johnson and Jane Austen, and enters to a new motif.

> You disturb and distract me from Samuel and Jane;
> O quickly release me! I hanker again
> For clues in the watermark, clues in the grain.

All examine, correct and tidy up the Manuscript, and present her to Caesar who signifies assent. She is placed on a bier in darkness and prepared for death.

The Manuscript emerges from darkness as a book, and Phillida welcomes her to the Library, 'Among the happiest places upon earth'. Dorinda warns Phillida not to lose the Library copy because there will be no other.

> No more, child: none. How many would you have?
> We print few copies of a book so grave—
> A score or so; some fifteen for reviews
> which the instructed Magians shall peruse;
> For Caesar one; one for your Library,
> Six for the others; one for the Author (free);
> And one in case—such things have been before—
> A customer should want one. What needs more?

Phillida exclaims there should be traffic, desire for commerce, for the gods to be glad that a new light should shine where darkness was. Colin of purer knowledge replies:

> None; 'tis the glory of the Absolute
> Not to deny, encourage, or dispute;
> But to himself to be himself displayed;
> Of whom herein we are a little shade.

And so with solemn music and an Epilogue, the *Masque* ends.

For Charles, the year 1927 was as the pageant of the Earthly Paradise in Dante's *Purgatorio,*[7] renewal, ecstasy, poetry and love. A student at the evening institute classes saw him and Phyllis walking along the road edge towards the building, 'and a radiance rising round them into the air, almost a golden mist'.[8]

He was also able to be on good terms with his family and in-laws. One of the few glimpses of his relations with Michal's family is at Christmas 1927.[9] He writes from St. Albans that while young Michael is being put to bed he will go and talk to his father-in-law, because Mr. Conway wants to talk about the budget. 'What a lot of people understand the Budget! Are Alexis and I unusual?' His father-in-law does the talking, 'while doing some paper hanging'. Charles is amazed at such a hobby. 'As if I should ever want to hang paper on walls! Or discuss the Budget—which I find my own father is yearning to do! Bless them'.

The Masque of Perusal, presented in the Library on 8 February 1929, is darker in colour, for the joy of his opening love for Phyllis had been overtaken by its pain, and the gaiety of the shared work of Amen House by something personal, less spontaneous and more strained. It has the new theme of the Graal (so Charles spelled it then), and the incarnation in the Graal's ritual of each virtue in writing and publishing. The Manuscript is replaced by the Book, afterwards the Thought. The Introducer, still Charles, is now called Tityrus (the name carried forward from *An Urbanity*).

The Book sighs and complains that it is a year since she was published,

> Since I was slain and raised and stationed here,
> And no-one has looked at me or needed me,
> And I wonder why I ever was brought to be.

She clamours for an answer from these masters of publishing. They all give unfeeling replies. She foresees herself second-hand, 'thrown and battered in a dingy shop'. Dorinda answers coldly,

> Be pulped then, being still more unwanted. Die.
> What man endures, that think'st thou to put by?
> *Alexis:*   Book, you are proud; what more would you be at?
> *Book:*   Not death, not life, but meaning! Tell me that!
> *(A complete silence)*

They fall back on routine, but Thought enters and the action becomes resultingly disordered. The curtains are drawn at last, and open again on Phillida in chains, blindfolded, Colin talking in Latin, Alexis demanding more and more books about less and less. The Thought wrestles with Alexis who is determined to make a book of it no matter what the thought is about:

The Thought:	Why do you publish?
Alexis:	Why? why not
The Thought:	By the dark slime where all shall rot,
	Why do you publish?
Alexis:	Why? why? why?
	As long as enough people buy!
The Thought:	By the sad lists that thicken so,
	Why do you publish?
Alexis (miserably):	I don't know.
The Thought:	What serves the Graal?
Alexis (falling down):	Alas, I fail,
	I care for nothing but the sale.

Colin tries to cure the dispair with clichés. The Thought fiercely demands of him, 'What serves the Graal?' and Colin collapses on top of Alexis. The Thought rushes to Phillida and cries, 'I break the chains: I cry, What serves the Graal?' Phillida replies, 'I answer: labour and purity and peace'. They all begin to escape from tumult and darkness, to recover lucidity. Dorinda cries out on 'you qualities of action', 'you fair proprieties', to be

>   as a light
> Wherein the steady hand begins to write
> What doing out of being hath required—

They all begin the Procession of the Graal, each respectively carrying ink-pot, pen, type, paper, periodicals. In turn they sing a chant:

> See the high arch once agen
> Flung from brink to earthly brink—
> As the Spear is, is the pen;
> As the Chalice is the ink;
> In each study, rhyme and tale
> Shine the hallows of the Graal.

> When the moment, rounded ripe,
> Speaks significance of worth,
> As the spirit is the type
> And the paper as the earth;
> Printing, publication, sale:
> Lo, the hallows of the Graal.

> Hark the summons to the wide
>   Periodical reviews;
> Hark the holy mystery cried,
>   Through the tumult of the news;
> Telegraph and post and mail
> Bear the hallows of the Graal.

Here, in *The Masque of Perusal,* are statements of a theology of work, as seen within Amen House and under Milford. Indeed, from the point where Phillida tells the Thought to question the staff why they work, the verse moves with a rare and exhilarating immediacy. All the masques exhibit this, something clearly different from the poetry in Charles's four published books of verse. At the time no one thought of it as more than an ephemeral delight, but fifty years later the masques seem valid still.

This was 1929 and Phyllis, he knew, had begun to slip from him. How could it not have been? She was ready to be interested, to give time to go to lectures for a while, but she had her life to make. He wrote one more masque, *Of the Termination of Copyright,* which 'owing to various hindrances' was neither acted nor printed. It was written for his own poetic need out of his own pain. The joy, the new wonder, the perfect end are there within, for he knew that these were true, sure and lasting, however one's own experience of them had been true, destructive and fleeting.

It is, consciously, the last of the series, and Tityrus as Introducer looks forward to the re-creation in other times and places of what has been known at Amen House:

> Hail to the Sacred Throne! And to you all,
> gallant companions, gathered in this hall
> for the conclusion of the brave employ
> when we became inheritors of joy,
> and a new wonder in the world was made
> since Caesar was not harsh nor we afraid;
> which if—who knows?—another century view
> shall we not live in other centuries too?
> in other houses have, through other years,
> heirs, sequences, successors, rivals, peers?

The scene opens in

> the soft interior of the Muses' heaven,
> where is the shadow of the perfect end
> and final judgement.

Here are Alexis, Dorinda, Colin, Phillida, Thyrsis (the Master of the Music) and a new character, Perigot, the herald of the gods. They consider together the book upon the Syrian noun, and find it had 'been written with a perfect will', was 'the cause and mother of high thought'. They therefore decide that, now out of copyright, it must be re-published. Their decision that

> the council of the gods decree
> to this good work full immortality,

is told to its patron, Tityrus, who must now resign all claim to it:

> Thou shalt be unknown.
> Not thou from it but it from thee is grown.

Perigot is then sent down to earth to find a copy, for those remaining

> (by loss, by wasting, or by fire
> are spoiled), and bring her to the holy house
> wherein a mortal publisher yet avows
> the Muses' service.

The scene changes to a wretched second-hand bookshop, in which the same godly characters are shown as humans gone to seed in the midst of untidiness and squalor. Thyrsis comes in with a sackful of books to sell, among them *Syrian Nouns*. Dorinda buys them all for five shillings, with Thyrsis saying sadly

> Ah! it wasn't like this long ago
> when that girl sold it me.

Perigot enters. The stage direction says that he comes 'putting the heavy air aside', like the young man John in converse with Gregory Persimmons in Chapter XI of *War in Heaven*. He asks for *Syrian Nouns*. Phillida, making up to him as at least a personable man, sells him for two shillings what he is there

> to redeem—at what price man may ask—
> the soul that duteously hath wrought its task.

Having bought the book, Perigot offers the staff each one's heart's delight. Alexis asks for the winner of the three o'clock race, Dorinda for the surest book to stock and sell, Colin for the one word missing from his crossword. Phillida doesn't know. Perigot insists, so she says vaguely, 'A little happiness and joy and peace'. Perigot gives correct answers to the first three, which they don't attempt to take seriously—this was how Charles himself saw so many people's attitude to religion. Perigot then tells Phillida,

> Between the worlds of godhead and of man
> another, less and more than either, lies,
> the way from exile into Paradise;
> there the immortals, though not wholly fair,
> know themselves better than they do elsewhere
>
> .   .   .
>
> there Caesar is and there are Caesar's friends.

and asks her, 'Maiden, to such doom art thou well resigned?' She cries,

> I will be all that they will have me be.
> O take and lift me to that ecstasy.

Then all cry,

> Have then thy will! Take on another past,
> expect another future, and stand fast;
> lift up thy heart to be called Caesar's friend.
> World of redemption, world of light, descend.

'The Carol of Amen House' recalls beginnings in the first masque; it recalls also 'peace and the perfect end'. The scene changes back to the Library, where Phyllida has been dreaming. Alexis comes seeking the file copy of *Syrian Nouns,* for Caesar wants the book to consider for reprinting. She replies that she hasn't a copy.

> It was sold—yes, I remember now—long ago
> I recall the face, but not in every feature,
> Of the man who bought it from me—a charming creature.

Much hand wringing at Caesar's anger follows, until Perigot enters with a copy. An estimate is asked for, whence follows a hectic and, to publishers, accurate, song of two verses by Alexis and Dorinda in which a cast-off (the necessary word count) is done.

Much lighthearted publishing leg-pulling follows, before it is revealed that Caesar has had an order for *Syrian Nouns* from the Foreign Office and the French government, and Dorinda murmurs,

> At times I'm on the brink
> of almost—*almost*—venturing to think
> the Presence* has a touch of worldly guile.

It is discovered that more than one copy is needed for republication, and Phillida is set to copy it out. Redeemed, she does not dodge the task, but says:

> And in the good time of the perfect end
> me of this charge may their high grace acquit.
> Here at my work, here on my watch, I sit.

A song follows of the vision all have seen, and Tityrus then hails the golden age, once on Tiber's banks, now on those of Thames. He cries

> But how can even beatitude endure,
> in spirits yet incapable of heaven,
> unless some aid, some word of help, be given?
> Tell us, you voices, ere you pass away,
> what star above this threshold shines to-day?

They cry that the star is of all the activities of their work and that its name is Love. Phillida is given the last line of the action, 'Love, beauty, joy; peace and the perfect ending'. Then Tityrus before the curtain speaks of the Library:

> with what of heavenly Love once entered here,
> which does not wholly die or disappear,
> but, being itself transmuted beyond thought,
> leaves memory with its old perfection fraught.

When he rises, the curtains open to reveal an empty stage. In anguish he cries, 'Where are the presences, and where the sound?' He turns then to invoke Caesar to recall the 'blessed Company' of the masques:

*Caesar (Milford).

> You graced the first beginning; now befriend
> with like beneficence the accomplished end.
> The tale is done; receive it and allow.
> Receive it, Caesar, for the end is now.

Formerly, at the end of each masque he has knelt to Caesar: this time he does not, but goes swiftly out. A vision has been celebrated in 'To A Publisher', in 'An Urbanity', in the Carol and the three masques. He has seen how earthly work in a City office can be related to the pattern of deity, Caesar, human and divine, the Graal and the Muses' heaven. He has offered it and now asks for it to be received, for he has said all he had to say: 'the end is now'.

Indeed it was. Phyllis never read or saw this third masque. Years later, in 1935, Williams wrote to her in Java (when he was staying a night with Dr. Bell, Bishop of Chichester, working on Bell's *Life of Randall Davidson,* later Archbishop of Canterbury): 'I have prayed (say they!) three times for you in Chichester; once, years ago, in the Cathedral while, at your wish, I wrote the Third Masque . . . and now again in the chapel . . . dear, best, truest, truest, truest. O how your head shone!'[10] At the time of their production it was thought that the masques were only for one time and one group; but when in 1955 the first two were staged at St. Anne's, Soho, London, with Geoffrey Cumberlege, the then Publisher, as Caesar but with none of the original casts, they were enjoyed.

At his office desk, Charles was at this time supervising the Centenary (1928) edition of Tolstoy's works, which was being edited by the difficult Aylmer Maude. Each volume had an introduction by a well-known, and therefore often temperamental or eccentric, author—Bernard Shaw, H. G. Wells and Rebecca West among them—and with each of these Charles had to cope. The Press was also represented at two Tolstoy exhibitions in that year.

Probably in 1929, he wrote to Phyllis, 'What a year! I don't really go back much—or only rather vaguely—before the end of last June. And the first Tolstoy. And then the . . . lecture. And the second Tolstoy.[11] Do you remember offering to take me to 'The Ghost Train'? Yes, you liked me a little then. But instead I took your arm—which to me was much like a weekend at Brighton—and we talked about Almighty God . . . it was only the second time in my life I had taken—even so remotely as that—a woman's arm. And certainly certainly only the second time that the idea of kissing her had crossed my mind—as it did at Victoria. And took four months to eventuate, blessed be He! . . . All is but a prelude. We begin something new—and that also is a prelude. Will next year be sharper, sadder, but as precious as this past?'[12]

Another letter of that time was still thinking of the happiness. Did she remember the Adelphi? 'I told you there once that you'd gathered up and transmuted and saved me from everything that had been unsatisfied'. He remembered how sweetly 'you said softly "I'm glad". . . . London's full of such places. O either side of Euston too, and many other streets. . . . Haven't you broken down every barrier between me and bliss? O my saint, my hero, my beauty. All the physical intercourse in the world is nothing to your single action. What's a drug away from you is the elixir of life with you. . . . Ingenuity—one of the things you, and only you, freed in me. You blessed ingenuity and gave it back to me redeemed: "the kingdoms of this world became the kingdoms of our Lord and of his Christ."'[13]

By then he had made his beginning as poet, playwright, critic, novelist and theologian. Yet 'The Dolorous Strokes [fell] on him day by day'[14] as the nature of redemption began to enter him. Was his discovery of love in Phyllis different from his discovery of it in Florence? His marriage and his poetry (all the published poetry up to and including *Windows of Night* is Florence's), and also his letters to Alice Meynell and John Pellow show the first discovery. At the time of his death Florence destroyed his letters to her, except those written during the Second World War, 1939–45. More evidence may yet come to light, but a serious look can be taken at what we have.

In Florence he found what all youth seeks and not all understand when they have found—a microcosm of reality. The physical, spatial creation was related to her, in detail and in purpose. So were the qualities of the creating purpose and love, and some of the means, as the act in religion and the word in poetry and art. *The Silver Stair* tells us this. Far more than just the relationship between them was carried visibly at some moments, when he saw in act or motion the authority of all act, all motion. This validity modulated every moment from awe to ease, but did not prevent sin or quarrels. The body—hers and his—and sexual love and life in it, were of primal value. By 1925, at thirty-nine years old, and fifteen years into the life of love, his powers and range had enormously developed, though not necessarily changed. The same was true of Florence, however she may have limited her development to the son Michael. One, or both, had failed to practise renewal in marriage. Small changes, new beginnings between them, had not been brought in or had failed to grow. Development in Charles had far outstripped his home relationship, although he may not have brought this into focus.

At his new level of development, he came into daily contact with a very able young woman who desired to learn new ways, new minds. She was indeed willing to learn, though not to be persuaded. This distinction he did not discover at first, though accurately later. At first, she desired to know and enter into all the new lives of Amen House. Unprofessional, not commercially trained, she was as new to them as they and their familiar life to her. Not Charles alone was affected.

He gave her the name Phillida in *An Urbanity* and then in the masques, by which the whole firm knew her ever since. But he discovered the new level of relationship with her personality in a new name, Celia. This derives from the Latin *coelum* meaning sky, heaven, and developing into the late Latin plural *coeli,* heavens; as in the Coelian Hill, on which the oldest church of Christ in Rome is built, St. John Lateran. 'Celia' has lasted as long as 'Phillida' and been translated into literature as the Celian moment. Celia means the capacities for good, for love, purity, intelligence, the instinct for deepening these capacities, for inspiring and enlightening its world. When he knew moments of these in her, towards himself or towards others, she was Celia and he named her so in his verse and considered her so in his mind and heart. When she was a young thing all could get on with, argue with, she was Phillida. In reading poetry, when he came on a rare line, a phrase, that gave the authority of its form in a new meaning to its own and other poetry, it was a Celian moment, as he used it in his Introduction to *The New Book of English Verse*. So did he in *The Silver Stair,* when he saw in an act or motion of Florence the authority of all act and motion. The Celian moment was more developed and commanded a wider range.

For Phyllis, however, Charles's Celian moments and poetic development were not the whole of life. She became restless and, not lacking courage, told him of her desire for change. He replied in a long and key letter: 'I don't know why, Celia, my child, it should, by a bad light and with lectures and poems and Samson and Palgrave to be attended to, give me pleasure to begin writing to you—at least, I do. It is the flight of the human mind to any kind of retreat from the conviction that it's utterly worthless. And Palgrave etc., merely accentuate the feeling. . . . We might talk about it a little—yes? Namely—this jolly old change of yours.

No—I don't know that I noticed it myself . . . But that your normal appearance and charm would explain . . . No, I reckon, effectively, from Tolstoy—the first Tolstoy[15]. . . . I don't think you will change to me until estrangement comes inevitably. O yes it does, bless you, sooner or later: except by a miracle. Well, vive Dieu! let us believe in a miracle. So I do, ten per cent, but not the other ninety. But, Celia mia, I don't mean anything bitter or angry or evil by estrangement. As indeed I needn't tell you, who know already one of the first conditions of the Way. If in ordinary things, death or marriage, and when I say this I mean romantic love accepted as Destiny—not destiny, or journeys or the mere lapse of time close much delight, how should not the real death and the final betrothal and the longest journey, but not, certainly not, the mere lapse of time there! But that you did notice a change I find it possible to believe. Separation and distance and differently maturing minds partly, of course, but not altogether.

It isn't knowing me. God forbid; in fact, He did. But it may be—I don't know—that your mind *has* rather been in a forcing-house these last few months or so. After all, no-one can even begin to think about (yes, they're both wanted) half the things we have talked of during that time without being a little deflected . . . Thought, interior enquiry, a real consideration? . . . my dear, you can't begin to think of it without allowing all kinds of possibilities which simply don't occur to people at all'.

The two of them existed in Amen House 'in a world where things are done and said and known . . . no question is ruled out and poetry is a normal thing and religion recognized as a normal fact, not an abnormal, and employers are cultivated and equal with you . . . it is a right and just world—not the last place nor within universes of it perhaps, but (in a way) its image'. The letter goes on that when he wrote the sequence of poems he called the Dianeme Poems[16] he wanted—not to present a crisis or propagate an accepted morality, but to discover the principle of that morality. Intellectual (therefore of course a limited) curiosity rode him. But this curiosity did not very largely exist among the people of the world. From such an interior occupation, from hints of a further concern more important than all, 'can you turn to share completely in the games and delights of the world?' He thinks not. ' . . . some difference has opened; another kind of self-consciousness'. A paradox of life is 'that, until everything is given up, nothing can be really known; nor anything found until all is lost'.[17] No one can say he did not try. But he has passed out of Broceliande, the place of making. He could not keep her. Poor man he thought this was his tragedy. Nothing prepared him for his real pain. He found in a few months that though he had lost her she would not leave him. As sexual intercourse or the study of their naked bodies had never[18] come into their relationship, there was no measurable beginning or end. His geological study of the body as a microcosm of the earth, the flesh, blood, circulation under the skin, bones holding the flesh, might have been diverted by sex—or might not. He was contemporary. Edith Sitwell, his younger by one year, wrote of

> the anguish of the bone
> Deserted by all love.[19]

He knew of no future development. Like his own Cranmer, 'the way he treads is turning into a rope',[20] which has bound him but does not yet begin to constrict him.

Her letters to him he put in an envelope addressed to Fred Page, in case of his death.[21] We know no more of them than this.

5

'Great Crooked Crags, Cruelly Jagged'

Within the Press, Charles and Fred Page handled the London firm's general literary output. What remained of the specialist departments, music, medical and the rest, had been separated out. From 1926 Ralph Binfield became their assistant, indexer and also runabout to the British Museum Library when it was necessary to check copy against the original text.

Charles read authors' manuscripts and gave H. S. M. his opinion of them. If one was accepted, he re-read it to raise queries with the author, corrected inconsistencies, misspellings and bad grammar, prepared the preliminary pages, and saw it through the printing stages, which at that time were three, galley, page and final revise. When the printed, bound and jacketed book finally appeared on his desk, he would sigh, push it into his shelves, and wait for H. S. M. to find a misprint in the Publisher's copy.

Much of the Press's output was reprint work: sets of good-selling classic authors like Dickens, or series such as the World's Classics or the Oxford Standard Authors. These Charles edited and proofread as new editions were called for, and also suggested new titles. Sometimes he had to find outside authors to write introductions (as he did for the Centenary edition of Tolstoy), or else do them himself, often in co-operation with the Clarendon Press staff at Oxford. Because of this editorial work over many years, in addition to his own interest, Charles had read the whole of Dickens, Scott, Thackeray, Tolstoy and Trollope (for the World's Classics), together with Shakespeare, Milton, Wordsworth, Byron, Blake, Keats,

Swinburne, the two Brownings, Tennyson and Hopkins, as well as the Bible and the Book of Common Prayer.

His editor's letters varied delicately with the work and style of the recipient: it was in this capacity that he wrote to A. E. Housman, saying that he had recently read his 'Introductory Lecture before all sorts of faculties at University College in 1892', and going on to suggest that, as the Press had begun to publish Robert Bridges's prose, it would like to consider Housman's also. 'It is not for me to praise Mr. Housman, but perhaps I may suggest that the qualities of your mind and style are the precise qualities of which at present men are very much in need; and that this republication would be a definite act against chaos and looseness and mess and in favour of strength and intellect and lucidity'.[1]

Robert Bridges, Poet Laureate since 1913, had spoken of Williams as a 'great living English poet' and 'by far the most interesting of the younger English poets'.[2] Bridges had previously edited G. M. Hopkins's poems, and when a new edition was proposed, agreed to Charles writing a critical introduction, an important step for him.

His perception of Hopkins's poetry comes from his own soul, that Hopkins was not, like Swinburne, 'the child of vocabulary, but of passion'. 'The very race of the words and lines ... present their unity and their elements at once'. 'For all the art of impulse and rush ... it is very evident that the original impulse was to most careful labour as well as to apparent carelessness'. As for wilder images, 'Such things are the accidents of genius seriously engaged upon its own business'.[3] In that last comment Charles describes himself also and speaks foreknowingly of his own future in writing of Hopkins's relation to Milton—their imaginations felt the universe divided within and without them while they recognized a single control.

He had to search for editors for prose and verse anthologies, or at times edit them himself. In 1925, for instance, the head of Amen House's Education Department had written to Oxford about a proposed anthology of Victorian narrative verse, that there was no need to engage an outside editor, 'Williams will do just as well'; and Oxford agreed, 'Yes, Williams can handle it as well as anybody'.[4] This job included the troublesome seeking of authors' permissions to use their poems, and the writing of notes and an introduction suitably adjusted to the needs of, for example, the Indian publishing branch of the Press, for whom it was being produced. Having suggested the abridgement of Sir Edmund Chambers's two-volume standard life of Shakespeare[5], he then did it in 1931-2 for the Clarendon Press.[6] He participated also in the publication of such reference books as Harvey's *Oxford Companion to English Literature*, (1932), the idea of which arose out of talk in his own office, and the later *Oxford Dictionary of Quotations*.

Though his deep knowledge of English poets and dramatists went back to Chaucer, he read modern poetry keenly, had contacts through his work with poets, and now began to meet them. Lady Ottoline Morrell, the well-known hostess, invited him to her literary parties at which he met T. S. Eliot, a fellow publisher at Faber's. Eliot indeed told Lady Ottoline of his pleasure at the meeting—perhaps he had suggested to her that Charles be invited.

In 1930, after thanking Eliot for a promised book introduction, Williams wrote about his recently published *Ash Wednesday:* 'It will not perhaps displease you to know that Mr. Milford and Hopkins and I all, separately and together, agreed that it seemed to suggest to us that our great-grandchildren would find it great poetry; but that by the way. Without asking for meaning or interpretation or anything, it did just occur to us to wonder whether there were any,—well, say, allusion—in the "three leopards" or the "unicorns dragging a gilded hearse" that one would perhaps be happier for recognizing. Dante or "the Forest Philosophers of India" (my God!) or anything? "Direct our eyes in the right direction", as Francis Thompson said to Patmore, "and we will see for ourselves". Or words to that effect. (We have looked at Dante, but unachievingly)'.[7]

Eliot, two years his junior, had won early success. He had formed one mould for contemporary poetry, while Charles was meditating on the Grail-Arthur myth and on Love. But in a poet's reading of Milton, or on Keats bluffing the world in 'La Belle Dame Sans Merci', or on Mrs. Browning, they were in full understanding.[8] Later, they were to go together to the production of *Hamlet* in the original full text—one of the great dramatic experiences of the 1930's.

The Press had difficulty in deciding upon an editor for its planned *Oxford Book of Modern Verse.* Lascelles Abercrombie had been first chosen but after four years had done little. Williams went to see him and, finding him ill with diabetes and unable to make the necessary decisions, himself suggested W. B. Yeats as the only editor whose name was guaranteed to sell the book. Oxford agreed, and Yeats got it out in 1936, after two years work.

Milford had by now published four books of Charles's poetry but had failed to sell them. R. W. Chapman, Secretary to the Delegates of the Press wrote to H. S. M. on 9 January 1929, 'How CAN we put CW over? Shall we try announcing him as the most unsaleable of all Oxford authors'?

Yet Milford in April 1929 published *A Myth of Shakespeare,* a verse play suggested by A. C. Ward of the City Literary Institute for a Shakespeare festival, which provided a mock-Elizabethan framework for excerpts from a number of Shakespeare's plays. 'It contains no thesis of Shakespeare's life, character or genius', Charles says in a prefatory note, 'except that he was a born poet and working dramatist. The scenes included were intended, quite mythically, to represent barely possible incidents in his life, passages read to or by his friends, or performances in his theatre'. With it Charles's unsaleability ended, for a second impression appeared in July. The *Myth* was admired by senior staff both in London and at Oxford, some of whom tried, but failed, to get it 'produced, say, as a prologue to the Stratford festival'.[9] On a different level, it got reported in the *Hertfordshire Advertiser* as 'St Albans Poet's High Adventure'.

In 1930, too, the Clarendon Press published Charles's *Poetry at Present,* sixteen essays on contemporary poets from Hardy to Blunden and Eliot, with a related poem of his own at the end of each essay. Nothing could be more tricky than to write about living poets. However, his first book of literary criticism emerged well. Housman 'says . . . that I have praised them all too much'.[10] Gibson wrote: 'I have now read all the articles with deep interest and much appreciation. I need hardly say how proud and pleased I was to find myself among the "significant" poets'.[11] Blunden spoke of 'your capital and original book . . . I am delighted with your subtly varied poetical art in expressing the qualities of the several Bards, myself included';[12] and Abercrombie said 'you have given me a splendid show . . . in a book which, in everything I *can* judge is by far the best thing of its kind I know'.[13]

Its publication by the Clarendon Press gave Williams standing as a literary critic, and as poet by juxtaposition of his own poems with essays on other poets. Moreover, it went to a second impression in 1931. Nevertheless, five years later Charles, suggesting a new edition, was to speak of 'this pathetic effort of my immaturity'.[14]

Other verse plays were written in the 1929-30 period and published in 1931 by Milford as *Three Plays.* All are presentations of the death of love, and the Arthurian poems with which they are interspersed relate to ways in which that death can be known: *The Witch,* for the Balham Commercial Institute, *The Rite of the Passion,* for the Three Hours Good Friday service of 1929 at his friend Henry Lee's London church, and *The Chaste Wanton.*

In *The Witch,* love dies uselessly, destroyed by pure evil. *The Rite* presents the Christian story dramatized as a happening in our own hearts, the endurance of death as Love's own purpose in order that the life of love might be renewed wherever needed in every human soul. In it the figure of Satan, not so much an actively malicious figure as the presentation of how evil things happen, is the forerunner of others in Charles's plays who in timelessness comment upon the play's action in time—the Skeleton in *Thomas Cranmer of Canterbury,* the Third King in *Seed of Adam,* the Accuser in *Judgement at Chelmsford,* and the Flame in *The House of Octopus.*

The title of *The Chaste Wanton,* he says 'is due, I believe, to Mr Gerard Hopkins, who dropped it casually in conversation as possible for a mock-Elizabethan play. But, before the amusement was begun, it or I had turned serious, and the title enlarged its meaning beyond its original scope'.[15]

The Chaste Wanton indeed carries in verse the vision of his love for Phyllis, its promise, its loss, and affirmation of its validity.

> This air will crystallize
> into some marvellous event; some new
> manner and mode of loving—so much good
> must find conclusion great as is itself,
> utterly past our knowledge.

This was his search in love. And when their parting comes, and she cries in his prison cell,

> I shall forget, I shall forget, the whole
> of this new life and strength!

He answers, 'Forget, but be it!'

In a letter of the time he wrote to her: 'What you have, Celia,—what you *are,* rather—is one of those curious and marvellous beings whose lure is the refusal, whose invitation is the denial, whose hand of union is the sword of separation. It is the type which hides in some of Shakespeare's boy-heroines (spiritual in you; theatrical in them). It is what I have meant by babbling about your virginal aloofness. It is, I think, not a common type (and incidentally it was always my childhood's dream, my adolescent vision). . . . Your abandonments and play do but emphasize it—but woe to the wretch who doesn't realise it. I think you might easily be, because of that, a delirium to some minds'.[16] He himself knew moments of this delirium. Yet out of it came one of his deepest thoughts. At the conclusion of *The Rite of the Passion,* when Jesus has died on the cross for love and risen again, in the last salutation comes the line, 'Yea, also this is Thou'.

His frequently-expressed meditation, 'This also is Thou; neither is this Thou', seems to have originated here.

Williams's literary output in 1930 had yet more to come. In 1925 he had written his first novel, *The Black Bastard,* and in 1926 he finished another, *The Corpse*. After they were rejected, he had put them with other manuscripts in a wooden box in his office and had tried to forget them. One day in 1929, helped by Jocelyn Harris who often typed his letters, he was having a clear-out of old papers when she noticed a script which, he said, could be thrown away. She remonstrated. He said she could do what she liked with it. So, having taken and read it, she sent *The Corpse* on his behalf to the then recently founded firm of Victor Gollancz Ltd. Victor sat up all night reading it, then accepted it, although insisting that its title be changed. His mind full of *Paradise Lost,* Charles called it *War in Heaven*. It appeared in 1930, the first of his books to be published at the commercial risk of a firm not his own. Victor wrote to Charles, '*War in Heaven* gave me a small but satisfactory profit, and a really gargantuan pleasure in the publishing of it'. He wanted another, 'as a reader and as a publisher. In fact, I itch for it, so don't delay a moment'.[17]

Norman Collins, who had left the Press to join Robert Lynd on the old *News-Chronicle*'s literary page, in 1930 started to send batches of detective novels to Charles for review. This suited him well, in enjoyment and in earnings. Detective stories were a taste he shared with Humphrey Milford.

There was also *Heroes and Kings*. Hubert Foss was connected with Henderson & Spalding, who had printed *An Urbanity* and the first two masques. The firm used the imprint of The Sylvan Press, and Foss suggested to Charles that they should bring out a new volume of verse in a limited edition.[18] Designed by Foss, with wood-engravings by Norman Janes, the eighty-page book was produced in a large-page (11¾" × 8") size on handmade paper using an 18-point Caslon Monotype face. It was bound in scarlet cloth boards, with a gold-blocked design front and back by Janes: 300 were printed and numbered, 250 of them for sale.

We may think that he had already used the best of his finished Arthurian poems in *Three Plays,* for he wrote to Phyllis, 'though the poems are not what I could have wished, still Tristram does derive from your Circassian and inscribed hands, and Lamoracke from a not unworthy fantasy of you, and the first Palomides is a lament for you, and the Percivale was written at your request, and the Taliessin is an aspiration for you'.[19] He had been searching for a method of treating Arthur otherwise than in blank narrative verse. 'And then the most happy chance by which you asked me to write to you about the Table one Saturday—and then my other poem about the Assumption of Celia—and there the method lay'.[20] 'The other poem' may be 'Taliessin's Song of the Princess of Byzantion'.

Heroes and Kings is not outstanding but contains some good poems. 'Flint Castle' is a rare one for him, a glimpse of unity in a fusion of words and landscape. It refers to Shakespeare's *Richard II,* Act III, scene iii, at

Flint Castle, and presumably to Charles seeing the castle on some visit. First, the elements were separate—air, earth and water. Then Charles says aloud Shakespeare's lines beginning

> the castle royally is manned,
>   my lord,

and a change, a fusion, grew in the elements as the

> syllables of verse unrolled.

> .   .   .

> natural as the air to verse
> grew the verse unto the air,

in the power of

> the many-heirdomed line
> the five accents half-divine
> which are England's greatest gift
> to the world.

A unity established itself in words, air, earth, ruins and water, and passed inward through his eyes, 'all their separations done'. Prospero here was finding power, not using it.

There are poems for Michal and for young Michael, as well as for Phyllis. Some of the narrative poems are surely too long. They are all still 'romantic' in the sense of being felt and written from his personal views, emotions and reactions. The advance to a deeper level of fact and vision is still to come, in *Taliessin Through Logres*.

In August 1930 Phyllis went on a riding holiday. She fell, broke her leg, and was taken to Petworth Cottage Hospital in Sussex. When the news reached Amen House, the concealed accumulation of three years' feeling broke out. Milford was distressed but calm. Charles was horrified at her pain and isolation among strangers.[21] But Gerry Hopkins—sophisticated, totally self-concealing, attractive character—revealed in his shock and distress a more deadly blow, that he and Phyllis loved each other.

For Charles, who had brought himself to relinquish her devotion and company for her need to find a life in the world of her own age, the damage can only be reckoned by his own capacity. He had known she was interested in Billie Somervaille, and with her brother saw a good deal of him.

This was an intelligible pain. But that she should turn from himself and poetry to another married man of his own age, more money and social position, a club in London, unremarkable abilities, fashionable literary judgment—this outraged both the good and the bad in him. At work, at home, in the streets, in trains, in bed, the wound burned and tore him. But as in the visions of the burning seraphs, love rose twisting, agonized, refining in the burning. Letters to Phyllis poured out of him. On 6 September 1930, the day after he heard the news of her accident, he wrote, 'Since yesterday morning I heard, my heart has been prancing like . . . like the high hills jumping. I don't mean my heart of imagination, but my literal and physical heart—more than even air-raids made it—and to such an extent that yesterday afternoon I went clean off into a kind of faint. Fortunately I was alone in the office. . . . It has made me frightfully proud to think that your injury can so strike at me (in so small a way), and I hope it may win the shadow of a smile in your eyes'. He told Fred Page and Daniel Nicholson, asked friends to write. Books, magazines were to be sent, if anything 'takes your fancy, your lovely and dear fancy, and that can be got—you will do so and "have it charged to my account", won't you? . . . It shakes and racks me to think of you, and all you bore from the fall to now, all the horrible detail, and all the time, the mere slow grinding time'.

He continued, 'At moments of crisis I can—for a second—become very nearly Christian, and when we heard from you Alexis* came up (being cautious now!) to ask if I had heard. And the notion of you, in your distress and pain and fear, having to write it all down *twice*—because you couldn't trust your lovers to behave like . . . lovers—and to leave off the natural outpouring of your most moving sorrow and love to him because you had to write to me in another kind of love—these two things distressed me . . . believe me, my dearest . . . if you are in critical times then you *must* send messages rather than give yourself *any* trouble extra. There are rare moments, darling Celia, when I know the Good and even desire it; and when I die I would not have it said of me, among the accusations, that I had interrupted anybody writing to her sweet-heart—much less you. . . . It should always be natural to Us to ask each other to do anything. After all—in the beginning and ever since—there we were! It was as near Fate as makes no difference. What were we to do but to ask one another to do things? . . . I hate sleeping while you wake. . . . O my book†—no, it hasn't come yet; only a sample binding which awed us'.[22]

*Gerry Hopkins.
†*Heroes and Kings*.

He kept down the emotional, dramatic level of the letters, knowing the fatigue of the patient. He tells her what she wants to know rather than details of his inner life. He has been to Downe House School and addressed eighty girls. He is postponing *Many Dimensions* (the novel whose Chloe is based on Phyllis); he is moving flats, to five houses away, at £125 p.a. rent instead of £80, so he must make more money, and she is not to say he must not spend any on her. Expenditure on her is necessity, not luxury. Day after day the attention went on. Her absence in Amen House, the sound of other footsteps, other voices at the door, never weakened in baleful power. He went on arranging visits to see her in hospital, sometimes with Gerry or Nicholson. He was in a turmoil or trance the next day.

What was he like at home? Moving flats must have helped, and he had always been a master at concealing his intimacies, loving or dark. But he denied nothing of the past, and forgot nothing. Three sonnets[23] written at this time, 'On Moving', treat the move as a setting for the Grail pageant. In Sonnet I he says:

> I see the cunning carriers and stout
> Bear in procession our belongings out,

He thought of Percivale who failed to question the purpose of the Grail pageant, and asks:

> Whereto serves the Grail?
> For these things are the outer mystery,
> The Holy Vessel which doth ever move
> in the care of the maiden-mother of my love.
> Watch, eyes; and question, thought.

This last line is the theme of the sequence and is repeated in each sonnet. Each person can be in his own capacities related to one of the three knights, Galahad, Percivale and Bors, who succeeded in the quest for the Grail, Bors being the married man. In Sonnet III he says:

> Being thyself their whole sodality,
> Be now, as Bors, content to watch and bless
> The pageant of the Hallows,—cups and books,
> Cushions and tables; last, her gentle looks
> Who is the centre of this business
> And sign.

He had always to recollect the terrible unity of man's life in God. He looked at his wife in these poems as he had seen her before he loved Phyllis.

Phyllis's leg failed to set and heal. Pain continued, the doctors were uncertain. One day she had a visitor, a friend from Lancaster House, who was married to a senior member of the Westminster Hospital staff. He came with his wife, and one of the Petworth doctors confided his uneasiness to him. X-rays were taken and sent to Westminster. A telegram returned authorising Phyllis to be transferred at once to Westminster Hospital. So she arrived back in London, ill and in pain after many weeks. The leg was re-set and different treatment used. She was in hospital until the end of October, when she was released to convalesce in the country before returning to work. The nearness of the hospital raised the tension in Amen House. Visits increased. One might meet anyone unexpectedly. As Charles commented,

'GH preferred not to speak of anything more than the normal friendship, since he will—in that sense—keep me at arm's length and forget the past, and pretend we are equally concerned with a distressed invalid. . . . He told me on Tuesday morning that he thought of coming, and I assented with goodwill. But it was impossible, just impossible, for me to go down on Wednesday and ask him how long and when he was coming. I'm not, really and truly I'm *not,* being silly or selfish or gloomy. I didn't shut myself up—I didn't even feel annoyed, not to speak of. . . . Alexis is a dear, and we are great friends, but we cannot occupy the same space at the same time—in any sense'.

She wrote seemingly to suggest that one of the 'young women' from his lectures might be cheering him up in her absence, for his letter goes on 'really, darling child, most exquisite irrationalist. . . . I will not ask you to compare yourself and "one of my young women" (whom, in the circumstances I am glad to be able to say I haven't had here for weeks—none of them), because you know very well that only an intellectual egotism gets any kick out the them. There is always something one couldn't bear physically. This isn't pigginess; merely difference'.[24]

Another letter links with this: 'I don't know what Michal makes of it all: there are moments when I feel I must speak of it. But more when I feel as if it had all been handed to me, so to speak, in a parcel—"do what you will, only be happy. And let it rest there; Why drag it into talk?" If it were so, I should think it wise. It is months and months since any kind of married intercourse took place—O ages. And I am not at all certain that this is not done for me. On the other hand, she may think my nature is *so,* and that's that. Only certainly all my loss of appetite and the rest was put down to your being away. Well, so it was. . . . There is no news to tell you, except that the arch of the stairs this morning was like your hand. That's new, but not news.' Fred Page sent his love. She is not to worry about Charles by day or night. 'There is no need. "I will finish the work thou hast given me to do", if and as far as I can'.[25] He added that he, having suggested her name, had secured her the job of making an index (a well-paid publishing extra).

At some unrecorded moment the inevitable happened. Fred Page told Michal of Charles's love for Phyllis, his extreme of passion, and that the firm knew about it, for Charles was living the relationship with letters, poetry and devotion. Fred had known Michal since before her marriage, when she was the dark brilliance of *The Silver Stair* and Charles was young and obscure. He was himself married, with one son, having had the same quiet home upbringing as Charles. Fred had put him in touch with Alice Meynell and so started his progress. Whether he was moved by jealousy of the Charles of 1930, or by a loyalty to the days of youth and pledges, no one knows. But the thing was done.

Michal took the news nobly. She to whom *The Silver Stair* had climbed was forced to experience it as the approach to love but not as love's glorious ascent. Charles wrote later of Page's 'devastation',[26] but at the first breaking of the news he wrote to Phyllis: 'Nothing whatever happens. Michal is exuding agape*—but under favourable circumstances . . . no; I lie. Not really very favouring. I cannot be cheerful enough to deceive—it *isn't* the word—to veil. The position is capable of outbreaks in any possible direction. I do what I can, and we haven't reopened the discussion, and *she* persists in regarding me as being good and so on to her—but I have a kind of volcanoish feeling. If agape lost hold for a moment I feel anything might happen—only nothing can. Nor (so far as I can see) can anything obliterate the fact that I committed myself to a perfectly definite. . . . However I don't like writing because the sentences don't seem to correspond with facts'.[27] Nor did they ever again, until he reached a further understanding of the depths in love.

Michal was now at least forty-four, not young, not feeling young. For twenty years poems about Charles's love for her had been published in book after book, for thirteen she had loved him and sustained the daily marriage. She had put up with sophisticated, learned and social people at the Press who meant much to Charles but little to her. She must have come to see the masques, and felt the strangeness, perhaps the danger. She may have thought Phillida a young harpy out for social advancement. At first (as he wrote in the last letter quoted) the principle of love which had been

*In Greek, 'selfless love'.

theirs held. Then the furies of middle age and helplessness broke in and made her heart, and their flat, a *doloroso ospizio,*[28] an abode of pain.

Slowly crisis became daily life, losing only the stimulus of newness. Charles had to live with the knowledge that his love had left him for a man he had to meet almost every day. Her presence was in the building; he might encounter her and Gerry at meetings or on the stairs. The knowledge of Michal's suffering was added to his own. She had lost her love and had no money to leave home with the child and make another life—even if she had thought it right. Michal, Phyllis and Gerry: each place and hour was that of the *Inferno,* 'void of all light, which bellows like the sea in tempest, when it is combated by warring winds'.[29] 'The hellish storm, which never rests'[30] drove him day and night, at each step in the passage outside his room, on the stairs, in each meeting, when he turned the key in his front-door, when the bedroom light was turned out. 'No hope ever comforts them, not of rest but even of less pain'.[31]

In his emotional and theological concerns, however, he did not lose touch with man in society, in the political and industrial affairs of the day. He must have found love exhaustingly wearisome, and welcomed the evening or morning newspaper as a relief. These were the early 1930's: the Great Slump, high unemployment and a National Government in Britain, failure of a disarmament conference in Europe, the rise of the Fascists under Benito Mussolini in Italy and of the Nazis in Germany. Then came major shocks to the status quo. In 1932 Rutherford split the atom, in January 1933 Adolf Hitler was ecstatically voted to power in Germany, and in 1934 Josef Stalin established his personal rule in Russia. Williams was greatly interested by the splitting of the atom, the basic unit as known of man's physical nature, and the study of its double character. He felt, too, that peace was increasingly in danger in a world of continuing social unrest caused by, and itself the cause of, rapid changes in society.

Writing did not ease him but it was an imperative. He would drop a sonnet on an august desk or scrappy typing table.

> Dorinda doesn't care for verse
> (not *really,* Celia), Colin's mood
> demands high poetry, not worse.
> At least he drops them back again
> quite silently, depressing doom![32]

No wonder, if Colin (Fred Page) had told Michal about Phyllis. 'On a Staff Meeting' is a glimpse of his day's work:

Celia, I listen, nurse my ankle, dream,
and watch the ash upon my cigarette.

He thinks of her and of meetings in other years when joy and hope were
in the gathering.

I meditate, while round me flows the talk
of commerce, banking, book-keeping, and French,*[33]

Phyllis would not let him altogether go. He wrote to her, 'I will contem-
plate you for hours together. I will make fantasies of others, so that I may
not make use of you. Say *dearest* again. Darling, I cling to our secret
life. . . . I drink you in by the meeting of our eyes; unless your arms clasp
me I am lost—and so are forty other people. True enough, but your letter
this morning moved me to tears'.[34]
A poem was written on the opening evening of a commercial institute,

Celia, they thunder and rush to and fro,
and stiller, as they gallop, grows my soul;

They talk of 'business economics'.

Lord,
have mercy on the creatures thou hast made;
be thou in all thy miracles adored
but be not I into such stars betrayed.
Yet all things in their motion curving back
trace equally their path unto thy end—
the wildest dream that does my brain-cells crack
and the fair sunshine of my newest friend.
Retired within my solitude I view
all, and know all are dreams and yet are true.[35]

New friends came in plenty. From Downe House came headmistress
Olive Willis and her pupil Ann Bradby (later Anne Ridler). Olive had
read some of Charles's work and invited him to speak at the school to the
senior forms. In 1930, Blake was one of his subjects and Bacon another.
She also lent one of the cottages she owned at Aisholt in Somerset to
Charles and Michal for holidays. On one of these occasions, four of her

*'French' means that Gerry Hopkins was at the meeting. As for 'meditate' I have been at meetings
where Charles seemed to be meditating, and would suddenly come out with an exact proposal.

senior pupils were with her in another cottage, and joined Charles and Michal for walks and talks which were a successful mix of pleasure and stimulus to learning. The poem 'Epilogue in Somerset', printed at the end of *Three Plays,* shows the spirit of that time. Anne, the daughter of Humphrey Milford's sister, was just about to leave school. She was deeply talented and capable, and already a poet. Charles, always willing to discuss scansion, poetic discipline or techniques with young poets, soon began a long friendship by writing to her about some comments she had made on English prosody.[36] Anne later on married Vivian Ridler, who became Printer to the University of Oxford; she has developed into a fine poet of our time. Joan Wallis came to him like Thelma Shuttleworth (who was married in 1931) via evening institute lectures. I, and later my second husband Charles Hadfield, came in by a different door, that of employment in the Press.

But Charles was not dependent on individuals. His student following, mostly (but not all) women, was a jest among the senior staff, who commented blithely on it. Referring to the union of the ways of affirmation and of rejection, he wrote 'some of this lay behind my own far-renowned Caution—or at any rate a consciousness that for me too actively to affirm anywhere would have less adequate results than both'.[37] But where he could usefully help, he did. Probably several young women dreamed that he was more absorbed in them than he was. He did not repel them but he did not need them. The danger inherent in student-admirer relationships has brought men to vanity and nothingness, but Charles had a quality that enabled him to walk in this fire and not be consumed. Many of his relationships proved indestructible and survived his own lifetime.

A letter of 28 June 1932 to Thelma Shuttleworth says that he and Michal are going on holiday: 'I shall read D H Lawrence and think out the next book'. This was to be *The English Poetic Mind.* They were also going to see the performance by the senior girls of Downe House, of his *Myth of Francis Bacon* (a very junior partner of his *A Myth of Shakespeare*), which had been initiated by Olive Willis.[38]

The previous three years must have put enormous strain upon his whole system. In the summer of 1933 he was taken suddenly ill with internal pain, rushed to hospital and operated on for what he referred to as obstruction, but was more correctly intussusception. He was seriously ill for a week and away from work for longer. In a shaky letter to Phyllis he wrote that he wanted to come to Amen House for a few moments and had asked Sir Humphrey. 'I think I shall sleep better if I see you for even a second or two. (So far as I can understand—but my brain isn't really working—

F.P.'s let off more *devastation** one way and another in the course of the
first 24 hours than one would think possible!)'[39] After he had been there,
Sir Humphrey wrote a private memo on 22 September to Kenneth Sisam
at the Clarendon Press: 'Mr Williams (pale and thin he has lost twenty-
four pounds . . . but cheerful) called this afternoon'.[40]

It must have been then that he lost the robust physique which shows in
his photographs as a young man, and became the quick, slim figure that I
remember. Once recovered, he did not ail but was energetic in voice and
walk, though the thick hair now showed a little grey. He stood well,
straight and easy, always in his familiar grey-blue suit, with black shoes
and grey homburg hat. He was—C. W.

---

*It is possible that this was the point at which Fred Page told Michal about his love for Phyllis, and
not at the time of her accident in 1930. But I think the evidence for the earlier date is stronger.

6

Five Novels

The years of putting manuscripts in the wooden box in his office had ended in 1930, when Victor Gollancz had taken *The Corpse*, re-titled *War in Heaven*, and asked for another. In June, therefore, Charles sent him *The Black Bastard*, then *Shadow* (later to be *Shadows*) *of Ecstasy*, saying 'it is only fair to warn you that it has been refused by several publishers . . . my own feeling is that I would make the alterations noted on the attached sheet, and then I think it might be quite bearable . . . I had rather not spend much time on it, nor do I think it would be much better if I did'.[1] His suggestions included cutting 'out all Mrs Considine' and the clergyman 'down to the barest need'. And in July, having had Gollancz's comments, he said 'I agree with you entirely. I think I know what is wrong with it, but I am not sure whether the book is worth putting right'.[2]

Charles laid it aside for other books. Eventually, much rewritten, he delivered it at the end of July 1932, saying 'I think this much simpler. And I'm sure it's much better than it was. It hasn't any high points, but I think the general run is fairly quick'.[3]

We do not know what Gollancz replied, but Charles then wrote 'Of course you're right. I don't care for this as much as the others—except that it was the first, the first of all the ideas in them. But I do a little wonder whether lots of people won't like it more . . . there isn't anything as obscure and supernatural in this as might put them off. After all, it could be done'.[4] *Shadows of Ecstasy* was published, the last of the five Gollancz novels, in

1933. Between it and *War in Heaven* came *Many Dimensions* and *The Place of the Lion* in 1931, and *The Greater Trumps* in 1932. Later he wrote *Descent into Hell* published by Faber in 1937, and began a novel which was never finished but he called *The Noises That Weren't There.* He mentioned it without the title in a letter to Thelma of 1940. It lingered on but he abandoned it in favour of *All Hallows' Eve* (1945), also published by Faber.

T. S. Eliot was to write of the novels: 'What Williams has to give is . . . the work of imagination, based upon real *experience* of the supernatural world, of a supernatural world which is just as natural to the author as our everyday world. And he makes our everyday world very much more exciting, because of the supernatural which he finds always active in it.'[5]

It is this finding of the supernatural in the natural that gives the novels their depth and speed, for situations and characters grow from a single concept. Situations such as the use of power by the Tarot cards, by the Stone of King Suleiman, by a possible Holy Grail, in place, time and the mind, all involve unprepared ordinary people who cope with the extremes of experience by the power that is in ordinary people, and are then made or broken. The books make an instant impact upon the reader; they are quick and enthralling, glancing sometimes at a possibility, sometimes penetrating it, and always carrying you and me and our everyday work into our origins and ends.

All five novels are akin. They all involve London, for London was to Charles the place of life, of work, of people and of things happening. In each of the five a situation develops where the qualities or abilities that people say they admire or want appear in their own social environment— philosophical principles such as strength, subtlety, innocence; or a talisman, a means of personal power, security or wealth. How would people, how would the author, react and behave? Without the ordinary limitations of physical and social life, what in fact would happen?

The situations are gripping, positive, clear and deep without obscurity. Williams uses no cynicism, and the analysis of character is accomplished in motive and action. The briskness with which the action moves shows that he enjoyed writing them. When we remember his search for a glimpse of that something other within all the actions of man, in this early 1930's period of loss when poetry was perhaps changing gear in him, the use of another medium was probably welcome. It also brought in useful money. When writing to Gollancz early in 1932, he hoped that *Shadows of Ecstasy* as well as *The Greater Trumps* would be published that year, 'In the purely financial reasons for which I write books, I was longing, and all but reckoning . . . on some possibility of those two to see me respectively through the year'.[6]

Though religion or the Christian faith are hardly mentioned, except in *War in Heaven*, the world of the novels is still the *Civitas Dei*, that is man in the city of God, as well as in the city of man. People make their own characters and by their own choices form the events. There is no function for a Superman in the *Civitas Dei*. Charles knew well the writings of William Law and later quoted in *The New Christian Year:* 'All outward power that we exercise in the things about us is but as a shadow in comparison of that inward power that resides in our will, imagination, and desires; these communicate with eternity and kindle a life which always reaches either Heaven or hell'.[7]

The first written and last published of the five novels, *Shadows of Ecstasy,* is well named. An Englishman, Nigel Considine, has become an adept in the secret transmutation of energy, so that he has lived through more than one life-span and shows no sign of aging. He is organizing an armed revolution throughout black Africa that will dominate the world, with himself as leader.

The other main characters are Roger Ingram, professor of poetry; his wife Isabel, intelligent and loving; Sir Bernard Travers, a well-known surgeon; and his son Philip who is in love with Isabel's sister Rosamund. The Zulu hereditary king Inkamasi, Caithness a priest of the Church of England, and two devout Jews who hold valuable jewels for the service of the Lord God of Israel fill out the book. All have some capacity for ecstasy, some sense of the perfect aim of their work: Roger, poetry; Philip, young love; Isabel, married love; Sir Bernard, fact; the two Jews, the Holy One of Israel; and Inkamasi, royalty. Considine will tempt them all to transmute their vision to the service of his idea, his power.

The African High Executive announces its purpose of removing all white people from Africa—the age of intellect is done and Africa must advance 'by paths which the white peoples have neglected and to ends which they have not understood'. Devotion to the arts and an exchanged adoration of love will effect the transmutation of energy and conquest of death. The High Executive has finance, arms and aircraft. Considine reveals his plans and power to Roger and his friends. For him, are Roger, Isabel and Inkamasi; doubtfully against are Sir Bernard, Caithness and the others.

African air raids on London begin. Crowds attack the old Jews' house and the jewels are stolen and brought to Considine for High Executive funds. However, one of his staff is consumed by ecstasy over the jewels. At the point of Considine's departure for Africa to take command, the man shoots him. There is a rush of action, and the book ends on an echo of Ariel's song of a sea-change.

In its rewritten form, the book's intricate action is sustained by clear, strong writing and well-planned detail. The style of Charles Williams's prose wakes action out of thought; it was an ability that made him also a dramatist. There is relation between such waking and his greater success with fictional wives than with lovers. Isabel Ingram, like Barbara Rackstraw in *War in Heaven,* are such wives as one would wish to be, loving, perceptive, practical, sustaining. Lovers give less scope for action, and thought predominates. It is often compelling, as in Philip's vision from the beauty of Rosamund, but perhaps easier to write. Charles himself was not fascinated by personalities as such, in life or fiction. His interest was in what they made of their lives, how they laboured or not to develop goodness in their own circumstances, how they noted or ignored glimpses of other worlds in what they read, heard or saw.

War in Heaven is the story of a struggle for a silver chalice which some historical evidence shows might be the Holy Grail, the cup which Jesus used for wine at his last supper with his disciples. At this gathering Jesus drank first from the chalice, and then told all those present to drink from it as his blood, sealing a new covenant with God that would bring new life for man in the forgiveness of sins. Jesus knew that he would shortly be arrested and crucified. The new life in man, however and whenever discovered, would grow from his bloodshed and death, his overcoming of death and return to a new life. This new life, and the promise of life after death, would be communicated to his disciples in the forgiveness of sins and in their eating and drinking blessed bread and wine together. The ceremony of love, death and new life became powerful in Christian worship, and also outside the Christian communities in followers of magic and occult practices. The cup itself was held to be charged with power.

In the novel, an old silver cup rests unregarded in a cupboard in the Fardles village church. Sir Giles Tumulty, archaeologist and expert in folklore, Gregory Persimmons, retired publisher and man of occult knowledge, whose son now runs a publishing firm in considerable dread of his father, and a Levantine who keeps a chemist's shop in a poor part of London, have all traced the history of the Grail to modern times and the possibility that it is in Fardles church. The rector, Archdeacon Julian Davenant, himself then picks up the trail from a manuscript in Persimmons's office, where at the book's opening a body has just been found, apparently murdered.

Attempts begin to buy, exchange or steal the chalice. Strangers break into the church, Gregory Persimmons tries to become intimate with the

Archdeacon. He lends a holiday cottage to Rackstraw, a member of his son's staff, with his wife and small son. A Roman Catholic Duke and a poet from Persimmons's staff come on the scene, and Tumulty has business with the chemist's shop. The chalice is stolen, the Archdeacon steals it back, and a car chase through the country ends in victory by a margin of minutes at the Duke's London house.

Gregory Persimmons wants a child as much as the Grail, and delights Rackstraw's small son by 'playing games' of seeing distant places and events in liquor held in the cup. Were Rackstraw's wife to be killed or paralyzed, Rackstraw would leave the boy with Gregory for a time—an opportunity for experiments with the power of the cup.

Every character in the book becomes included in the struggle for the Grail. As each person becomes more involved, his desires and instincts become stronger and clearer to him—to worship, use, possess, protect, or destroy. Only the Archdeacon more and more desires to serve the Grail in the Grail's own way of life. Police and local authorities join in. Persimmons has earlier annoyed the police, and an inspector now links his activities at Fardles with the dead man found in his son's office. The story moves to a climax in the chemist's shop, where 'everything makes haste to its doom', and the Grail's consummation in love at the celebration of Communion in Fardles with the church Grail.

The Observer wrote of the book as 'This astonishing battle between the incarnate forces of good and evil. . . . It has the elements of a great mystery story, of keen satire, and, above all, of a sweet, sorrowful apprehension of beauty, horror and death. . . . The book is at once an illuminated missal and a guide-book to Hell'. The *Morning Post* said Charles Williams had written a most remarkable religious novel in the tradition of such works of G. K. Chesterton as *The Ball and the Cross,* and at least their equal. ' . . . a moving, vivid tale, imbued with a deep knowledge of and passion for Christianity, a real sense of mysticism, and, at the same time, with a keen sense of humour. . . .' And Naomi Mitchison, very humanly, wrote in *Time and Tide* that it was 'the sort of book one must read in a day, for it is unbearable to go to sleep before it is finished!'

Many Dimensions, written in 1930, carries a presentation of Phyllis, not only as Phillida, but as Celia also. Charles Williams writes to her in the hospital on 'the labour which, according to my promise, I have created from your Sweetness' touch. Chloe—I *am* sorry about the name—but it wasn't done on purpose, and only you and I will know'.[8] Sir Giles Tumulty, the archaeologist of *War in Heaven,* has bought or stolen 'a circlet of old, tarnished and twisted gold' in which is set an engraved stone, all that is left of the crown of King Suleiman. The engraving is the Tetragrammaton or the four holy letters of the Hebrew Name of God. The stone has supernatural powers. It can be divided, and every part, or type, keeps the power of the original. Whoever holds one in his hand can in seconds be anywhere he wishes. Transport will become obsolete, and time uncertain. Other powers to fulfill wishes are discovered. The stone becomes a matter for international action between the British and Persian governments, with archaeologists and Airway chiefs, the National Transport Union, and Lord Arglay, the Lord Chief Justice, with his secretary Chloe, holding urgent meetings, and all in heated private agitation.

An old Persian says that the stone is the End of Desire. Desire shapes men, and End can mean fulfilment or death. The more a person gets what he wants, or sees that he can get it, the more his central personality is revealed. The novel works through crises in the lives of characters, all of whom seek to obtain or protect the stone—businessmen, men concerned with government and law, a young man wanting to pass examinations, domestic people, and the sick wanting health. Only Chloe discovers that she wants the Stone of King Suleiman to have its own will, freed from any man's desire or protection.

One by one the holders of a type or division of the stone find the end of their desire, before Chloe provides for the original stone the path for its return to a greater world. As she holds it in her hands, before Lord Arglay's eyes, 'the Stone withdrew through a secluded heart',[9] and the book turns to her death and its conclusion.

Gerald Hopkins, also working on a novel, asked Charles Williams once, 'Do you ever wonder suddenly what the whole damn book is *about?*' Charles wrote to Phyllis, 'No', say I, 'I always know—it's about the Holy Grail or the Stone of Suleiman or attacks by negroes. "Back to matter"! is my cry—certain types of matter, bien entendu'.

The Spectator said the book was 'exciting, mysterious, and . . . profoundly satisfying', and also 'illumined by an unwavering flame of moral beauty'. The *New Statesman* made the good remark that 'As we read we feel that this is not fiction but the truth', but the *Morning Post,* flummoxed, confined itself to, 'Mr Williams is doing remarkable work, and his future must be carefully watched'.

The Place of the Lion and *The Greater Trumps* do not have an Arglay-like character, observing but not wholly involved. *The Place of the Lion* is based on Plato's theory that corresponding to this world's realities there are in another world ideas or archetypes of these realities. In the book, the ideas are more dangerous than the material things. Charles divides operative perception between Anthony Durrant, an editor on a literary paper, who shares rooms in London with Quentin Sabot, and a young bookseller,

Richardson. Anthony is in love with Damaris Tighe, who is afflicted with scholastic conceit. She is writing a thesis upon Pythagorean influences on Abelard, and lives in a small town north of London (likely to be St. Albans).

Curious things begin to happen in the neighbourhood. A lion is seen in the fields, huge and unafraid; a butterfly of unearthly size appears, then a snake and an eagle. Human capacities begin to be outstripped by new forces. Fire becomes impossible to extinguish, bricks and mortar lose their quality, and lines of houses collapse. Roads shift and ripple.

Anthony, becoming anxious for Damaris, discusses with local people the theory that the world and its people are created by 'the entrance of certain great principles into aboriginal matter. We call them by cold names; wisdom and courage and beauty and strength and so on, but actually they are very great and mighty Powers'.[10] In mankind the proportions are more gently mixed, in animals less so, in the archetypes not at all. ' . . . matter is the separation between all these animals which we know and the powers beyond. But if one of those animals should be brought within the terrific influence of one particular idea . . . the matter of the beast might be changed into the image of the idea, and this world, following that one, might all be drawn into that other world'.[11] Nothing would escape. Is this happening? Is the abolition of man and his world proceeding in one inexplicable disaster after another? Anthony considers the principles of creation, and God's redemption of the original breach made by man. He decides to see what he can do. A narrow victory for man and his world results. Moving from an experience of the fire of philosophical power, the strength of philosophical reasoning, against which 'poor personal desire could no longer govern or separate',[12] Anthony reaches comprehension. His mind goes inwards, to the moment "when man knew and named the powers of which he was made'.[13] In a field he faces the beasts and calls them by the invocation of their names as Ideas, and by command. They gather, and disappear. Anthony thus rescues his friend Quentin from the lion of brute strength and Damaris from the stinking pterodactyl of self-absorption. Human order returns to the town.

This novel deeply recalls the world of friendship as Charles had known it with Harold Eyers and Ernest Nottingham. There he had found that ideas and principles, meanings, humour and love held the young men in a heightened joy of reality. To him, 'those exchanges [were] of the nature of final and eternal being. Though they did not last, their importance did . . . no separation could deny the truth within it: all immortality could but more clearly reveal what in those moments had been'.[14]

The book was published in 1931 under the imprint of Mundanus Ltd., one used by Gollancz for an early but short-lived experiment in the parallel issue of novels in paperback, with a hardback edition for libraries only, at 3s and 7s 6d, respectively. The Mundanus blurb-writer let go: ' . . . the theme of the book . . . is far more original than that of the other two*; and in either of those does the prose rise to such superb heights of a rhetoric which is at once Gothic in its rich splendour and Greek in its restraint. . . . This is a work of genius: and because we wish for it the widest possible public, we include it in the Mundanus list'. Hugh Fausset in the *Yorkshire Post* agreed, 'If the power of genius is to mirage spiritual realities, this is a work of genius, and one, too, which brings the mystery of the supernatural home to the hearts and minds of ordinary men and women'.

Charles sent the manuscript of *The Greater Trumps* to Gollancz on 2 March 1932, and on the 5th got his reply: 'My dear Charles: I absolutely adore it. The snow storm is the very finest thing you have done. Five hours you kept me up, reading every word of it. But, alas, we shan't sell it—it is the most difficult of the lot. . . . P.S. Agreement on Monday'.[15] The book was published later in the same year.

The basic character is Lothair Coningsby a widower, a Warden in Lunacy, and so a senior legal officer. His son Ralph, daughter Nancy and sister Sybil live with him. He has been left by legacy an ancient pack of cards, with the proviso that on his death they should pass to the British Museum. Nancy is engaged to Henry Lee, who has a grandfather Aaron. Henry and Aaron are of gipsy origin and objects of suspicion to Lothair. During a visit, Henry is shown the cards, with their four suits corresponding to earth, air, fire and water, and recognizes that they are uniquely significant. He shows Nancy their power, by making her hold the suit of deniers, and so slide them through her fingers while thinking of soil and mould that particles of grit and earth appear on her hands and fall in a little pile on the table.

The Coningsby family spend Christmas with Aaron and Henry in Aaron's house on the downs south of London. At night on the road they are stopped by a weird old woman, Joanna, Aaron's sister. With her uncouth servant Stephen, she wanders the country, thinking she is the goddess Isis, always seeking the body of her dead child, torn in pieces. Sybil calms her, and she disappears in the darkness.

In the house, Aaron has a secret room holding a table with an intricate gold top, patterned with interlinking squares and circles, upon which little

---

War in Heaven and *Many Dimensions*.

gold figures dance gently and unrestingly. The origin of the designs of these ancient figures, which denote in their dance aspects and powers of human life, has never been proved but is thought to lie in the oldest pack of Tarot cards. Aaron and Henry realize that Lothair's pack is this long-lost original. Were cards and figures to be brought together, the complex dance could reveal unknown secrets in the working of man's life.

The old man whispers to Henry of power that is therefore almost in their hands, once every combination of figure and card has been studied. To find it, they need one other person to fulfil the correspondence without which there is no truth. Henry sees that with Nancy, he and she as the Lovers pictured in the cards could 'be aware of the dance' from within, and so gain a far more powerful knowledge than study from observation would bring.

Coningsby will not part with his legacy. Therefore he must die, but without the violence which the cards forbid. Nancy must not know—or not until she, from closeness to Henry's vision, comes to see his death's necessity. How should he die? Aaron finds the only way. 'He has the Tarots—can't he be given to the Tarots? Is wind nothing? Is water nothing? Let us give him wind and water, and let us see if the obstinacy that can keep the cards will bring him safely through the elements. Don't shed blood, don't be violent; let's loose the Tarots upon him'.[16]

Henry finds Nancy serious about the cards and the dancing figures, and ready to join with him. He feels sure that, even if she should discover his destruction of her father, she will 'acknowledge that his spirit denied something greater than itself and perished inevitably'.[17]

After lunch Lothair goes for a walk. Nancy has a rest, sleeps, and awakes to a hurricane and snowstorm, with her father still absent. Terrified, she searches the house for Henry, and finds him out of doors, at the end of the terrace. Through the ferocious storm, in which snow and mist make huge shapes that strike and overthrow her, she struggles, and as she does so, she guesses the truth. His hands are causing the storm. Reaching him, she drags herself up by his arms and hands. 'Don't do it', she cries. The cards of wind and water slip from him and are gone, leaving only 'the four princely chiefs', and a whirlwind out of control.

Sybil finds Lothair almost overcome. When he realizes it is she, he struggles to help and strengthen her. On their way back they find Ralph Coningsby helping Joanna with Stephen, and all find their way to the Lees's house. Nancy has realized that Henry has been killing her father and that she, by causing the loss of the Tarot cards, has made him unable to control the storm. She stammers out to Sybil the whole story of the cards and the gold dancing images. Sybil calms her, and persuades her to go to

Henry in love and with him discover whether the dancing figures can call back the elements into control.

Nancy rouses Henry to try, leading him instead of being led, and together, using the Greater Trumps, they still the storm. Nancy is thereby brought to new life. 'There had come into her life with the mystery of the Tarots a new sense of delighted amazement; the Tarots themselves were not more marvellous than the ordinary people she had so long unintelligently known. By the slightest vibration of the light in which she saw the world she saw it all differently; holy and beautiful, if sometimes perplexing and bewildering. . . . Nothing was certain, but everything was safe—that was part of the mystery of Love'.[18]

Joanna seizes Nancy in the secret room and is about to kill her as a sacrifice when Lothair breaks into the circle and rescues her. Sybil confronts magic and violence with the terrible truths of love, Lothair with strength and justice. Joanna seizes the Tarot cards, looses the set of swords that bring fire, and so destroys them all. Sybil brings the dance of golden figures to an instant's pause 'to receive the recollection of . . . sovereign being' and the end comes quickly with the blessed return of human ability.

Reviewing *The Greater Trumps,* Clemence Dane wrote of Williams's 'extraordinary gift for involving the reader in a whirl of magic happenings, making him implicitly believe every detail'.

Each of the five novels has a similar structure: there is a study of the practice of romantic love, allied with this, is a showing of the working out of the principles of co-inherence, exchange and substitution; a demonstration of the power of evil, the greater power of good, and the necessity of choosing what, in the end, you want—for when you get it there will be no return. As unstated background to it all is the Christian faith.

This structure holds each novel together—the magic provides the excitement and the opportunity for the highly-charged dramatic writing at which Williams excelled—but only that. What is important is the evil in men's hearts that uses it for their own purposes. Yet love practised, and good chosen, triumph in the end, and some of the triumph is due to the inner strength of the kind of man or woman who knows a theology of work, and so can act positively in a crisis.

The last three novels, *Many Dimensions, The Place of the Lion* and *The Greater Trumps,* were all written, and *Shadows of Ecstasy* re-written, between early 1930 and February 1932, a period that includes both his great publishing year of 1930 and the Phillidan crisis. The theology of romantic love, held to at all costs of suffering and loss, was the principal theme of his life then. Parallel ran that of the theology of work.

The former theme is least in *Shadows of Ecstasy,* because it was drafted earlier. In *War in Heaven,* written before the first masque, the theology of romantic love is in the married love of Lionel and Barbara Rackstraw with their child. At the end Lionel asks the stranger for 'Annihilation. . . . I have not asked for life, and I should be content now to know that soon I should not be. Do you think I desire the heaven they talk of?' And the stranger replies: 'God only gives. . . . Wait but a few years, and He shall give you the death you desire. But do not grudge too much if you find that death and heaven are one'.[19] Then, in church with Lionel, Barbara 'was happily distracted by the sedate movements of her child, till of a sudden the words of the Lesson recaptured her: "And God said: Let us make man, in Our image, after Our likeness . . . in the image of God created He him, male and female created He them". The very sound inclined her ever so slightly towards her husband; her hand went out and found his, and so linked they watched till the end. And the priest-king's voice closed on the Gospel: "Behold, I make all things new."'.[20]

Chloe in *Many Dimensions* moves through her work relationship with Lord Arglay that is also much more, and her love relationship with Frank Lindsay that is also much less, to become, by a supreme act of substitution through 'a secluded heart', the mother of love. Though Charles drew the character for Phyllis, and saw the capacities of Chloe in her, he also recognized that she did not yet fulfil them. He did not see himself as Lord Arglay, but he did see qualities of relationship to ideas or events which he recognized in himself. Indeed, the Lord Chief Justice stands out with the dignity of a man desiring not the benefits of God but the human discoveries of good in the emergence not of will but of law. He has an awareness of the theology of work that had touched Charles Williams.

In *The Place of the Lion,* Anthony Durrant is the serious man who can act in a crisis, and his redeeming love for the self-centred Damaris Tighe (who, however, has herself been serious in her work) is the underlying strength of the story. 'Something . . . still held. As, in the renewed and full pseudo-realization of what she was and what she was doing by her work— hers, hers, the darling hers!—she moved to rise . . . something for one second held her down. It held her—that slender ligature of unrealized devotion. . . . The years of selfish toil had had at any rate this good—they had been years of toil; she had not easily abandoned any search because of difficulty, and that habit of intention, by its own power of good, offered her salvation then. The full flood receded . . .', and she suffers her first true intimation of love, of which she 'knew little, but that it was blessed, innocent and joyous', of the earth yet originating in heaven.[21]

Lothair Coningsby in *The Greater Trumps* is the man whose work has given him the ability to prevent collapse. Because of his legal training, because, ironically, Williams makes him a Warden in Lunacy, he is the man of sense. It is his daughter Nancy who triumphs in love—in saving Henry Lee from himself and his grandfather, and in becoming Joanna's lost child in substituted love.

More than any other of his books, the early novels have produced speculations about Charles Williams's desire for power and capacity for cruelty. Much of it springs from those who do not follow Williams's own critical rule of attending to what words actually say and deriving conclusions only from them. Fortunately, we now have more source material.

The manuscript of the drama scribbled in 1902 when he was sixteen and a half,[22] shows a juvenile idea of power—the Prince's campaigns and victories, the number of his armed forces, lists of his household and plans for his country (including a canal 500 miles long). It is the kind of fantasy of power that most of us have in youth and carry over into adult life, till we slowly allow it to be replaced by reality. Perhaps, however, few are so sensible as to keep no traces of 'If only. . . .' Certainly to the vivid and ranging imagination of a young man like Charles, they would come easily enough, and persist longer.

Fifteen years later, bubbling with ideas, emotions and words, he had to show for them one book of poetry published, another accepted, and a minor editorial job. In 1917 he married, so taking one leap forward, and joined the Order of the Golden Dawn, so taking another.

Marriage took him further into love, religion, poetry, and to *The Outlines of Romantic Theology*. The Golden Dawn took him into a wider world of people he would not otherwise have met, of study of new ways of power, and of participation in rituals. It could well have been the Masons; it happened to be the Golden Dawn.

Thus when he began to write novels the two levels of his life combined. Their underlying structure derived from religion, romantic love, and his work; their superstructure from his interest in the workings of material and magical power; their excitement from the clash between the two. Some of the story bases are, one cannot help feeling, a trifle corny: an African High Executive (surely a throwback to 1902 with a touch of Rider Haggard); the Stone of Suleiman; the Tarot cards. Platonism and the Grail are far better. But the corniness does not matter, for it provides the accidents of the stories, not the essence.

Interestingly, *Shadows of Ecstasy* (written in 1925, the year after *Outlines of Romantic Theology* and five years before *Many Dimensions*) is much more about power and less about love and work than any of the others. Between the two periods had come Phyllis and the first masque. In the final version of *Shadows of Ecstasy,* the aim of Nigel Considine, the central man of power, is survival. The whole power of the transmutation of energy, of sex, love, poetry, religion, skill, is to be put to the end that he shall not die—not that he shall live well. So Considine becomes, not only a fraud, but a bore. Roger Ingram, professor of poetry, is Williams's choice: 'He took up his work again, but as he made notes for a special address on *The Antithetical Couplet from Dryden to Johnson* he was humbly aware that this work was part of a greater work'.[23] The magic workers of the other novels are not dissimilar: none have ordinary skills or occupations; they do not paint, play the violin, make furniture, farm the land, work in an office or a factory. The Lion and Snake in *The Place of the Lion* destroy all they meet, the Butterflies disappear—they do not make a life or worship God.

So Charles, in these novels, worked through such involvement as he had with the fascination of magical powers and rituals. Consciousness of them remained, until in *All Hallows' Eve* he rejects totally the very nature of magic (see p. 30). His concern had moved deeper and deeper into perception of the nature of poetry and love.

The years during which he had fantasized, studied and thought about power left a residuum. There was a touch of authority that showed itself in the occasional use of 'We' in letters, or the bestowal of classical names—Althea, Irene, Lalage—that separated their recipients a little from the everyday world of themselves; there was a touch of it, wholly good, in the tasks he set some people whom he did not see every day: tasks of learning poetry by heart, reading, copying, keeping one's temper, or recalling dogma. Some have used the word 'sadism', taken perhaps from D. H. Lawrence, for the small punishments he might have exacted for failure to do the duties—having to recite a set piece, or standing someone in a corner for a minute or two, or pulling hair.

He seems to have credited himself with more sadism than ever appeared in practice, and such as it was, he firmly controlled it in love. On 29 October 1930 he wrote to Phyllis, 'I am sadistic towards you, but within the sadism is mastery, and within the mastery is government, within the government is instruction, within the instruction, service, and within the service? Answer that'.[24] Later he wrote: 'Why are there some of us who like things better in the mind than in fact? Most people do, to an extent; which is why anticipation is so often pleasanter than the thing. But some of us particularly do it. But this is rather off the point, though as a cerebralizing sadist I could discuss it for hours.', (Don't, unless you have, look up sadist in the Dictionary; it will give you a wrong idea of me) . . . I wouldn't hurt a fly unless it made it perfectly clear that it liked it. And then only a little. And then only for the conversation'.[25]

Insofar as there are explanations for such oddnesses of behaviour, an obvious one is that he lacked intellectual and especially poetic intercourse with his equals. I think that at times he raged and despaired at its lack. He was driven by his nature, his two-worldly mind, his experience of love. He had possession of worlds of pain in his wife, and too little possession of his love who had left him. Students and colleagues—except, in certain ways, Milford—provided only part of the satisfaction he needed. Friends like Harold Eyers and Ernest Nottingham had died. Full companionship had died with them and not been replaced at his more developed level. Upon meeting him, almost everyone made some such comment as 'I've never known anyone like Williams'. Such separateness stimulated others, but Williams himself needed intellectual and poetic contest. Opposition, rivalry, brought out a particular brilliance in him.

His first four books of verse show that his persistent study of unity in creation had led in sexual life first to a deeper sense of polarity, his masculinity and Michal's femininity, and then to a deeper meaning—perhaps that which St. Paul called 'being renewed unto knowledge'—of a necessarily undefined union between both qualities. Yet the polarity is still there, the need to get some reaction from members of the opposite sex. The small actions in which he sometimes indulged were efforts to rouse those who sought his company to think, pay attention, do some real work for themselves. As they occurred only with some of his women friends, he clearly knew which reacted as he wanted, which put up with them, and which would resent them.

One of his friends' experience was different and served a different end. In *The English Poetic Mind*, he had quoted Wordsworth's

> hope that can never die,
> Effort, and expectation, and desire,
> And something evermore about to be.

He goes on: 'The difference between the satisfactory and the unsatisfactory poet is in the last line. The good poet has patience and power to wait till that 'something about to be' has been brought about, however many minutes, hours, or years he may spend in effort and expectation and desire. Unsatisfactory poetry happens when . . . the poet is content to write something down before the extreme moment of expectation has been reached, before the line has formed itself. That formation comes in a state in which the thought of spoils and prowess, of reward or fame, is equally blotted out, for nothing but poetry matters'.[26]

There were times of burden and exhaustion when Charles Williams sought for days to achieve a conclusion in poetry, or for an essential word which was eluding him. The rituals he had shared in the meetings of the Golden Dawn had been concerned with developing power in oneself, and whether he had believed in these or not they had remained in his mind. One of his young woman students, from the Balham Commercial Institute at Tooting Bec, worked in an office not far from Amen House. Her path to her office met with Charles's every day. He walked along with her, and embarrassed her by his vigorous unselfconscious talk and manner. She could not take it easily or superficially, and told him so. Here was a glint of contest. He suggested she should come to Amen House after work and sit in his room until he was free to go to his lecture, then they would pick up other students and go along together. She was engaged to be married, had no desire to philander, and noted that Charles always phoned Michal on departing.

In a cupboard in his office there was a ceremonial sword, remaining probably from Golden Dawn days. In silence Charles cleared a space and brought it out. He once called it a hazel wand, the ancient wood of water diviners and metal discoverers, the image in his poetry for measurement or training. He taught her to bend over, in silence, and in silence he took the sword and made smooth strokes with it over her buttocks. He did not hit, nor touch with his hand. She was fully clothed. All was in silence. Afterwards, she said she did not like it. He replied, 'This is necessary for the poem', and refused to allow the episode to be mentioned. Sometimes he would write on her hand or arm with the tip of a metal paper knife or darning needle, or he would slightly prick or make circular movements or patterns, but causing no pain. All was done in silence. After he had finished he went on with the conversation as before the ritual. He at no time showed any sign of tension, pleasure, climax. She behaved as a victim, with eyes shut; he knew this and was content. She herself thought that the writing on flesh was symbolic of a union of word and flesh. The same happened at every subsequent meeting, became more insistent in later years but led to nothing more. Once, later on during the war when he was living in Oxford, he wrote to her, 'I'm stuck in the poem, come on Friday, tell me the train'. And the same silent short ritual took place. He would not talk beforehand, being sunk in concentration.

Before Phyllis left Amen House, he wrote a rambling letter which reveals his own ambivalence about the body and sex. We have all, I suppose, known in ourselves or others possible heights of joy and union, possible depths of darkness and violence. Control, and so positive fulfilment, can only come through the daily choosing of love.

Phyllis had asked about Manichaeism. He wrote: 'Manichaeism regarded matter in itself as evil; it held that the pure and original light-substance was imprisoned in matter and had to be freed. . . . And good heavens above, a very reasonable idea! At least I have disliked my body often enough. . . . And when I was half your age, Celia, I disliked it a great deal more—for less reason. Then it was merely fastidiousness; now, it is a darker knowledge. But disliking it is one thing and calling its matter evil is quite another. . . . Our bodies go wrong; they torment us with diseases and irritate us with desires. They are subservient to our minds but not obedient. They see the right things at the wrong times. But the Church, with the Incarnation to start from, was obviously committed to a contrary dogma from the beginning. Matter might be permeated with evil; it was not itself evil. It might be the means of divine revelation; it might be a black cloud. But man was not *merely* to get rid of matter; it, or something that was produced out of it, was to be with him in the heavenly places, where the Divine Body had Itself ascended. . . . Of course the Church . . . had to do something about the poor dear unfortunate body. I don't say it has succeeded very well, but it has tried. . . . For it is quite clear, on this hypothesis, what matter ought to be. It ought to be the *significant* presence of God. . . . (Why does) to many people romantic love seem so intolerably *significant?* There are many loves and many friendships and places of beauty and delight—but this one shining *meaning* occurs very rarely—once in a life perhaps. I mean literally once, even with the beloved. But that is what all matter ought to be, everywhere and at all times. . . .'[27]

There we can leave it.

7

Poetry and People

In his mid-forties, Charles Williams had reached a change of angle in his life. His awareness of it is perhaps marked by the subject of his last letter to John Pellow. It answers a query from John on whether to use a literary agent: 'I think they're honest enough. Curtis Brown[1] took a part of me under their wing some time since, rather unprofitably for them, since I won't let them touch H.S.M. or Victor.[2] But they've always treated me very fairly. And it does save bother'.[3]

He worked hard, in or out of the Press. His lunches were scanty—a sandwich, a glass of sherry or his favourite hock and soda-water, coffee and a cigarette—for eating and drinking were of little interest. The Press's work and his own were partly interchangeable. Often he worked through the lunch hour and also took work home. He certainly wrote poetry in office hours, or dashed off a review of a thriller, but he never spent undue time going down to Oxford to consult someone, as other staff did, or met authors over long lunches instead of at brisk office interviews.

His day did not stop when he slammed papers into drawers, put on his coat, gloves and hat and went downstairs, listened and glanced in case Phyllis might be coming out of the Library, had a word with anyone passing on the stairs, said good-night to Sergeant and Miss Cox the telephonist, crossed the square with his easy quick stride, turned into the home-going crowds in narrow Warwick Lane and made for the tube station. Once or twice a week he would be lecturing, and not get home till ten. He and

Michal would talk, and young Michael too if he were awake; there would be a meal; and then Charles would get out his books and notes for writing and Michal would settle down or go to bed.

He told Anne Ridler that he reckoned to write nearly 7,000 words of prose in a weekend, or maybe 10,000 with the luck of no interruptions. Though their relationship had been re-established on the basis of saying nothing about Phyllis, such concentrated work at home suggests that he and Michal found being alone together difficult. Each was conscious of the effort the other willed to make. Charles often exclaimed in letters, 'My wife is very good!' and he meant just that.

He too was good, or tried to be. An undated sonnet of this period runs:

> Why must I play the hypocrite in the bed
> to which my metaphysic wedded me?
> Because an ancient fondness haunts my head
> and will not let my toilèd limbs go free;
> because I have not strength for cruel truth;
> because I did love in my ghostly style,
> and having woke her passion in my youth
> dare not her long troth now with grief defile.[4]

Below his daily work, he continued, without dodging the effort or drugging the consciousness, a search for meaning in the experience of Love, and of his particular experience of love in rejection, that extended his mind deeper into poetry. At its full significance poetry released or made a passage for a living power which could be experienced by man, just as that power needed men's words to release it into the world. Poetry, God and Love: if these concepts exist, some change must work in our lives. It was this change he wanted to examine, and part of it is the change of experience into poetry.

Williams's ideas on poetry are mainly set out in (chronologically) *The English Poetic Mind* (the substance of which was delivered as a special course for the City Literary Institute at the London Day Training College in 1931); *Reason and Beauty in the Poetic Mind;* the choice of poems in and the notes and introduction to his own anthology, *The New Book of English Verse;* a contribution to the World's Classics volume of *Shakespeare Criticism 1919 –35;* the introduction to the World's Classics edition of *The English Poems of John Milton;* and *The Figure of Beatrice* as it concerns the poetry of Dante.

The English Poetic Mind (1932) and *Reason and Beauty in the Poetic Mind* (1933) were, like *Poetry at Present,* published by the Clarendon

Press. Although the author could put no academic distinctions after his name on the title pages, the books seem to have been accepted without hesitation. Their publication under a distinguished imprint indicated acceptance by academic Oxford seven years before the war obliged him to move there in 1939.

His approach to published poetry is not, in the ordinary sense, a critical one, but instead, one of seeking to discover its hidden wealth and then that wealth's relation to us. In his lectures he told us how the voicing of a grief or love or despair can strengthen the mind by lucidity and lead to a vision able to make sense of it, and give daily ability to hold to it and even grow into it.

> I cannot be
> Mine own, nor anything to any, if
> I be not thine.[5]

If those lines from *The Winter's Tale* show a true glimpse of what love is, then being thine means that one must be the best of oneself, and of whatever thing one can be to any man, and conversely that the beloved must so love that by being hers he can be his best. Poetry is indeed for enjoyment, but also for living, a great country full of wealth still largely undiscovered.

He wanted now to make advances upon the hidden Genius of Poetry, not only in style or immediate meaning but in the life of the Muse itself— that power which in sacred places in the worship of the Greeks made the hairs on the spine rise at its approach. He once said to me, tilting back in his office chair after reading a scene from *Antony & Cleopatra,* 'If you were offered the choice of never feeling that shudder at great verse again or never drinking a glass of wine again—would you hesitate?' As he writes of poetry, he undergoes experience and his sentences lift themselves by their own vitality into creative power. Words are so deeply penetrated that their partaking of a divine nature is shown potent in the verse. A great line speaks of mortal change, and its own movement is change taking place. And so it is of conflict in the mind, of unrealizable grief, of new being.

In his Preface to *The English Poetic Mind* he says: 'Shakespeare, Milton, and Wordsworth may have been moved by any personal cause or aiming at any moral or metaphysical purpose conceivable—it does not matter. I have been concerned with the poetry only as it exists, and with its interrelation ... poetry is a thing *sui generis*. It explains itself by existing. There has been a great deal too much talked of what the poets *mean*. They also are mortal; they also express themselves badly sometimes; they also sometimes fail to discover quite finally the exact scope of their desire....

We know so little unless they tell us; we feel as they direct us; we are disordered and astray unless they govern us. Poetry is a good game—let us take it lightly. But it is also "liberty and power"—let us take it seriously'.

The book begins with the chapter, 'A Note on Great Poetry'. 'Poetry, one way or another, is "about" human experience; there is nothing else it can be about. But to whatever particular human experience it alludes, poetry is not that experience. Love poetry is poetry, not love; patriotic poetry is poetry, not patriotism; religious poetry is poetry, not religion. But good poetry does something more than allude to its subject; it is related to it, and it relates us to it . . .

> Let this immortal life, where'er it comes,
> Walk in a cloud of loves and martyrdoms.

that awakes in us . . . a sense that we are capable of love and sacrifice. It reminds us of a certain experience, and by its style it awakes a certain faculty for that experience. . . . This sensuous apprehension of our satisfied capacities for some experience or other is poetry of the finest kind'.[6] Lesser poetry, or verse, 'may remind us that we have some capacity or other, but it does not communicate a delighted sense of it, nor therefore can it join that sense to the equally delighted sense of words'.[7]

The book then moves to the progress of Wordsworth, as the poet most articulate in his own poetic progress; from him, to a close tracking of this 'sensuous apprehension of our satisfied capacities' in Shakespeare as his poetic capacities developed; then to Milton and this progress in his genius; to Wordsworth again and the reasons for his fall from highest poetry, his 'abdication of the pure poetic authority in his verse in favour of some other authority'[8] and an appreciative chapter on the lesser poets. The last short seventh chapter sets out Charles Williams's conclusions and vision for new developments in poetry.

Williams's crisis of love in mid-1930 preceded the lectures upon which the book rests. It is not surprising, therefore, that central to it is Wordsworth's crisis in the tenth book of *The Prelude* when Britain declares war upon the French Revolution which he had greeted with such hope—'Bliss was it in that dawn to be alive'.[9]

> Not in my single self alone I found,
> But in the minds of all ingenuous youth,
> Change and subversion from that hour. No shock
> Given to my moral nature had I known

> Down to that very moment; neither lapse
> Nor turn of sentiment that might be named
> A revolution, save at this one time;
> All else was progress on the self-same path
> On which, with a diversity of pace,
> I had been travelling: this a stride at once
> Into another region.

Upon which Williams comments: 'There fell upon him "a conflict of sensations without name". Things were changed "into their contraries". In the poets, the poetic mind is the most intense and enduring thing for good or evil, and they must feel such a conflict, such a revolution and subversion, in their genius. That genius is their soul; the wound is dealt to their soul'.[10]

Williams had begun his Preface by saying: 'The following essays are based on two convictions: (1) that *Troilus and Cressida* is of a great deal more importance in a study of Shakespeare than has generally been allowed, and (2) that the central crisis of *Troilus* is in direct poetic relation to the culminating crisis in Wordsworth's account of his own history in the *Prelude*'.

Indeed it is: 'The crisis which Troilus endured is one common to all men. . . . It is that in which every nerve of the body, every consciousness of the mind, shrieks that something cannot be. Only it is. Cressida *cannot* be playing with Diomed. But she is. The Queen *cannot* have married Claudius. But she has. Desdemona *cannot* love Cassio. But she does. Daughters *cannot* hate their father and benefactor. But they do. The British Government *cannot* have declared war on the Revolution. But it has. The whole being of the victim denies the fact; the fact outrages his whole being. This is indeed change, and it was this change with Shakespeare's genius was concerned'. There follows:

> This she? no, this is Diomed's Cressida.
> If beauty have a soul, this is not she . . .
>
> .   .   .
>
> this is, and is not, Cressid.
> Within my soul there doth conduce a fight
> Of this strange nature, that a thing inseparate
> Divides more wider than the sky and earth;
>
> .   .   .

'Troilus sways between two worlds. . . . Entire union and absolute division are experienced at once: heaven and the bonds of heaven are at odds.

All this is in his speech, but it is also in one line. There is a world where our mothers are unsoiled and Cressida is his: there is a world where our mothers are soiled and Cressida is given to Diomed. What connexion have those two worlds?

Nothing at all, unless that this were she?'[11] Here, in terms of poetic experience, is 'This also is Thou; neither is this Thou', which later he was also to call 'the inclusive-exclusive thing'.

Reason and Beauty in the Poetic Mind is a more specialised continuation of the earlier book. Its purpose is set out in the Preface. 'The four corners of this book lie in the following points (i) the use of the word Reason by Wordsworth in the *Prelude;* (ii) the abandonment of the intellect by Keats in the *Nightingale* and the *Urn;* (iii) the emphasis laid on Reason by Milton in *Paradise Lost;* (iv) the schism in Reason studied by Shakespeare in the tragedies. Add to these the four middle points of (1) the definition of Beauty by Marlowe in *Tamburlaine;* (2) the imagination of it by Keats in the same two odes; (3) the identification of it with Reason in *Paradise Lost;* (4) the humanization of it in the women of *Troilus* and *Othello* and the later plays; and the ground plan will be sufficiently marked. The studies are meant as literary, and not as either philosophical or aesthetic criticism. They do not attempt to consider what the poets ought to do, only what they have done, and that from the special point of view of their explicit use of those two words, or of their implicit attention to them.'

The book is original in the proper sense that it comes pure from its single origin of knowledge, understanding, feeling, experience. The knowledge was wide and deep, the understanding disciplined in daily work and study, the feeling exact, the experience true. *Reason and Beauty* opens the great poets to the reader's own life.

In his own kind of criticism of poetry Charles found a unity of his talents and work—literature, the Grail myths, religion, love, daily life. His many kinds of writing are all held in it, 'une unité de plan et une unité d'espirit'.[12]

To Phyllis he wrote: 'I once read a book in which it told you how to write it all down "in burning words". I could have told him a better way— or rather the Psalmist could—"I kept silence . . . but it was pain and grief . . . while I was thus musing the fire kindled; and at the last I spake with my tongue". But that mid-life silence has killed some poets. It is a fantasy, that I could find it in my heart to believe that Keats and Shelley died when they did because of some interior wound, but Keats had consumption and Shelley was drowned because a boat overset? I know, I know—it is silly. And yet look at the others. Look at Shakespeare—*Measure for Measure,*

Troilus; they are wounded, the very work stumbles. Look at Milton, preserved through a long silence, but even there the Muse has been hurt and hardened herself against it. *Samson* is not quite knowledge—not quite. And had the young poet of *Comus* lost *nothing* by the time of the *Paradises?* And Wordsworth—"him even"? He too wasn't the poet he was meant to be—not quite. He was wounded, and though his outer part recovered his inner (his poetry, his genius) lay in trance. . . . Might not one believe that Shakespeare, divided in himself, found himself divided again as he laboured over *Troilus,* trying to make his rational mind *do* something, and failing, and knowing he was failing? Keats too—*Hyperion* begun and abandoned and begun again? "Milton is death to me"—yes, Milton no doubt, but something else was thwarting him. He called it several things—other people and Fanny Brawne and so on. Could Fanny ever have satisfied him? I will never say a word against her; Keats had no shadow of a right to talk as he did, but yet if. . . . However she couldn't'.[13] He looks at Tennyson, Browning, Pope, Coleridge, Byron, Patmore, Blake, and the lesser Arnold and Hardy.

'And what *does* happen? Ah, that is precisely what we don't know. From somewhere or other a catastrophe falls on them. In Wordsworth it may have been the French Revolution, and in so far as he ceased to be a great poet it was because he had never recovered from the wound. They lie there, all these great poets, by the side of the Wounded King in the Castle which is the Graal Castle and the place of pageantry and birth, but *not,* no *not,* the Spiritual City where the Haut Prince saw That Which Malory called Joseph of Arimathea but which may have been a greater Master singing a Mass of our Lady, of the New Creation, immaculate, seen here only in glimpses as the Graal itself was seen, in glimpses and veiled. . . . Wouldn't it be lovely to begin to describe the *life* of genius, the movements of the Muse in herself, not in the individuals whom she uses. We should take only real poetry, perhaps only great poetry (on the *securus iudicat* principle). Tolstoy said art was the deliberate communication of emotion; I doubt it. I would rather say art was the creation of detached potential experience. Does the artist want to communicate? Not primarily; he just wants to hang a star in heaven, though if no-one says to him "My dear, how marvellous", he will pretty soon tire'.[14]

In criticism Charles had two aims, to search the writer's poetic life, and to create, to know his 'imagination producing out of actuality a thing satisfying to itself',[15] as he felt the words of poetry rising to weightless flight, dying their verbal death. He felt in this an intimation of the deeper search he had pursued in all things. 'It doesn't matter whether Shakespeare thought normal life worth living: did his genius succeed in living? and by what manifestations of the strength and subtlety of that mode of being which is poetry. "What the imagination seizes as beauty must be Truth"— in what sense? Do we come back again to Power? It is truth because it is powerful—fruitful? If so, then the Troilus-Wordsworth crisis might really destroy the sense of power, as it did in Wordsworth. It's curious that Bacon didn't fight his accusers; they say he didn't dare, and perhaps that's partly true. But I think there was something more to it; I think he fell recognising destiny. A very great man'.[16] 'I want to know what his (Shakespeare's) genius is doing in *A & C*.* Meditating the other night on the poetic mind I evolved two remarks (1) that genius desires always to serve itself and nothing else—no view of life; it desires to live as largely and deeply as it can (2) that Shakespeare in turning at the end to comedy threw over the *parti pris* of tragedy. His genius was freeing itself from *all* views, and *therefore* returned to comedy. I think this is true, because I rather feel that if one was *utterly* free one would be "comic" rather than "tragic". . . . Prospero's speech "I'll break my wand"—is this "I'll give up writing"? *Could* any poet say so (unless he was in love)? Mightn't it rather mean— "I'll break all imposition of views; life shall be just life?"[17] In Charles's lectures and his conversations he said, even insisted, that genius rejects enchantment, magic. It can, and therefore knows it must, achieve without it. 'But where in this progress does *A & C* come? What, precisely, was his genius doing with itself? He has passed the great change long since—perhaps it is the mark of a second change. . . . Perhaps this is the point at which he is freeing himself from tragedy—In *Troilus* he tried intellect, failed, cut deeper, got to beings, went on, and in *A & C* began to get to *being*. Umph! very badly put. Still, it is an idea. . . . It's all rather hazy, I know. But I'm tired of their personal Shakespeare with his personal history and views; let's have a poet for a change'.[18]

In poetry and in religion, Charles could not tolerate silly talk about great minds. Young people, then as now, often thought they knew better than the great. What mattered to Charles was whether the young person had really done some thinking. He came down emphatically if one were not enquiring but declaiming. A letter to Phyllis begins: 'Nonsense, Celia. Do you really mean to tell me that you seriously think minds like Augustine's and Aquinas's and souls like St Francis and St Teresa and Blake really believed that Christ was playing a puppet show? My dear, they didn't. They did (rightly or wrongly) believe that the humanity of Christ underwent a strain to which our own are mild, endured it, and wore it down. They thought he was tempted again and again, was crucified, and died.

Antony and Cleopatra.

They thought the Godhead itself was mysteriously ignorant of itself (no, I think that's heresy) or anyhow that the Godhead was veiled from the Manhood. It may be silly, but no religion could last for five minutes that had a mere prancing pretender at its head. The Gnostics were driven—some of them—to something like that; but they passed. No. Celia, examine your own admirable mind and tell me if you believe that the imagination of Dante accepted something you wouldn't accept for a minute; and that not in the mere accidentals of science but in his very vision of the universe. . . . Be grateful you've a mind that dare look at it and for it and into it. This is the Nature of very Being in itself, and not as a problem but as a power'. She had uncomfortable moments of wondering whether she ought to think so much about silk stockings, lipstick and pretty clothes. He smiled at this. 'The aim is to hold all things lightly, so that possession and desire may not chain you. . . . Enjoy Him in His creation—silk stockings or whatever. The more one considers them so, the more, and the more naturally, do they become insufficient to the mind. Unimportant, they are delightful, important, or so held, they petrify. . . . Remember, in the end he does it Himself. "Be still then and know that I am the Lord", the Voice proclaimed to Israel: and stillness is the means by which He works. It is in this sense, I believe, that his yoke is easy'.[19]

He wrote his thoughts to Phyllis, but he knew that she was not vitally interested. She liked him to write but has said that she didn't 'always read every word'. He knew this, and did not mask it to himself. When she was superficial or foolish, he told her so. She wrote that he did not really need her. 'Don't be such a little fool', he replied. 'If you're talking about what I need, you're talking about *my* needs and not yours. You may not like them or want to bother with them, but I can only need you with *my* needs. You want me to need you in your own way. Like my grandmother. Loving—good loving—is one thing; but needing is another'.[20]

The double knowledge made him write in another letter: 'From such an interior occupation, from hints of a further concern more important and profound than all, can you turn to share completely in the games and delights of the world?' Perhaps he is asking Phyllis, perhaps himself. 'Yes—as others can see (I think—I am not sure); but no, certainly, as far as you are concerned. There is no question of superiority, but some difference has opened; another kind of self-consciousness. In a way, it is a pity, I know; one signals helplessly from a sinking ship, and no one sees. And the ship *will* sink'.[21] He could look without illusion at his emotional future.

His letter went on: 'This may be all bosh of the purest kind. But I doubt it. And I believe also that, later on, by the practice of the presence of God, another kinship and understanding arises. It is not the least of the paradoxes of life that, until everything is given up, nothing can be really known; nor anything found until all is lost ... Which sounds like a demented Theosophist. 'Tisn't, "tis an even Christian."'.

He believed strongly in secondary causes. 'Do something towards love even if you can't do it wholly in love, if you are bothered with inhibitions *et al.* In each of us is something we cannot give to any mortal, only to Love, though we desire to give it. To escape into pictures of pure Love is still to escape'. But he grew into another thought. He had sometimes hugged the feeling that he couldn't write, had been betrayed, had an everlasting grudge, that Celia had stopped him being a poet of any value. 'I still wonder—in my more eccentric moments. In my centric I say: "Nothing but you can stop your being what God ordained; but, by God, you can"'.[22]

Phyllis left the Library during 1933 and moved to Production under Miss Peacock. I took over as Librarian, carrying on also with my other Press work. This lowered the temperature, as Sir Humphrey perhaps intended. Later in the year Gerry Hopkins staggered Charles (a rare feat) by publishing, also with Gollancz, *Nor Fish nor Flesh,* a novel which was clearly about Gerry, Charles and Phyllis. Charles spent several ten minutes in my Library in emphatic disclaiming, correction and wrath.

Phyllis had moved lodgings and now shared a flat with a member of the Music staff from Amen House. Though both young women led a brisk social life, it was a hopeless situation for Phyllis and she had the good sense to cure it. In September 1934, Billie Somervaille came home on leave from Soebang, Java, and Phyllis also took her holiday leave. One afternoon at work Charles was told, perhaps by Sir Humphrey, that Phyllis would leave the Press on Friday and marry Billie on Monday. She would then go to Java. Charles sent Gerry, on holiday, a note. He rang up Charles, or sent a telegram, to 'stop her'. Charles, shaken but clearer minded, said nothing could or should be done. No one knew or could judge more clearly than Phyllis what she truly wanted. The crisis was acute but invisible. Gossip flew round. Phyllis married Billie in September in London. She asked Charles if he would like to come and meet Billie after the wedding. He struggled in long confusion of mind and said no. Phyllis had been for ten years in Amen House, and now was gone.

The shock meant in fact no new break for Charles. He had been living in it for five years, seeking to find meaning in it as in poetry. He pressed on with the search, though the pain and loss of every hope of sight or sound of physical reality at times made him near to fainting at his desk. This new level of pain brought him deeper thoughts on words and meaning. He meditated on the word 'glory' in the sense of substantial being, as used in

the Church rituals, and as he had known Phyllis, not as a mere blur of
light. He had seen her progress to a substantiation of that light. It was that
physical sight in the wrists and other joints and bones that needed study
in art and theology, for philosophy and deeper perception.

Another loss followed with the death of Daniel Nicholson, the man
nearest to being a friend of Charles since those deaths of 1915 and 1917.
After Nicholson's funeral Charles wrote in a poem to Sir Humphrey:

> They buried the dead; Celia and I, long since,
> buried the living; our hands beat on our coffins;
> but there was always air, for God and Caesar
> ruled; in any government but yours,
> ill might—it is blasphemy, have conquered good.
> They buried the dead, and we grow old; my verse
> is mightier and darker: still the latest holds
> the Emperor's image—the Emperor in Byzantium;
> and the Vessel that holds us: but if for a while some minds
> delay upon my verse, and the forms within it,
> they muse on the Emperor sitting on the throne
> over the Golden Horn, and say 'what is he?'
> And I: 'It is . . . if it is . . . it has relation
> to Justinian, and Shakespeare, and the Spirit.[23]

In August 1930 Charles had learned of Gerry Hopkins's love affair
with Phyllis, and in September 1934 she had married Billie Somervaille.
By February 1932 he had finished writing his first five novels. Then he
brought out *The English Poetic Mind* and *Reason and Beauty,* studies of
poets in their poetry. Given the turmoil of his mind and emotions, it seems
natural that his next books should be, not novels or poetry or verse plays,
but historical biographies.

They seem to have originated with Olive Willis of Downe House
School. Out of Charles's talk on Bacon given there in 1930 came a performance of his short *Myth of Francis Bacon* in 1932. This led in the same
year to a commission for a full biography of Sir Francis Bacon from the
publisher Arthur Barker. Charles wrote to Victor Gollancz in confidence:
'I've told no-one but Oxford and my wife yet, so let it remain quiet. You
won't therefore have to fear my producing any more fiction for a few
months yet!'[24] Bacon, so great in mind and so intricate a many-levelled
character, was bound to fascinate Charles.

He wrote four historical biographies for Barker, identical in format:
Bacon (1933), *James I* (1934), *Rochester* (1935) and *Henry VII* (1937),
and the short *Queen Elizabeth* (1936) for Duckworth in its well-estab-

lished 'Great Lives' series. Bacon 'a very great man'; James I of England
and VI of Scotland, 'a small concealed man who outwitted many'; Rochester, a poet who found a love who worked with him in the presentation
of his imaginations, the world of sensation, and finally of conversion;
Queen Elizabeth, a woman who knew the heart of man, crooked and sublime, and rose with it to greatness; and Henry VII, a man hidden in his
work, securing national unity under the crown after the long civil wars.
Just as in his two books on the poet's mind he had sought to explain poetry
by poetry, so in his choice, certainly of the four Barker books, he sought
subjects whose work could only be understood by understanding them,
men whom one had to examine through layer upon secret layer—men,
indeed, with a make-up a little like his own. The quality that touched him
in each appears and flickers through his writing.

Charles Williams's own qualities made him sensitive to the greatness of
great men. He knew well how small ordinary people are. The constriction
of that smallness pressed on him all the time. The fact that he recognised
in each a divine glory and a relation of glory peculiar to each person made
no difference to his judgment on human and historical affairs. He saw
clearly that outstanding men stand out. His figures reach us as great men,
and we understand their stature. But even rarer than this was his understanding of two bases of the structure of sixteenth- and seventeenth-century
society—kingship and religion—which have been written about by
authorities whose hearts have never understood either. He could decide to
condemn or refuse either in its relation to people and events, but he understood what they meant in themselves. He enters into the crises of great
men as if his own life moved through them, as indeed he saw that their
lives and those of all great images moved through his.

He had a strong sense of history, but not too heavy a sense of a period
to obscure the movement of processes common to past generations and to
the present. As the historians Acton and Creighton have said, every age
is modern to itself; and Charles, a working poet, Christian, husband,
experienced in rejected love, shadowed by advancing threats of European
war and risings of 'the people', was not separated from men of five
hundred years ago. A modern lecturer said Charles was a great biographer
in his pursuit of the details and the realities, in making himself feel part of
the age. He had a special understanding of, and feeling for the age of the
Elizabethans. He entered into its enormous intelligence and consequent
demands, its sense of the supernatural, for good or bad, its poetry, its scope
and colour and darkness, its conflict between glory, self-protection and
necessity. *Bacon* and *Queen Elizabeth* explore and glimpse it, *James I*
lived through it and into the new century. *Henry VII* was its begetter as

the father of Henry VIII, Elizabeth's father. *Rochester* is the life of the bright spirit of the age that arose from its ashes. In Chapter V of *Rochester*, Williams gives in five short pages a brilliant presentation of the philosophical transition from the sixteenth to the seventeenth centuries. He did more than understand his subjects psychologically. The extraordinary complexity of domestic affairs in the career of Bacon, and of foreign and religious as well as domestic affairs in the lives of both Elizabeth and James, are brought into perspective and intelligibility. *James I* has been called by David Mathew, a specialist in the period, the finest book ever written on its subject. The public certainly thought it a good one, for it went to a second impression.

Bacon and *James I* are full-length biographies, *Queen Elizabeth* is provokingly half-length. But the same wholeness of grasp is there in the central sketch of the queen as in the full studies of the figures on each side of her. Charles's presentation of a real woman of the past compares well with his presentation in the novels of imaginary women of the present who tend to the stilted and awkward. More and more he understood things and imagined them less. The study of Bacon goes beyond imagination almost to the point of an exchanged life. He speaks of Bacon's 'astonishing energy'; he felt the drive of it as he felt his own. 'Energy is only caught by energy' he says of Rochester's attraction to Hobbes, Elizabeth Barry, and Burnet. Where his subjects expressed themselves on paper, too, he could penetrate to true understanding, as with Bacon on law and perfection, James on kingship, Rochester on the fruition of life.

There was a movement in Bacon's life to which Williams was peculiarly sensitive by reason of the movement of his own—the slow, late approach step-by-step through a career to great place, the experience of it by a deep, intelligent personality, and its loss. Not that Williams desired great place, but he desired some accommodation of the outward world to his inner throbbing power, some fuller life than an office job and the laborious publication of books read by a comparative handful of people. He had approached that kind of happiness during the years of the masques and of his several publications of 1930–32, and then had felt it fade. Though the matter was less than Bacon's loss of the Lord Chancellorship, the process in the personality was the same, and the path was the same. How piercingly he understood Bacon's mind, with its attention and enormous understanding which was ever more solitary and ever less related to the tragedy of his career.

Before he began *Rochester*, he had told Anne Ridler that the book would not be about Lord Rochester at all but about Charles Williams. That would destroy all hopes of sales, but life would be better served.[25] This was a moment of truth. Rochester had that in his life which Charles had longed for. They were both poets, both wrote plays. Rochester loved Elizabeth Barry the actress. His Charles II wanted harems of sensation, not of women. Rochester got bored with harems of sensation and fled to monogamy of the spirit. Elizabeth 'answered his approach with a capacity for action both within and beyond love. They set to work—most happy!—to make something'.[26] To Phyllis Charles had written: 'It was as the maker of prose and verse, a coadjutor, a way into it, a corporeal analysis of it, that I wanted you, and God knows I made myself enough of a nuisance saying so'.[27]

The book gave trouble. 'How this damn book is ever going to reach 75,000 words I don't know. . . . We have reached 17,000, and all the best bits except the Repentance . . . it mustn't barge in on literary criticism. My present motto is: *Keep Milton out;* if he gets in, we're lost'.[28] The critics of *Rochester* annoyed him. 'The *Listener* says my style is "sprightly"— which is a change. Sylvia Lynd says it is cloudy. I say it is at its *Hamlet* period—or perhaps *Othello*—a little rampant, a little muddled, but (like the Holy Ghost) Proceeding'.[29] On *Elizabeth* the Roman Catholic magazine *The Tablet* said Williams didn't understand the catholic doctrine of the Sacrament,[30] which, again, did not disturb him. Of *Henry VII* he wrote that 'I shall throw over every effort to bring this in or that in, or deal wtih diplomacy in detail; I have but one purpose—to write seventy thousand words all more or less about Henry. The real title of the book ought to be 'The King without a Face'.[31]

Throughout the later Phyllis period, Charles had published no poetry except that in *Heroes and Kings* and *Three Plays*. He wrote poems continuously, however, and much of his output survives, though unpublished. But so deep a change possessed him that he was absorbed interiorly in surviving it and finding its meaning. His absorption in the poets deepened, and his recovery came through their work in him. Housman wrote to his sister when her son was killed that 'it is the function of poetry to harmonize the sorrows of the world', but Charles demanded a more significant personal function. The poetry he wrote during this time is mostly immediate, a way of survival of mind and soul. So too had been the novels earlier: 'Cards, clergymen, murder stories, oh yes, but "little simple acts of love"— no'.[32]

As part of his work at the Press, Charles had suggested W. B. Yeats as editor of the *Oxford Book of Modern Verse*. The latter's introduction to the book was little more than a series of notes upon the poets chosen. His last sentence about eligible poets he had omitted 'as apparently born out of time' is odd, and could well include Charles. But when Victor Gollancz offered Charles the chance to make his own anthology, *The New Book of English Verse,* (for which only two rules were laid down '(1) that it should contain nothing which was in the *Oxford Book of English Verse* or the *Golden Treasury,* and (2) that every poem included should be of poetic importance'), he was able to write his own introduction.

In it he set out his poetic values and ideas with penetration and clarity, a lucent sense of change and hidden awarenesses. He included verse which contained a critical comment. 'The criticism of poetry by poetry is never quite the same as criticism in prose, and English poetry has always possessed a high capacity for reflecting, and reflecting on, itself'. He spoke of cant, 'the great and everlasting enemy of Poetry,' in pre-suggesting reactions to poetry. It is when versifiers use 'language without the intensity it should convey and concentrate that Cant begins to exist'.

The Celian moment is given its just illumination in Marvell's poem 'The Match' (p. 330). It is the moment of passion which makes visible the actual and the potential in 'all love and Nature's store', the last line of the poem. Charles traced awareness of the Celian moment through English verse from the early Elizabethans, through Donne ('An Anatomie of the World'), to the stone and shell, geometry and sound, of Wordsworth's vision, and to Coleridge. Presentation of the state without its definition he found in Shakespeare's late plays, *Pericles, The Winter's Tale, Cymbeline, The Tempest,* 'on the topmost consciousness of poetry'. But 'If there was any poet who could show us more—there was one, and he was Dante'.

He sent some pages of the introduction to *The New Book* to Phyllis with a letter, 'committing us both to mere good hope that we shall not separately be annoyed or angry ... I should like you to read it through from the beginning because then you will come upon what I have called "the Celian moment" in its proper order. You will know that it is, for me, a definition of all that the great vision of you was, as much as I have here turned it into what, could one have one's way, I should like to become a phrase habitual to English criticism. Indeed it seems to me that it was the most marvellous visibility of the potential and the actual in you—in your beauty, your power, your goodness, your intelligence, your love—that was your peculiar greatness. ... You were, in fact—I wrote you a poem about it, didn't I?—at once the stone and the shell of Wordsworth's vision— geometry and sound—exact definition and reverberating loveliness. ... If you say that all this is my own hobby and not the *you,* I shall hope you are wrong. God bless you, loveliest and dearest, and always so'.[33]

He did not have it all his own way in *The New Book of English Verse.* There were associate editors, Lord David Cecil, Ernest de Selincourt and E. M. W. Tillyard. They had arguments on Coleridge selections, and on

Clare—after Charles had gone through 700 pages of Clare. 'We have determined, and sworn by many of Our secondary gods, such as the making of Our biographies (but not of Our poems), the loves of the strange women that visit us (but not of Our household), the verses of Our childhood, the intelligence of Mr Belloc, and the cut finger nail fragments of Celia (but not the nails on her fingers), that after We are 60 We will never offer an opinion upon poetry'.[34] Which oath he kept, at least in this world.

The New Book, a substantial volume of 828 pages, was published in London in 1935, and in New York by Macmillan in 1936. It did not prove a good seller.

It is not surprising that he held most contemporary criticism of poetry in non-interest and despondency. The 1930's were a time for the handling of verse by self-conscious people, many sincere, all ready to throw away the historic, religious and poetic past, and closely explore the upper levels of feeling. Not only critics did this, but commentators on, and teachers of, poetry. 'In answer to your question', he wrote to Anne Ridler in 1936, 'I assert that probably even Shakespeare sometimes left his notes at the *Globe* or gave his typist the wrong scene. Even Napoleon made errors.... "A thousand difficulties do not make one doubt", and "the heart has reasons of which the brain knows nothing," et *ainsi de suite.* Thus reducing quotations to explanations—a shocking and disastrous thing; but I take refuge with God, and subordinate all quotations to the Word: Who perhaps will justify, and rather more than justify, will avenge on his Day all quotations against their users, and they will exhibit analyses of their syntheses, and be catastrophic, except by their tenderness, and their tenderness will control their explosiveness, and they will be poised in a silence, like the Word itself before Herod; and perhaps this is the doom which has already fallen on many readers, teachers, professors, and critics, and they sit on their chairs, academic and other, saying to the words, as Herod to the Word— "he had heard many things of him and he hoped to have seen some miracle done by him. Then he questioned him with many words, but he answered him nothing". Could anything better describe many of those who write on Shakespeare? or (even better) Milton? They have questioned him with many words, and he has answered precisely nothing. So (let us go on) "Herod with his men of war set him at nought, and mocked him, AND ARRAYED HIM IN A GORGEOUS ROBE, and sent him again to Pilate". And now they part Miltonic garments among them, and for the Shakespearean vesture they cast lots. But I allow there is a mass of goodwill; still, so there was among the Pharisees'.[35]

He often spoke at this time of a conviction that he was, unknown to himself, starting a new career. Certainly a new mind now entered his life through his Amen House work—Søren Kierkegaard. This Danish religious, social, satiric, fantastic writer, who had died in 1855, was then hardly heard of in England, though known on the Continent. At the beginning of 1935 Alexander Dru, who know Kierkegaard's work in Danish, approached the Oxford University Press with a proposal for the publication of a ten-volume edition of Kierkegaard's works in English, with an introductory volume by himself.

The letter was handed to Charles Williams, who sent Ralph Binfield to the British Museum to find out what of Kierkegaard had been published in English. He found one work only, a volume of selections that had appeared in the University of Texas Bulletin in 1932. Charles, on behalf of a somewhat startled Press, suggested that it might consider its own volume of selections. Dru thereupon became indignant, and Charles wrote soothingly: 'We are of course a little hampered here by not having any of Kierkegaard's actual work before us. . . . Kierkegaard is no doubt frightfully important but we would not promise to publish a manuscript by St Thomas or Socrates without seeing it'.[36]

Charles did, however, see enough in English translation to realise that here was a writer who spoke to his condition, in recognition of the suffering nature of love, in acceptance and concealment of some degree of personal crucifixion if one tried to live in relationship to God as love. As he spoke of cant in poetry, so he recognized man's escape from love into personal feeling and will as cant. 'To the Christian love is the works of love', Kierkegaard wrote in his *Journals.* It has often been said, but he went on: 'To say that love is a feeling or anything of the kind is really an un-Christian conception of love. That is the aesthetic definition and therefore fits the erotic and everything of that nature. But to the Christian love is the works of love. Christ's love was not an inner feeling, a full heart and what not, it was the work of love which was his life'. At last, Charles felt, at last the words had sounded on modern air.

Charles eventually recommended that the O.U.P. make a start upon publishing, not selections, but complete books by Kierkegaard in translation. He spent much time with Dru and eventually piloted the first volume through the press: *Philosophical Fragments,* published by Oxford in December 1936 and in the United States by the Princeton University Press. Many others followed, and, thanks to Williams,* religious and philosophical thinking in Britain and America was profoundly influenced.

---

*Charles also lectured on Kierkegaard in his evening classes. These must have been among the first in England to be given to general audiences.

Kierkegaard gave Charles's mind a new stimulus which brought with it the strength of recognizing a truth basic to himself. He read that God is love and therefore man lives in terror and anguish. 'God is perfect love just the same, nothing is more certain to him. . . . But he must put up with suffering. Then in the course of time, when he becomes more concrete in the actuality of life, comes more and more to himself as a temporal being, when time and its succession exercises its power over him, when in spite of all his effort it becomes so difficult to live on with the assistance of only the eternal',[37]—every word described Charles's own life to himself—'I said to God: . . . allow me to withdraw myself. Thou art love; and when I perceive that a near relationship to thee (in the pain of that unlikeness of mine) will continue to be sheer suffering, thou wilt in "grace" permit me, yea, thou wilt aid me to slip away a little further from thee; for this I understand, that the nearer one comes to thee, the more suffering there is in this life. . . . So I thought to myself. And yet it did not come to pass'.[38]

8

The Feeling Intellect: *Cranmer*

I had come to Amen House at the beginning of 1933 to edit the *Oxford Dictionary of Quotations*. It was my first job, after three years at Oxford University and one at Mount Holyoke College, Massachusetts, and it entailed working with Charles Williams in his capacity as a walking encyclopaedia of literature. I had a little office next door to the Library, with walls lined with shelves full of slips carrying quotations cut from every other relevant dictionary—the groundwork of our own. I thought I knew a great deal, but I had no idea of the world I had entered.

Those mid-1930's were rich publishing years, while in the world outside Mussolini invaded Abyssinia in 1935, and in 1936 civil war began in Spain with active involvement from English left-wing militants and writers. Middle-aged people remembered 1914 and saw another war approaching.

The great *Oxford English Dictionary*, begun in 1879, had been completed in 1928 and defined 414,825 words in twelve volumes. It fathered a diminishing series of derivative dictionaries, headed by *The Shorter Oxford English Dictionary*, published in two volumes in 1933, and reprinted three times before a second edition in 1936. Harvey's *Oxford Companion to English Literature* came out in 1932, with a second edition in 1937; *The Oxford History of England* was appearing in fifteen volumes, each by a period expert; and the two-volume *Early Victorian England* was published in 1934. When in 1936 Humphrey Milford was knighted, the honour seemed to us to seal not only past achievement, but present exhilaration.

I was so proud of my publishing firm that I could imagine no better life, in spite of the then normal Saturday morning working. I earned £4 a week and could not have been happier. All the peculiar scholarly and companionable joys of my University days at Oxford and Mount Holyoke were enfolded there, in the beauty of Amen House, with the standards of work demanded and attained, and the books around me. In September 1936 Charles Hadfield joined the Press, and like others was often in the Library. Recruited to start installment selling of the great Dictionary, he became head of Juvenile department two years later.

From my own experience I can understand Charles Williams's stability within the firm. Phyllis had gone from Amen House, giving him more time, and freedom from having to cope with her immediate presence and office contacts. He could not escape his choice to love and serve her for ever, though she had removed herself to Java and another man's bed. 'Whither shall I go then from thy Spirit: or whither shall I go then from thy presence? If I climb up into heaven, thou art there also. . . .'[1] But the place of his choice was good, and in its life carried elements of exchange and co-inherence and intelligence which were of the nature of love. He involved himself in Amen House activities, wrote articles for the house magazine *The Lantern*, helped with rehearsals of the annual play, and coached the actors, *quorum pars minima fui*. In my time I remember *The Devil's Disciple, Many Waters, Leave it to Psmith,* and *Berkeley Square.* Ralph Binfield was the producer, valiantly supported by Charles. Lynton Lamb, the firm's illustrator and designer, was also active. We acted one play in a men's prison, under Hubert Foss's leadership. Charles must have known and talked to every member of the staff. As with others, he was extraordinarily good to me, in talking, teaching and listening.

When I came to read Charles's letters to Phyllis, I was not surprised to find that I was a poor substitute for her in the Library, but indignant that Sir Humphrey didn't think I was so ready to work. Charles also wrote, after a *Quotations* meeting 'arising out of some damn quotation that I have forgotten, Alice Mary announced suddenly, to my extreme surprise, that she didn't think I had a heart. At first I thought this was a mild joke, but she rather repeated it, with enough tone to make me think she half—or wholly meant it: I just hadn't a heart. Haven't I? Have I only a stone? and did you always know this, and feel it? It lies a little on my mind. . . . I wondered a little if it was because I never mention you now to her, or to any. . . . Yes I did, directly you had gone, for a time. But I can't now. I am becoming—on that single subject—as silent as ever you were. I have never found it so difficult to work at my hack jobs. "She's gone; and all is something less worth while". Faintly I see something of the great meaning (the force we knew before) of those words—

> Since Cleopatra died
> I have lived in such dishonour—'

He ends the letter with an old name, 'your Urban'.[2]

He set me to read Dante's *Divine Comedy*, after having insisted that I start, not with the *Inferno* but instead with the *Paradiso*, so that I should grasp the aim of the whole journey, the celestial glory that moved the verse and drew the travellers onwards from the fearful beginning. In my daily work I came to see the authority and goodness of Charles's attitude to life, and I was blessed so to know him, though I could not help his loneliness. It was a time when he was writing to Phyllis, 'When I came down to the Press on. . . . Saturday morning I wasn't in any turmoil. Only something had stopped. There was, at last, no reason why I should be there or not be there: do you see? In my repeated quotation—solitudinem facitur et pacem vocatur: "there was a solitude and it was called peace"'. 'There was no reason, so far as I was concerned, why I should be anywhere at all rather than anywhere else. I had wondered about many things, but hardly that quiet complete shock of cessation. But do not think that cessation meant a cessation of you'.[3]

He was also writing to Dorothy Sayers, on business perhaps but wild and wonderful letters. To T. S. Eliot after an evening meeting, he wrote, referring to Nicholson,[4] 'I have not known so happy and easy a time since the dearest of my male friends died two years ago'. He made a date with Eliot for a talk on 'a few modern poems on the Grail story'. But he once said that he did not like Eliot's verse more because he liked the man. 'The English poets have not waited for Eliot to tell us about the Waste Land, nor English theology to learn from him'. Perhaps he found the meaning spread thin in Eliot's highly effective verse.

He became friends with the Bishop of Chichester, Dr. George Bell, whose *Life* of Randall Davidson, Archbishop of Canterbury, was printed in 1935. Charles was in charge of the book's progress, and the bishop became much attached to him: 'I value your eyes and your mind intensely', he wrote. He and the Bishop of Coventry (Davidson's last resident chaplain) thought Charles's appreciation of the Archbishop 'a brilliant piece of work, and extraordinarily true'.[5] Charles wrote to Phyllis while he was staying with the bishop at Chichester: 'I am staying here for the night, talking about the life of the late Archbishop, and (incidentally) about St.

Thomas and the basis of Romantic Theology. One of these days . . . Chichester may be Canterbury. I should mildly like to dine at Lambeth before
I die; still more, I should like to hear Romantic Theology declared and
defended from the Throne of Augustine. The thesis was metaphysically
formulated before the Celian Star rose, I reluctantly admit, but it was the
full Celian sun that uttered to all of me the identical words of Christ: "I
am come that ye may have life, and that ye may have it more abundantly".
Which certainly was the gift Celia bestowed—a full well in a thirsty land,
though in those days we did not teach theology to Bishops, only to each
other'.[6] Dr. Bell was a leader in the growing movement of religious drama,
and he noted Charles as a potentially useful author.

Meantime Phyllis was finding oil company society in Java very different
from Amen House in London and ideas of romantic theology. Had she
been happier in her new life, Charles might have had occasional relief
from pain. But since she had chosen Billie, her world had changed from
one at least aware of co-inherence to one founded on status and so upon
separateness. Social events were related to status, conversation at coffee and
dinner parties was chat based on knowledge of status. There was little to
interest her in the countryside around Soebang, though she used and
explored the markets. Billie was as popular as he was immensely kind and
loving, but nevertheless Phyllis felt herself an outsider in the only available
society, half despising it and half despising herself for doing so. She wrote
a sentence to Charles, probably without calculating its effect: 'Am I still
Celia?'

Charles, after learning of her love affair with Gerry, then her marriage
and departure from the Press, had gone down through the earth's crust of
his nature from one layer of experience to a deeper. Was he now called
upon to go deeper day by day, below the crust down into the mantle? What
ungauged pressures, what drowning floods had Milton found when he saw
his friend Lycidas under the whelming tide at the bottom of the monstrous
world?[7]

Another man might have decided that he could do no more. He had only
to write a gentle letter about devotion to Billie. 'Mein Herz schwimmt in
Blut', brooded Bach.[8] Charles replied in a deep sigh from the soul, 'The
answer is that you are. Quite clearly, quite certainly, you are all that I
ever said. I always saw *you*. There is no room or corridor in which you
did not—and, to my heart, do not—abound in grace and virtue and bene-
ficence. . . . Dear Celia, you are an exactitude of vision. Be exact'. The
letter goes on: 'I cannot bear that you should think of those letters, those
poems, as being *past*. They are—as much as you will have them be—from
me now'. He recalled Abelard, who wrote to Heloise when she was an

abbess, lost to him: "Inseparable comrade", I thought of you—inseparable comrade'.[9]

He continued to write while she was in Java, for two or three years. He brooded on why she had thus renewed the relationship, with its torment for him. When I came to study his letters, I thought it best to speak to Phyllis about the situation and ask her why she had written so. She replied, 'To be honest, I'm not sure I can recall just what I felt or that it is possible after so many years to rethink my unhappiness of that traumatic time. Maybe I'm thinking what I might have felt or justifying what I felt and asked. . . . I think you must leave it that I felt there was some reciprocal relationship above the "sexual" torment that must exist somewhere—though I think the truth is that it didn't'.

Fortunately, Charles's home life seems to have improved in the mid-1930's. Young Michael was no longer a source of contention. The cancellation of family engagements was transferring itself at monthly intervals to Michal's pains in her back, but when she was well she was a good intelligent companion. Charles was always surprised to find that people valued him, as the time when young Michael fell ill with pneumonia. One of Faber & Faber's staff was seriously enough concerned to write to Charles and later to send Michael a book. Nursing had to be continuous and Charles wrote of sitting up in a dark room at 3 A.M., not allowed to smoke. Michael recovered, and then his mother became ill and Charles was involved in more nursing. A friend offered him a loan in this time of crisis, but he replied, 'it does not mean that I am fundamentally bothered about money; it is all going to be very inconvenient but I don't honestly think that I am sufficiently conscious of it to make it a matter of Exchange'.[10]

The day's work increased with the deepening of his own ability. We can imagine the relief underlying his next letter to Java: 'It has been a very full time—in all but the single essential—since you went. You knew that Caesar moved F. P.* into Noel's† office, and left me alone here? I gather I indicated that I thought this arrangement had points, and he approved: he told R. C. G.‡ he thought people regarded us too much as a single entity. So here I sit, having cleared up a good deal, and sing my solitary song. (O Celia, the things they wouldn't put in of Wordsworth's at Q!§ O and Marlowe. I needed your sword by mine then. . . . You know, darling,

---

*Fred Page.
†Burgess.
‡Goffin.
§*The Oxford Dictionary of Quotations* weekly meeting.

I really did *want* you for our ally there.).... Shall I go on? shall I tell you how I went to Oxford yesterday to speak on *Henry V* or go to Liverpool next month for the same purpose? or that Duckworth's have asked me to do a *Queen Elizabeth* for their *Great Lives*? or that *James* has sold 900 copies?... Well, you don't expect me to be cheerful, do you. Not when I read your letters.... Am I likely to laugh last? do I want God to avenge me on you? would you want it? I've always wanted you to be happy— only to let me go away or keep away if I couldn't bring myself to increase your happiness. But I never really expected you would. There is a line in Henry V which seemed to have a reference: "Therefore take heed how you impawn our person". It's a superb line, isn't it?' He repeats how dull it is at work. 'And it ensures no stability of middle age.... And now, insepa-rable comrade, what do we do about substituted love? Mightn't it be useful?'[11]

Kierkegaard's clenched grip on difficult reality must have helped Charles never to give up, take to drink or distraction, but to move one step after another into the real world of principles and meaning. He wrote to Phyllis: 'There appeared to me to-night... a sudden sense of cool and quiet delight: rising in the secrets of the heart, delicately making itself manifest, and as gently withdrawing. Compared to which and similar satisfactions how poor are the fevers, the excitements, the restlessness of superficial things and our unsteady emotions. And yet almost the whole world, yes, even Christendom itself, by the emphasis it lays on those things tends to keep our attention fixed on them. Holy indifference is the first step even towards enjoyment—well, not the first step but the first sure step, the first real ascent'. He must distinguish between taking this Stoically (as an end) or Christianly (as a means). Nor is it detachment. The powers of the soul are withdrawn to be redirected.[12] His poetic comprehension sought new air, new food, and his mind broke through to new levels of life.

Charles had showed Wordsworth's power in *The English Poetic Mind*. A key by which he opened a way out of darkness into strength lay in the lines:

> All shall be his: and he whose soul hath risen
> up to the height of feeling intellect
> shall want no humbler tenderness; his heart
> be tender as a nursing mother's heart;
> of female softness shall his life be full,
> of humble cares and delicate desires,
> mild interests and gentlest sympathies.[13]

'Shall want* no humbler tenderness'—how often he praised Wordsworth for this phrase. Chatting in the evenings, washing up, remembering
his wife's preferences and ways, and thinking out little pleasures for her—
such humbler tendernesses could only come from a touch of the feeling
intellect. The state was not aimed at or worked for, it was discovered in
his self-centred, struggling heart, through his obstinate pursuit, against
inclination, of

> that which moves with light and life informed,
> actual, divine, and true![14]

The key was 'the feeling intellect', in the full meaning of both opposed
words. Charles shrank from no feeling, he accepted all intellectual examination. But for a time he could not find a way of uniting them in his own
experience. One afternoon in 1935 he talked to me in the Library about
his work, the lack in it of full fusion of intellect and heart, and his search
for a phrase that would bear the life of the emotion or the fact, and not
just describe it. Later he dropped a sonnet on my desk.

The Prelude, XIV, 225-7

> Since I thought of this to-day and with you
>   I will make for you the first statement; while
> I wonder yet a little if it is true
>   and by what force it may be seized, or what guile:
> whether pattern may be joined to pattern now,
>   and the formal passion of the physical shape,
> the perplexing equations of hand, spine, and brow,
>   whose other terms, beyond the *equals*, gape
> emptily, be balanced.

The last two lines are pure Charles Williams and heart-feeling,

> the frame of flesh with the feeling intellect blending,
> and all richness, and no ruin or rending.[15]

In a later letter of 29 May 1935 to Phyllis in Java, he goes further. He
had been thinking about her form and what he believed about it, and sent
her a verse with the note that the line which started his thought is the
second:

> Say Celia, and speak the doctrine;
> utter the epigrams of articulation,

---

*In the sense of 'lack'.

in the flesh of Circassia the joints of Celia;
the glory in the power, the power in the kingdom,
in the heart-breaking manual acts of the Pope,
in the Lateran—the Phillidan temple of Celia.*

The letter goes on, ' "the epigram of articulation" means the anatomical articulation of your joints and also the articulation of speech; and your frame is an intellectual utterance—a compressed epigram—of all articulation of both kinds'. She had thought of compiling a Word Book. 'You might bear "articulation" in mind, though I do not think it has been much used—surprisingly. A theory of poetry as joints occurred to me the other day'. He said that he might work on it, perhaps in some Taliessin poems.

He begins to see a change rising in his deepest thought, of articulation as words and joints in our physical form and so in our thinking and making, in our society and laws. He writes of it to her in the same letter. He remembered an evening, and considered poetry, and a point between her thumb and forefinger, 'and then, as will happen when you and poetry are combined in my mind, the idea took on a sudden enlargement. For, I asked myself, why are sensations one thing with you, and another thing—or (at) least run the risk of being another thing—outside you?' With her, the nerve moves with the Lateran church, with Logres and the Grail, but other sensations are separated, are Circassian without its membership of the Empire. 'The world of physical delights properly is in touch with beauty and the self-awareness of the soul and the reason why you have been all that you have been is that there was this utter unity in you'. But her life with Gerry and Billie obviously prevent her continuing this, 'and precisely this effort of mine to create a unity here is, by its nature, bound to failure, anyhow as far as your nature—and perhaps your apprehension—is concerned'.[16]

'It isn't what one wants but what one wills that procures fruit. And I have never seen the division so clear'.[17] He must study the real spiritual beauty of Celia, and, for the study of articulation, turn to 'the parts of Libya about Cyrene or what not. This at least would avoid something stultifying in the very effort itself'. The call of poetry in word and thought is to be final. The meaning within the word and the body, human and corporate every hour of life must be studied, and not his longings.[18] He wrote to her, 'Did I tell you I was talking with Eliot and John Hayward,*

---

*See p. 74.
*John Hayward had in 1926 edited Rochester's *Poems*, and Williams came to know him while he was writing his *Rochester*. In the Acknowledgments to that book, he thanks Hayward not only for 'many kindnesses', but also for 'life's chief happiness—friendship'.

and we touched on the Troilus-Niphates crises? I referred to the moment when the thing by which we lived becomes poisoned—as Othello said— and Eliot said he didn't quite get it. So I said—"O—Keats and Fanny Brawne", and he said, so charmingly and seriously, "Ah I don't know that state". But Hayward and I agreed that we did, only too well'.[19]

A letter from her arrived before this one was sent and provoked a rare written burst of temper. 'I will not discuss it now. I am too angry at heart to do it properly . . . I love you; I am tired of saying I need you; and anyhow we mean quite different things by "love", and they never meet. Goodbye. O I hate, hate, everything—the world and myself and you—I hate it for months, and it grows. Blessing, be blessed'.[20] It is almost 'this thing of darkness I acknowledge mine'.[21]

He wrote in letters to several people, including Anne Ridler, of his leaning towards the Pythagorean theory that the world was founded on mathematics, though not mathematics used only scientifically. Blood, brain and fact made the triangle which defines every man, and which he saw based upon the line of the arm. He had been working on this in his Arthurian poetry. Since it was uncommon to native thought, he had given it to the Saracen knight Palomides and presented it first in a draft of a poem, 'The Coming of Palomides', which he sent to two or three of his friends. The triangle is equilateral there, or isosceles, but he imagined each person to have an individual scalene triangle of his nature,

> triple angles, triple sides,
> and that proceed which naught divides
> through their great centre.[22]

Union would be not physical or mathematical but metaphysical.

In 1936 he would be fifty. He meant to offer H. S. M. the opening of his main Arthurian work in that year, but, as we shall see, it was postponed by *Cranmer*. In all the years since *Heroes and Kings* in 1930, he had been absorbed in poetry, deepening his knowledge of poetry's life and power. *The English Poetic Mind* and *Reason and Beauty in the Poetic Mind* were as if he were prospecting for gold, in words, phrases, lines,

> 'something . . . strange and admirable'[23]

> 'My desolation doth begin to make a better life'[24]

He was seeking his own method of finding unity in the sound, meaning and form of the poetic line—listening to words, and lines, and his own remoter mind.

During this time, working at Amen House, he had also been coping with his son's and wife's pneumonia, writing his first theological book, *He Came Down from Heaven*, a verse play, *Seed of Adam*, and a novel, *Descent into Hell*, which was in proof by July. The pressure on him was lightened suddenly with an invitation from the Friends of Canterbury Cathedral to write the play for the Canterbury Festival in June 1936, next after T. S. Eliot's 1935 contribution, *Murder in the Cathedral*. Subjects were to be chosen from Canterbury's history, and for the festival audience that had been built up, the play was to be short and popular in appeal. Religious festivals of music and drama had been popular in England since Anglo-Saxon days. Acted representations of the events of the Christian year, especially of Passiontide, Eastertide and of Christmas, had been included in the famous play-cycles of Chester, York, Wakefield and others.

The revival of English religious drama has been well told and documented by Gerald Weales in *Religion in Modern English Drama*.[25] From the 1890's onwards, feeling for a visual, living presentation of religious and spiritual truths had grown steadily. Chichester, Canterbury and Chelmsford were leaders of the revival—and Dr. George Bell with whom Charles had once stayed the night (and talked probably half of it) had been Dean of Canterbury before becoming Bishop of Chichester. E. Martin Browne led the Religious Drama Society from 1929 as chief actor and organiser, with Dr. Bell as President. In October 1932, Dr. Bell had called a conference on religion and drama, and Williams and Martin Browne had been there.[26]

In his autobiography Martin Browne says that his first memory of Williams was an evening lecture on Milton given in a bare schoolroom, when a spare, short-sighted man 'set the room aflame. I have never met any human being in whom the divisions between body and spirit, natural and supernatural, temporal and eternal were so non-existent, nor any writer who so consistently took their non-existence for granted'.[27] Martin Browne suggested Williams's name as a possible author for the Canterbury play after Eliot's.

The invitation reached Charles. As usual, he was instant in response and speedy in work. He called the play a masque, though the word did not appear in the sale edition, which the Oxford University Press agreed to publish. On 14 October 1935 he wrote a minute to Sir Humphrey about business details: 'The thing altogether only lasts 1½ hours—about twice as long as the once sacred Masques'. There would, he said, be about fourteen performances, and an acting edition* would also be needed.

---

*This, titled *Cranmer of Canterbury,* was printed by H. J. Goulden at Canterbury.

He suggested a 10 percent royalty on the general edition, with an advance of £50, and at the end slipped in a note to say that he had been meaning to offer Sir Humphrey the first series of his Taliessin poems in 1936. Canterbury had 'cropped up', but he still had them in mind for the autumn; 'My Life Work, and will come out in bits over what decades remain, and I had proposed to publish (with you, if you would be so kind) the first few next year'. He ends 'I think Canterbury might help them'.[28]

Thomas Cranmer of Canterbury is the first published book of his new verse. The subject—a religious man of words and by then, of faith and fear, a lover of people and of order—suited Charles's mind. Years of loss and pain had affirmed in him the validity of the images he had lost, the personal love, the woman. He had come altogether to hold to the way of affirmation of images, meaning by that phrase belief that man could find God in human activities, emotions and thoughts. The other way of finding God, in the negation of images, in seeking Him behind or above or in deprivation of them, he understood and appreciated, but went no further. Thomas Cranmer was a man who affirmed his images, even to choosing death for holding them.

Five years of thought, work and experience, he must have felt, could be sunk into *Cranmer* to make clear the relevance of his ideas to plain men. Plain men—does he not know how they are inspired, driven, enlightened, haunted? How their virtues and achievements haunt them, their selves betray them—how their insight and their faith can save them after all is lost? He saw possible a treatment of time in which the simultaneity he knew to be valid in experience could be presented on the stage. Could intellect, wisdom, feeling, also be the triangle poetry, theology, body? Drama was the medium for it, compressed, clear, fast and deep, and producing new style.

Written in two parts, with time sequences moving into one another, the play is the story of the Cambridge scholar and ecclesiastic who became so useful an adviser to Henry VIII that he was made Archbishop of Canterbury in 1533. Thenceforward he supported the king in throwing off the supremacy of the Pope, and in annulling his marriage to Catherine of Aragon and later that to Anne Boleyn. He had responsibility for widening the use of the Bible in English and, under Henry's successor, Edward VI, writing the basis of the Book of Common Prayer. When in 1553 the Catholic Mary came to the throne, Cranmer was tried, sentenced and degraded for heresy. He then 'for fear of death' recanted several of his beliefs, but renounced his recantations and was burned at the stake in March 1556 at Oxford.

A reader, like a member of the audience, must become a person living within the social and political framework of Cranmer's time. In recollection of the penalty for heresy—to be tied alive to a stake, surrounded with piled wood, and there burned till dead—he or she should read the opening prayer written by Cranmer himself in happy years, and in eternal things unknowingly valid.

> God, the protector of all that trust in thee, without whom nothing is strong, nothing is holy; Increase and multiply upon us thy mercy; that, thou being our ruler and guide, we may so pass through things temporal, that we finally lose not the things eternal: Grant this, O heavenly Father, for Jesus Christ's sake our Lord. Amen.

When he begins to write his Communion Service for the Book of Common Prayer, he speaks to the crowd:

> You ignorant rough creatures, you rocks and heaths
> who will have the mystery of Christ to be no more
> than an unintelligible monster, risen
> from your and your fathers' past. . . .[29]

By this unintelligible monster from the past he is to be broken and destroyed. Yet 'how the sweet words ring their beauty'. And near the end he found truth:

> Can life itself be redemption? all grace but grace?
> all this terror the agonizing glory of grace?[30]

Where was sequence in this knowledge? Simultaneity enlightened understanding.

Williams needed a new dramatic figure to express, not explain, his idea of simultaneity in action. A chorus had been the usual means of linking an audience with an author's intentions. But a chorus, he thought, could not be made to work these out. So he introduced the Skeleton, invisible and unknown to the actors except, at moments, to Cranmer himself. Yet he is operative in their thoughts, leaping in and out of crowds, court and council, holding the audience in time-conscious suspense. The scene in which Cranmer is writing the service of Holy Communion is a crisis. He writes from his heart: 'It is very meet, right, and our bounden duty, that we should at all times and in all places, give thanks . . .' and the Skeleton agrees to the audience:

> Ah how the sweet words ring their beauty:
> *it is meet, right, and our bounden duty.*
> but will you sing it with unchanged faces
> when God shall change the times and the places?[31]

Then the singers come in with Cranmer's Communion prayer: '. . . here we offer and present unto thee, O Lord, ourselves, our souls and bodies, to be a reasonable, holy and lively sacrifice. . . .'[32]

Simultaneity brings Christ, is another medium for Christ. Cranmer's quiet early life, his promotion to high office, to danger, enmity, recantation, repentance, total loss, all singly and all as one bring him to Christ.

> I can reach from heaven no succour, nor earth to me.
> What shall I then? despair? thou art not despair.
> Into thee now do I run, into thy love . . ..[33]

A line of the 1552 scene,

> the grace and peace of the perfect end[34]

recalls (in another aspect of simultaneity)

> Lo, peace and the perfect end!

in the Carol of Amen House sung in the *Masque of the Manuscript*. With Charles's re-calling of the masques opens again the knowledge of pain— 'the rope begins to constrict'—'Hope is beginning to feel a little choked: Faith soon. Love—we shall see presently'—'a hot iron to my heart'—'my heart stops'—'each limb. . . . begins to jerk'—'each jerk/of the limbs lurks in the brain'—'dream into dream/cast, sweat into sweat, fear into fear'.[35]

The bishop urges Cranmer to consider the command of Queen Mary about God, the witness of the learned about God. The Skeleton adds:

> Consider anything with a remote resemblance to God
> that is likely in the least degree to save you from burning.[36]

A pause, and Cranmer recants of necessity to save himself. He finds this will not save him. He is still to burn. And faith and truth rise up in him, above his fear. The Skeleton, knowing Cranmer as he knows all men, knows his deepest truth and faith,

> I am the only thing that outruns necessity,
> I am necessary Love where necessity is not.[37]

So Cranmer, like Charles Williams himself, in the end stands by words and their meaning:

> Therefore I draw to the thing that troubles me
> more than all else I ever did—the writings
> I let abroad against my heart's belief
> to keep my life . . .
> . . . the writings, all writings wherein I denied God's will,
> I altogether reject them.[38]

E. Martin Browne, who acted the Skeleton to Robert Speaight's Cranmer, wrote later that 'The Skeleton, as a part, gave me a satisfaction more complete than any other in my acting career . . . the Skeleton made the maximum demand on my peculiar capabilities, as well as a humbling demand on my understanding'. Charles Williams felt his performance. He wrote him a sonnet two days after the play opened:

> 'Must you show me the Skeleton then, not only in art
> by one part played and other parts designed,
> but by the bony fingers probing the heart,
> chilling and determining the pretentious mind?
> Must you show me, I say, the way I hate to go,
> Yet lately drew in a chart, of such neat lines?[39]

Dr. Cavaliero writes of Williams's use of the Skeleton in *Cranmer*: 'The key figure is of course the Skeleton, the Figura Rerum or shape of things, the knowledge of God as fallen man experiences it. He derives from Satan in *The Rite of the Passion*, there designated "dark viceroy of the Holy Ghost"; and his function is to be developed in the succeeding plays. These figures of remedial providence are Williams' unique contribution to twentieth century drama, a remarkable instance of the embodiment in dramatic terms of a complexity of theological associations. They reflect his interest in the writings of Kierkegaard, and are the outcome of his preoccupation with the springs of action and the nature of tragedy, as found in the biographies and the two books on the poetic mind. In these he posits that men and women can only truly act when their fortunes conflict with their natures, so that they are compelled to deny their self-sufficiency. Man exists, as it were, in dialogue with his circumstances. In *Cranmer* the fact of the opposition between fortune and nature, the Impossibility, is personified in the Skeleton, the divine providence that is adverse fate, "Christ's back". The Skeleton does here for one man what such figures as the Accuser and the Flame* do in later plays for many'.[40] Poet and critic, W. H. Auden, said: 'Williams succeeds in what I would have thought was impossible, namely, in creating a symbolic figure who is not an embarrassing bore'.[41]

The play was very successful, with happily gratifying audiences. T. S. Eliot came out and exclaimed in conversation 'lunch . . . tea . . . dinner . . . supper—or breakfast at any time' for him and Charles to talk. A group of staff, including Helen Peacock, Fred Page, Ralph Binfield and myself, from Amen House went down to Canterbury for a performance, and I came back dazed with the play, the staging, music and some new world in the poetry.

Soon after the festival, *Cranmer* was performed in London at the St. Pancras People's Theatre, a professional reportory theatre for whose magazine Charles had written articles and poems. After this, the play was not performed in public for a long time though it was printed and could be read. It was next produced by E. Martin Browne at the Union Theological Seminary in New York in 1959-60. There the students' reaction included: ' . . . the magnificence of the author's poetry. . . . The force of this play rested upon the speaking and hearing of words that rang and sang and danced in our ears. Running, falling, spinning, dancing are verbs that we hear over and over again. We seek after God, but God chases after us! It is significant that the play ends with the word 'speed', while the actors race from our sight'.[42] Later in 1980 a London church put it on, St. Luke's Church, Broomwood, in conjunction with Broomwood Methodist Church. Dr. Brian Horne from London University, then secretary of the Charles Williams Society, wrote of the performance: 'My doubts about whether the play was "performable" were quite dispelled by what I saw. . . . The play is *very* powerful. What I had not realized was its *scale*'.

Charles did not regard *Cranmer* as a religious drama. He says in an article of April 1938[43] that religious drama is concerned with the relations of man with God. Thomas Cranmer was subjected to political and social compulsions in the name of religion, which is not the same as God.

Charles was always aware of contemporary verse, and his job required ability to assess it. He went to Oxford in July 1936 to talk to W. H. Auden about an *Oxford Book of Light Verse* that Auden wanted to produce and edit. It was the kind of book which, when taken seriously, Charles thought tended to increase the superficial reading of poetry. Auden, however, thought differences in poetry were more clearly shown by light than by serious writers. Charles considered this grading by manner or author was

*In *Judgement at Chelmsford* and *The House of the Octopus*, respectively.

a move downwards, into second- or third-hand teaching. However, Charles noted about the interview that 'my own inclination . . . is that it would be quite a good idea to collect Auden's name. He is still generally regarded as the most important of the young poets at present, and likely to be more important if he develops'.[44] The Press agreed, the book was commissioned, and published in 1938.

Auden met Charles only twice, at Oxford and soon afterwards in London, yet wrote of the meetings: 'For the first time in my life [I] felt myself in the presence of personal sanctity', and 'I had met many good people before . . . but in the presence of this man—we never discussed anything but literary business . . . I felt transformed into a person who was incapable of doing or thinking anything base or unloving'.[45]

Williams's sixth novel, *Descent into Hell*, published by Faber in 1937 after Gollancz had refused it, moves in levels not always human—but supernatural and natural were both close to him. Clear and sombre, the book searches the idea and working of the concept of substitution in the people of Battle Hill, a place identified by Charles's friend John Pellow as a part of St. Albans, where he had lived in childhood and youth. There centuries blend with many visible remains of Roman, mediaeval and later times, and so occasionally in the book the dead move among the living.

A verse play is being rehearsed in the grounds of a big house, and the characters in the novel move in and around—a young woman has a recurrent terror of meeting her double in the street; an unemployed man commits suicide in hopelessness of life and finds he has gained no relief, lost no consciousness; an old woman, wise and sensible, slowly approaches death; the historian Wentworth, musicians and actors in the play enter into the rehearsals, with accompanying love affairs; the poet Peter Stanhope studies and considers the verse.

Substitution is part of the way of life of exchange and co-inherence which developed as Charles Williams's metaphysical base. He finds two natures in it, positive and destructive. Charles held that man had chosen originally, in the fall of Adam, to have the right to destroy himself, but could not restore the damage. Only the Crucifixion of the Creator as man did that, and included every man, through the web of all created souls, in Christ's sacrifice and risen life. In love, one can take a burden of fear or anxiety from another person and bear it without misery or damage. But in care for oneself alone one can evade reality and fasten on illusion and self-protection, taking oneself for the whole world, and one's illusions for common reality.

These two ways are worked out through the book with great clarity. There is no explaining; all is experiencing, each person growing towards inward life or death, to increasing capacity for joy or increasing protection of the self. Christ is not mentioned, nor outward religion. But through the streets of the little town, and through the music, costumes and action of the play and the players, the characters move in a real, metaphysical world.

While writing *Descent into Hell*, he had said to Phyllis in an undated letter: 'I am serious about the novel—a new strange fantasy in a new style'.[46] Reviewers were puzzled. The *Times Literary Supplement* did not understand why Wentworth went to hell.[47] Charles wrote to Phyllis Potter: 'hardly a single one of them has suggested any unusualness. I presume that the whole reviewing world is absolutely acquainted with the general idea of substituted love. I am blanketed with courtesy and the general recognition of extremely able writing'.[48] He must have smiled as he wrote that, even though the standard to which Charles like most authors felt reviews of his books should attain sometimes seems over high. Nevertheless, the reviewer for the *Manchester Guardian Supplement* did say firmly of *Descent into Hell*, 'it is one of the most deeply religious novels I have ever read, unflinching in its exposition of the "universal rule" that in order to find freedom and joy we must bear each other's burdens'. But Faber's had not got its money back in March 1940.[49]

Poetry lives in Stanhope's play: 'the process of the theatre was wholly reversed, for stillness cast up the verse and the verse flung out the actors. . . . The words were no longer separated from the living stillness, they were themselves the life of the stillness, and though they sounded in it they no more broke it than the infinite particles of creation break the eternal contemplation of God in God'.[50]

Maybe this vision of a playwright's achievement caused him to use 'Peter Stanhope' as a pen-name on the title page of the later *Judgement at Chelmsford* and sometimes in letters. However, he had a trick of using fictional names, as occasionally 'Arglay' from *Many Dimensions*. One cannot wholly like the characterization of Stanhope—it seems to need salt and vinegar.

Charles enjoyed writing religious plays, and his enjoyment shows in the vigour and humour of the verse. His mind so held the tension of the feeling intellect that words sprang into action, not explanation. *Seed of Adam, The Death of Good Fortune, The House by the Stable* and *Grab and Grace*, all written in response to societies' requests, followed *Cranmer* as fast as he could fit them in. He developed a compressed yet free style that well held levels of meaning. Anne Ridler, in the 1948 edition of *Seed of Adam and Other Plays*, which contains all four, has written an excellent introduction to his technique. His characters never speak as outside the action, they hardly ponder, and never explain. They know, things happen to them, they act and the result follows.[51]

In 1936, when *Cranmer's* summer was over, he wrote for Phyllis Potter, director of religious drama in the diocese of Chelmsford, and her company, his first Nativity play, *Seed of Adam*. What was latent in Charles came out in dramatic strength and humour. This enchanting short play has been one of his most successful. It moves swiftly between Adam, as power in the world and also as man the father of Mary; the three kings who are wealth, adoration and desire; hell; Mary; Joseph the military and dutiful young man; a small chorus; and the Archangel. Three inventions stand out: the character of the Third King, in the line backwards to the Skeleton and Satan and forwards to the Accuser and the Flame; the negress Mother Myrrh who symbolises hell and yet acts as midwife to Mary, utter negation helping to bring its total opposite to birth; and the conversion of the weary cry, 'to-morrow everything begins again' into Joseph's joyful words to the first man at the stable door:

> Father Adam, come in; here is your child.
> here is the Son of Man, here is Paradise.
> To-day everything begins again.[52]

Evelyn Underhill came to see it, and at some time in its activity Charles made two friends, Isobel Douglas and her daughter Margaret.

The crispness and spring of the verse give the plays their own character. One doesn't get much religion, but one gets an enormous, instant idea of God. 'Where another writer might present the supernatural as a construct of belief and fantasy, Williams always seems to be offering it as observed fact'.[53] When he used allegory, his principle was that the idea must spring from the allegorized person, and not the person from the allegorized idea. Images, ways of knowing God, of refusing Him, he made real and instant. 'The tube platform, lounge, street, the thing is then and there happening and that's why it is obscure'.[54]

> Blessed be he who is sown in our flesh, grown
> among us for our salvation: blessed be he.[55]

The edge of the pit is there. So is the step back.

The originality and popularity of these plays caused some clergy to respond with thankful appreciation, others with doubt and dislike. He wrote in an article: 'Art then provokes true emotions, and consequently does not represent them—which is where all theories of deliberate communication in art break down'.[56] Nowhere more so than in religious drama.

Charles put his idea of God in a letter, oddly enough about money and his wife's pneumonia: 'The root of the whole matter is that I grow more sure that the Omnipotence exists and more sure that It was never more correct than when It remarked pensively that Its ways were not our ways. Though I don't think it need have been proud of that'.[57]

Judgement at Chelmsford was a casualty of the war in 1939. It was commissioned to celebrate the twenty-fifth anniversary of the diocese of Chelmsford in the county of Essex, to be produced by Phyllis Potter, and to be put on at London's Scala Theatre from 23 September to 7 October 1939. But, as the correspondence over it shows, delays kept on developing while the play was being cast and rehearsed as war approached, until the first days of September 1939 cancelled it along with much else. It was, however, put on at the same theatre from 14 to 28 June 1947.

This pageant play, composed as a series of historical episodes, develops the new sense of time expressed in *Cranmer*—'the aesthetic of sacramental time' as William Spanos calls it.[58] Charles wrote in a note on the play that it 'combines all its Episodes into a complete whole. Each, therefore, must be understood not as a separate incident, but as an incident related to all the others and to the final climax'.[59] Each episode, he goes on to say, has two sides, historical and spiritual. It is an event in the history of Essex people, and a piece of evidence brought to a judgement of the church's fidelity to its local mission. The whole pageant play shows a movement of the soul of man from the things of this world to the heavenly city of God, and its action is a movement of redemption of human nature and of time by Christ's love, exhibited with speed, humour and commonsense. The equivalent of the Skeleton is here the Accuser, 'designated', says Dr. Cavaliero, 'by a nice fusion of celestial and demonic associations, "the dweller on the threshold of love". His role is to be a devil's advocate within the self, a conception less mythical than existential'.[60]

Phyllis Potter, who lived at Great Waltham near Chelmsford, was in charge of rehearsals. Charles was often asked to watch them and to alter or cut a line or so to help the actors. He could, of course, go only on weekends. Michal reasonably took objection to this, and probably to the atmosphere of possession which all dramatic companies and directors develop towards the author, along with the assumption that the author's family cannot properly appreciate the work. Some element of hero-worship appeared, not by Phyllis Potter, but by some member or members of the cast, and Charles enjoyed it. Michal held Phyllis Potter responsible and tackled the situation with her own immediate dramatic ability. Charles, ever carrying emotional guilt towards Michal, agreed with her at once. There was a tremendous row, then came peace and rehearsals proceeded.

Playwriting seems to have co-ordinated his springing ideas. Exchange, substitution and co-inherence were now the basis of his thought. He did not regard them as his 'message', but as facts which had shown him meaning in his life, work and emotions. The 1930's questioned Christianity, and he agreed that no creed was finally expressed. He himself had been a child of Christ from infancy, but not a presuming child. He had examined the basis of his belief, had exclaimed that it was impossible to humans, and discovered that it was therefore, if not divine, then superhuman. He enquired further, and as he wrote in *Outlines of Romantic Theology*, he observed and experienced a total holding of human life in the Christian story of the Incarnation. Meditating as he walked the streets, or spent evenings, nights and weekends with his wife, he found the clearest significance in great poetry and in the experience of love, the Word and the human life of Christ.

His religious foundation never cracked. By its implications of the experience of the sufferings of His creation by the Creator, he was able to think deeply, clearly and unfumblingly into the art of words and poetry, words not entirely human. From there, in his forties, he came into the fullness of his gift and saw that poetry and human love were not the limit. Divine bearing of human life went through the whole range of our existence, in every man to his capacity and willingness. Exchange* meant that every man lived through Christ's human life, aware of it or not, and so through all other men.

Difficulties, joys, daily life itself can be lived, solved, enjoyed, by acceptance of Christ's experiencing their nature and bearing of the worst, penetrating the best. If I love, or will to love, and to help the beloved—or one in need—I can do it, not through myself which leads to feelings of helplessness or of how much I am doing, but through the life, death and resurrection of Christ the creator. Charles felt and knew a co-inherence of both ways of exchange and substitution, a reflection of the Creator's method to aid us. Physically we all live from others, and co-inherence brings us into the act of creation which holds all mankind in a web through Christ's life in us. Well he knew Hopkins's lines on 'The Blessed Virgin Compared to the Air we Breathe':

> we are wound
> With mercy round and round

*See p. 32.

> As if with air: the same
> Is Mary, more by name.
> She, wild web, wondrous robe,
> Mantles the guilty globe,
> Since God has let dispense
> Her prayers his providence.
>
> .   .   .
>
> O live air,
> Of patience, penance, prayer:
> World-mothering air, air wild,
> Wound with thee, in thee isled,
> Fold home, fast fold thy child.[61]

The year 1938 was to be his '*Annus Mirabilis*', holding the publication of *Taliessin Through Logres* and *He Came Down from Heaven*. It also brought the return of Phyllis, with a two-year-old daughter, seeking a divorce, and doing part-time work at Amen House.

9

Taliessin in Arthur's Logres

Charles wrote of his Taliessin poems that they were from an 'unfinished cycle, of which a part appeared in *Heroes and Kings*, which proposed to begin with the distress of Logres, to speak of the vision of the elect soul, of the establishment of Arthur, of the transmutation of the Table at the coming of the High Prince, and of his achievement. Outside which (as some tell us) man has no concern'.[1] In a sense this comment was true of Charles himself. The more one reads the poetry for itself alone, the clearer becomes the language, the more illuminating the images.

In his last, unfinished book *The Figure of Arthur*,[2] Charles outlines three strands to the Arthurian Grail myth as it has come down to English readers. First is the Bible story in St. Mark's gospel of Jesus Christ's last supper with his disciples, and his trial and crucifixion the following day. At supper Jesus broke bread and gave it to his disciples saying 'This is my body', and he took a cup, gave thanks, and passed it to them all to drink, saying 'This is my blood of the covenant, which is shed for many'. The cup came to be called the Grail. In it, Joseph of Arimathea was said to have caught drops of blood from Jesus' body after it was pierced with a spear by the Roman guard to ensure death before the first hour of the Jewish Sabbath.

In the myth this cup was preserved. It produced experiences of power and holiness on which minds and bodies fed, and round it grew a great poetic and religious imagination. The Grail moved from Palestine across

147

Europe to the western part of Logres (an older name for Britain) to the castle of Carbonek. King Pelles was keeper of the Grail and also the Hallows—the nails and spear used at Christ's crucifixion—but he was wounded in the thighs by a blow from the spear catastrophically used by Sir Balin le Sauvage for his own preservation. The wound would not heal, and the wide territory of Carbonek became neglected and called the Waste Land.

Second is the story of Artus, now Arthur. Britain had become part of the Roman Empire in the first century A.D. Over the next two centuries Christianity spread throughout an empire whose borders were slowly being eroded by barbarian invaders. The year 312 saw the first Christian emperor, Constantine, who in 330 moved his capital to Byzantium.* The last of the legions was withdrawn from Britain in 429. Rome's justice, and its military and administrative skills were not wholly lost, for they were passed down in the families who had thrived under Roman rule. But the prosperous, orderly province of Britain was open to the invaders. At the beginning of the chaotic sixth century a leader Artus arose in the south of Britain. He trained a force which harassed the invaders in small engagements. Finally, at a date narrowed down by the chroniclers to between A.D. 493 and 516, at Mons Badonis, he and his forces inflicted a crushing defeat on the attackers, and established peace in his southern area for thirty years, a leader's lifetime. Peaceful life, Christian worship, places of learning were revived.

The Grail story and the Arthur story had spread through Northern Europe. References to them in monastic records or inscriptions on old carvings are known from the seventh century. The Norman conquest renewed the interchange of ideas between Britain and Europe which had been one of Rome's gifts. Continental abbeys, princely courts and alehouses were glad of new tales of heroic and Christian themes, translated into the local tongue by scholars and monks. By the twelfth century there was Arthurian carving in Modena Cathedral in Italy, and collections of Arthurian and knightly tales by Chrétien de Troyes and the romantic Marie de France. When Geoffrey of Monmouth wrote his *History of the Kings of Britain* in this century, he wrote for a public familiar with Saxon and Norse mythology: the devastation in Celtic Britain, the half-magical wise man, Merlin and his sister Brisen, Arthur's crowning as King, his marriage with Queen Guinevere, his famous capital of Camelot, his campaigns in Britain and Europe, Sir Lancelot the champion in all contests, and the treachery of Arthur's illegitimate son Mordred.

*Later Constantinople, now Istanbul.

The High History of the Holy Grail carried on the Grail side of the story and brought the King nearer to it, but still there seemed nowhere for the myth to go. Then, perhaps by its own power, it breaks through to its achievement. In the fifteenth century, in prison, Sir Thomas Malory wrote his stories of King Arthur, and in his presentation of the birth of Galahad, begotten by Sir Lancelot under a drug or enchantment on Helayne, the daughter of King Pelles, Keeper of the Grail, he brought together the Court and the Grail myths. Here is the third strand.

The Court became more and more defined. Ways of the soul in ideals and imagination were grasped less in themselves than in the offices of King, bishops, knights or hermits of outstanding courage or dedication. To this Court came the young man Galahad, who in himself included both sides of the myth. After Galahad was welcomed at court and the king knighted him, the Grail appeared, veiled, over the great table at dinner. The knights demanded both the honour of seeing it unveiled and to go on quests to find it so.

The King could not refuse. The Table was scattered and broken. Malice and envy in the person of Mordred raised civil war, while the Grail after long journeys revealed itself to its three chosen knights, of sanctity, vocation, and love in daily life: Galahad, Percivale and Bors the married man. They came to the Chapel of the Grail where the Holy Communion was being offered, with the Grail as the Cup. Galahad was assumed into the spiritual life, Percivale became a monk, and only Bors returned to the desolate Court. Mordred destroyed the kingdom and the King, and was himself killed. Only haunting beliefs remain, of Joseph, the holy thorn, and the Grail in Glastonbury, of Arthur's grave, and of Arthur's return at England's peril. Williams's five chapters of *The Figure of Arthur* take us to this point.

Through Charles's teens and early maturity the myths assured him with their penetration and vision. They told him no quaint story. Through his life, finding the myths contemporary, he was within the moments of their action and experience. He wrote to Anne Ridler that 'the coming of the High Prince to Camelot and the vision of the Grail might correspond—to a kind of life—just ordinary life—as one thing. I say "one thing" because Unity and so on might imply too much. But there passes over the waters at times the wind of a tendency to say "this is *life*"—not a single name given to a million detached bits, but as the name of the unique whole lot. And I wondered if this hint of unity might not be the apparition of the High Prince, the Infant, Dom Galahad. Anyhow in the poem it should, psychologically, be'.[3]

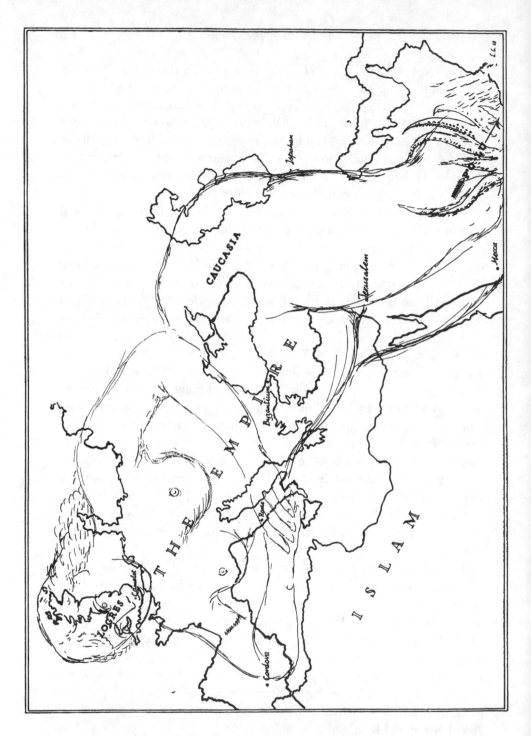

Lynton Lamb's drawing for the endpaper of the original edition of *Taliessin Through Logres*, 1938

150

Thinking and writing his Arthurian poems became a triple 'articulation' to Charles: of the relevance of the myth to life; the finding of the exact word to catch the flash of his vision; and of relation of the human body to the principles and forms of the physical universe, in both of which the Spirit lived and moved. In A. E. Waite's thinking and teaching, Charles had known diagrams of the body from ancient teaching as the sum of human qualities under the Creator. But those qualities had been too fixed, and the Creator too separate from them, for Charles's choice. To him, the Grail, or the presence of Christ, was potentially everywhere and in all times. Its world was, and is a 'world where the Incarnation and the Sacrament (single or multiple) happen',[4] simply, at any time, completely. In Amen House the Emperor may have been God, he was also the Emperor in Byzantium, he was the law. Sir Humphrey was the publisher, and King Arthur, and final necessity; the cast of the masques was also Amen House staff at work and the court of King Arthur. Charles was Taliessin the King's poet and captain of horse, bold and clear; also, as something of an outsider by birth and background to most of the editorial and music staff, he had affinities with Palomides, the Saracen at King Arthur's Christian Court.

The presence of a Saracen was one of Charles's poetic necessities: the inclusion of opposites. Saracens were nomadic peoples of the Syro-Arabian desert—hence Arabs, or Moslems, and non-Christians. Moslems (followers of Mahomet who died in Mecca in 632) denied the divinity of Jesus Christ, and held that God is pure Spirit; He created flesh but was not defiled by taking it Himself. To be free of clinging unduly to the body, they held that death in combat ensured a man's soul of heaven, and this belief made them reckless fighters.

The first volume of Williams's wholly Arthurian poems was published as *Taliessin Through Logres* in 1938 by the Oxford University Press. The world of the poems[5] is that of the Byzantine or later Roman Empire, now Christian. Britain, (Logres) is a member with the nearer parts of Europe. In the poems the Empire is imaged by a reclining woman's body. Logres is the head, or conscious direction and intelligence. Within Logres, Camelot is the capital city and place of the King's court and administration of man's daily life and work. It is also, Charles told me, the seat of life without direct revelation of joy, therefore of love in loss. Carbonek is the place of the castle of the Hallows and their keeper King Pelles, of direct communication in dedication and spiritual insight, and of possible catastrophe; to the west of Carbonek is the forest of Broceliande, with wild country, lakes and streams running down to the western coast and ocean.

Broceliande is the place of making, of all impulse, of the subconscious—not to be ignored but to be alert when journeying through it.

Beyond Logres across the southern sea is France. Her breasts are the great universities which nourished the growth of Christian civilization in doctrinal and philosophical thought in the middle ages. Rome is the centre of organized religion and the place of the Pope, where the hands of the figure cross below the breasts; Byzantium is the navel, or point of union in the Empire's capital, centre of law and authority and of the church in St. Sophia, meaning Holy Wisdom; Jerusalem is the womb, the origin of Christian faith. The province of Caucasia, the buttocks, is natural, uncomplicated joy and beauty, the basic manual work of the world, essential balance in the body and in all thought and life. Sarras, city of the soul, is everywhere by achievement, and so not marked on the map. It is implied in the poems for convenience to be an island city in the western seas beyond the forested coasts of Broceliande.

Outside the Empire is Ispahan, centre of Moslem thought which rejects matter, and so is placed at the rectum, place of the body's rejecting. In the far seas is the place of chosen, willed and operative evil, P'o-Lu, an island towards Java, on which unwary ships may be storm-driven or cast away in calms.

The endpapers of the original edition of *Taliessin Through Logres* picture this form of the Empire and its provinces. Lynton Lamb drew the design at Charles's exact direction. Both were very pleased at the result. Lamb liked the visual idea, and Charles saw his imagination in 'The Coming of Palomides':

> to mind and blood the fact's intense
> incredible obedience.[6]

Geography appeared to adapt itself to the vision.

Taliessin Through Logres begins with two prefatory sentences. The dedication reads 'For Humphrey Milford under whom we observed an appearance of Byzantium'. In the life in Amen House under Sir Humphrey, work and personalities had expanded into possibilities and levels of common experience which were part of the relationship of the City in Man. 'Observed' is used with two meanings: (1) in Amen House, where the staff had become aware of this expansion, and (2) in the wider and future world, where people reading C. W.'s books would, like student astronomers, observe the movement of his mind through intellectual skies.

The second sentence is from Dante's *De Monarchia*, I (iii): '*Unde est, quod non operatio propria propter essentiam, sed haec propter illam habet ut sit*'. (Therefore it follows that the operation does not exist for the sake of the essence, but the essence for the sake of the operation). A person exists for a greater purpose than himself, and his life's work is to find and enter into it. The purpose of romantic love is not simply to obtain personal satisfactions, but to bring a man and woman into the life of Love.

The order of the poems is strictly Charles's decision. The first poem, 'Prelude', begins at the point in the mind when original faith becomes old fashioned, and reason takes over. Facts are the sole standard, and become contentious and misleading. Areas of man's nature are neglected. Taliessin, as he grew up, took ship for Byzantium to learn life and wisdom. He comes back a poet, feeling the instincts and intuitions of poetry and man. He knows the fearful experiences poets have explored, and feels his own power but also the dangers of life. He is heart-free and chooses to join King Arthur's men, to exercise his poetic gift under discipline and training of work among other men. He knows the long servitude of Gareth, young son of the King and Queen of Orkney, now in King Arthur's palace, 'for cause of obedience set to the worst work'.[7]

In the offices of the Oxford University Press at Amen Corner, in the roaring streets of the City of London, and in the Abbey or the little quiet house in St. Albans, the poet studies his world in his poetry. In 'The Vision of the Empire', 'The Calling of Arthur', he sees the wholeness of it, the complex and satisfying order, the beauty of its people and its working, the wisdom learnt in its history, and the vision in the power of Christ's sacrifice whereby all men are one, in St. Albans' great Abbey or the little City churches where office workers often went to a service before work began. He sees that morals spring from facts of the body, of geometry and creation.

> Strength articulated itself in morals
> of arms, joints, wrists, hands;
> the planes of palms, the mid-points of hid cones,
> opened in Lombardy, the cone's point in Rome.[8]

These are the hands of priest and communicant certainly, but perhaps also the hands and wrists of a desk-worker ever before his eyes. He knows by servitude, 'needful and needless'. He sees evil chosen, self-will set against God, and what it is to be a lost soul in a lost world.

Man is not belittled in his poems, the poet is not superior or hostile to his kind nor to his time. The

> candles of the solstice
> that flared round the golden-girdled Logos. . . .[9]

which St. John saw in the heavenly City shone through the cavalry of Taliessin in the victory of 'Mount Badon' and at 'The Crowning of Arthur'. Merlin, 'presaging intelligence of time'[10] knew the moment when the kingdom and the power and the glory chimed. The choice is with each one of us as with the King at his crowning.

> the king made for the kingdom, or the kingdom made for the king?[11]

Is love made for us or are we made to learn love? So Sir Bors, the married man, received love in his marriage and offered what he received, and thereby ' . . . the wealth of the self is the health of the self exchanged'[12] in increasing capacity through life.

Morals were much to Charles, religion and love were more, but verse was the deepest power of all. When he was free to sink himself into poetry he did not need Arthurian or divine language or subject. 'Taliessin in the School of the Poets' speaks of the nature of poetry, the life work of a poet in the observation and learning of this nature, and the knowledge of the union of the creator as man and as word.

Yet there, in his central love, he suffered the power and agony of hell:

> . . . the stemming and staling of great verse,
> of poetry plunged into the void
> where Virgil clutched at clumps of song
> when that master of poets died.[13]

This agony comes in Williams's verse when there is the deepest struggle with the creative power. To him it was in the life of poetry, or in the life of love, as in the poem 'Lamorack and the Queen Morgause of Orkney'. It speaks of how Lamorack knew love as a dolorous blow, as hungry, extreme, convulsed, unchangeable, as a schism of primaeval rock with itself. 'Her hand discharged catastrophe'. Sent to explore the coast of Orkney for the King, Lamorack recorded:

> Ship and sculpture shuddered; the crags' scream
> mingled with the seamews'; Logres' convulsed theme
> wailed in the whirlwind; we fled before the storms,
> and behind us loosed in the air flew giant inhuman forms.[14]

Charles knew this state in himself and in verse. He had pondered in *The English Poetic Mind* on Wordsworth's solitary apparition, 'this

stone—this sea-beast—this cloud'.[15] He knew that poets must force the
terrors to speak, and speaking, to explain their being. Lamorack experienced the worst and knew what he suffered. He loved without hope. Yet
love remained his fact. The poem ends:

> I am the queen's servant; while I live
> down my eyes the cliff, the carving, the winged things drive,
> since the rock, in those fleet lids of rock's hue,
> the sculpture, the living sculpture, rose and flew.[16]

The poet advances again into the nature of poetry in 'The Coming of
Palomides'. This is the figure, the Saracen, the stranger poet, whom
Charles Williams seemed at times to link with himself. Wordsworth's
dream of the Arab riding fast over the sandy wilderness with a sea deluge
gaining on him, carrying a stone and a shell, Euclid's *Elements* and poetry,
had been a primal concept to Williams. The Arab said that Euclid was

> The one that held acquaintance with the stars,
> And wedded soul to soul in purest bond
> Of reason, undisturbed by space or time.[17]

Williams had been meditating for years on geometry in the body, reason
and intelligence in flesh. This vision of Wordsworth, the use of the word
'wedded', had supported his thought. Perhaps the link with Palomides,
akin to Arabs, came from this.

In the poem,[18] at the summer palace of Mark King of Cornwall and
Queen Iseult, the King invites Sir Palomides to show 'a trick of the Persian
music-craft'. Palomides begins:

> Blessed (I sang) the Cornish queen;
> for till to-day no eyes have seen
> how curves of golden life define
> the straightness of a perfect line,
> till the queen's blessed arm became
> a rigid bar of golden flame
> where well might Archimedes prove
> the doctrine of Euclidean love,
> and draw his demonstrations right
> against the unmathematic night
> of ignorance and indolence!

Above the golden line of the arm,

> fiery circles leap
> round finger-point and shoulder; arc
> with arc encountering strikes a spark
> wherefrom the dropping chords of fire
> fashion the diagram of desire.

The first diagram is complete:

> lo, on the arm's base for a sign,
> the single equilateral trine!

Unions first seen by the intellectual power of geometry open a new world to the intellect and senses. The intellect sees within the three sides of the triangle

> that proceed which naught divides
> through their great centre, by the stress
> of the queen's arm's blissful nakedness,
> to unions metaphysical.

The body is perceived to be a unity of authorities,

> obedience in the mind, subdued
> to fire of fact and fire of blood;
> obedience in the blood, exact
> to fire of mind and fire of fact;
> to mind and blood the fact's intense
> incredible obedience,
> in the true equilateral ease.

The doctrine of Euclidean love had entered English poetry.

Williams pursued this study and meditation in his thinking and in his letters, but not in *Taliessin Through Logres*. Here he keeps to his main theme. The kingdom of King Arthur is set up, but the effort to maintain justice in the state and love in the mind is exacting, and without exchange is inadequate, as everywhere and at all times. William Morris, Charles Ashbee and our nineteenth-century socialists are reflected in the troubles of Sir Bors, member of the King's council of administration, himself responsible for the western area of the kingdom. The new government, the reformers, are learning that justice requires just men, rule requires loving men, work and pay require honest men. In 'Bors to Elayne: on the King's Coins', coming home after riding all night from London, Bors finds Elayne his wife feeding the farm hands, and sees in her 'the sole figure of the organic salvation of our good'.[19]

Economics and money are necessary studies, or tools, but have no salvation in themselves. The Archbishop on the King's council says of money:

> 'the everlasting house the soul discovers
> is always another's; we must lose our own ends;
> we must always live in the habitation of our lovers,
> my friend's shelter for me, mine for him.
>
>   .   .   .
>
> What saith Heracleitus?—and what is the City's breath?—
> *dying each others life, living each other's death.*
> Money is a medium of exchange.'[20]

Bors is in anguish over the necessary harshness of order—'What without coinage or with coinage can be saved?'[21] He looks for every man to know the love which carries his wife and himself and their workpeople, 'in your hand the bread of love, in your head lightness of law'.[22] The turmoil of minds and good wills in the 1890's of Williams's youth is alive in the poem. But in the next, 'The Star of Percivale', is seen

> a new direct earth of sweet joy given
> and its fusion with a new heaven, indirect joy of substitution.[23]

The first half of the book is concerned with the people in the world of the court—knights, young men in training, armourers, carpenters, priests, musicians, stablemen, kitchen and farm workers, sweepers and dung-men, noble ladies and their families, women doing domestic service, needle-women and others. Poems show Taliessin conversant and concerned with these, indeed with one who thinks she has fallen in love with him. He gently deflects her. He is shown supporting court discipline and practice, using it always as a base of appropriate philosophy and love,

> heaven's best skill
> to treat the world's will but as and at the world's will[24]

as he moves the person forward on her or his necessary way.

Then comes a change. Williams gets down to the real business of poetry and the Grail. He places next the poem 'The Sister of Percivale', which concerns Taliessin falling in love. So far the poems have shown him a poet, a man of intelligence and action, making his life in the world with other people. Now this, though necessary, becomes secondary. His poetry moved on to explore the experience of love, its divine link with the Grail, and the meaning of both for man.

Taliessin was lying on a wall, doing nothing, between the worlds of sensation and of spirit, making poetry, watching a girl draw water from the well. Percivale and his sister Blanchefleur and Lamorack his brother arrived at the castle gate. A trumpet sounded for their arrival. Alerted, in the first sight of Blanchefleur he saw in one figure the woman and the nearest to the Divine Presence that man can bear. The hemispheres of the known world and the guessed unknown met. Horizon had no lack of horizon; the circle closed. He saw union of body and spirit, though he could not at once express it. Images from sight and sound riot in the poem.

'The Son of Lancelot' explores the birth of love—in the Arthurian story, in human life, in the mind and in poetry as the *mens sensitiva* and the feeling intellect. The wise man Merlin sees by magical skill the whole Empire. He sees how men lack the working of love, and are dependent on tradition, reason, force and self-defence. Government has deteriorated, Moslem raiders are attacking the coasts and seizing areas of land. The Empire's centre is weakened, its leaders distracted by dreams. The Christian faith showed men the discovery of love as substitution, when the sinless Jesus bore the penalty of men's sins on the cross for love. The nature of love is shown to be the substitution of the loved one for oneself in one's own desires and motives. In the Arthurian myth the idea is worked out in the story of the birth of Galahad. Sir Lancelot, the King's chief knight and general of his forces was also the faithful sworn knight of Queen Guinevere. A false appeal from her for help called him to the Castle of the Grail in Carbonek. The Grail was here in the care of the wounded King Pelles, whose daughter Helayne served it. Under a drug or enchantment Lancelot lay with Helayne, knowing her as Guinevere, and begot Galahad, the figure of love in the myth. Lancelot was almost destroyed by his act when he recovered and knew what he had done. His honour was lost, his fidelity broken, and without these his life was worthless to him. He leaped out of the bedroom window, and ran half-mad as a wolf-man in the woods for nine months.

Galahad was born with Brisen (Merlin's sister) as midwife, and carried to a convent where Taliessin's love Blanchefleur was portress. She took him in to safe keeping. The Emperor ordered a full attack on the enemy raiders, and the recovery of occupied territories; Lancelot was healed of his madness. Joy, energy and love returned to King Arthur's household.

But love has its own nature, which is to be learned by every man. The learning and the working in the soul do not at first make life easier. Lancelot was almost broken by substitution, Palomides rejected co-inherence and insisted on not being like other people. In love, poetry, intelligence and

honour he knew his worth. Slowly it separated him from everyone. Not
until he accepted a total change, to be christened, to undergo the working
of love in Christ, did he recover. When he came to die, he thought back
through his life, through ancient learning and worship, through his love,
his friendships, his tournaments and his passions; he did not know conclusions, he recalled only the paths, but he knew now that these were blessed
because there was love, and 'The Lord created all things by means of his
Blessing'.[25]

He did, and He has much to answer for. Charles Williams, thinking of
war, blindness, damaged marriage, and lost love, knew that the fact of
eternal love does not alter human conditions. Galahad's birth did nothing
to alter Lancelot's loss of honour, of fidelity, of meaning in his life.

The tragic myth now has its potentiality for development, and so for the
tragedy to be healed. In 'The Coming of Galahad' we find the King, the
Queen and the whole Court welcoming Galahad and acknowledging him
as heir to the King—man's best effort acknowledging the authority of love.
After the ceremonies, Taliessin takes his harp and goes through the palace,
which in the poem is also the body, the world of matter and of exchange.
The yard slave, Gareth, has seen the Grail, veiled, in the air over the great
dining table, visible for the first time in the Court. Taliessin and Gareth
speak of sanctity and poetry, stone and shell of vision and fact:

> 'And I among dung and urine—am I one
> with shell or stone,' Gareth asked, 'in the jakes?'

Taliessin answers:

> And what makes the City?
>
> . . .
>
> consent
> to be nothing but the shape in the gate of excrement,
>
> . . .
>
> question and digestion, rejection and election,
> winged shapes of the Grail's officers
>
> . . .
>
> Sir,
> without this alley-way how can man prefer?
> and without preference can the Grail's grace be stored?[26]

He talks with all the kitchen workers, searching the nature of the body and the facts of experience.

Galahad has been recognized. Now the worlds change. God is here, in man's life, time loses its implacability,

> rites and runes
> are come away from sequence, from rules of magic;
> here all is cause and all effect.[27]

From our roots vigours of joy drive up. We are not slaves of our past, of rules of magic or fear. We are capable at all moments of new love since 'time's foster-child', Lancelot's son, has come to the whole being of man, and in our body sits in the Perilous Chair, a seat kept for the knight of the Grail, till now unknown.

Three steps in the myth remain. First is the healing of the wound of King Pelles who lies helpless from the Dolorous Blow in the castle of the Hallows at Carbonek. The poem's title, 'Percivale at Carbonek', tells us that Percivale is recording the scene, though he is not otherwise named.

Galahad comes with Bors to the entrance arch of the castle. The Grail appears in the air, angels welcome him and rejoice. King Pelles' people gather to acclaim him; Pelles awaits the curing of his wound. All goodwill comes with Galahad. The astonished angels hear him sigh, see him kneel. He knows his blessed mission, but he knows also the misery of his father Lancelot in fathering him for this act of reconciliation. Lancelot only knows that he has been false to Guinevere. Charles Williams wrote of this: 'Only once does the Joyous Prince weep, and that is when he comes to Carbonek, the place where he was born, and Lancelot went mad. Galahad doubts if even eternity is quite worth it'.[28] The poem uses the concept of love asking pardon from fallen man for the pain and effort of living the life of love.

Galahad asks Bors, a relative of Lancelot, to take pardon from the fallen world of Camelot to the devout world of Carbonek. Bors asks what he and his world should forgive.

> 'Forgive Us,' the High Prince said, 'for Our existence;
> forgive the means of grace and the hope of glory.
> In the name of Our father forgive Our mother for Our birth'.[29]

Bors replies with an assent to life and birth, and leads Galahad into Carbonek for the healing of King Pelles' wound.

In the last two poems Williams draws the myth on through the final two stages of development which are missing from the mediaeval versions. First is the earthly conclusion of King Arthur's kingdom, represented symbolically in the journeying of his true knights and servants to Sarras, carrying the recollection of the ferocity of their enemies and the death of their friends. The effort of a union of heaven and earth in Logres is withdrawn to the city and castle of Carbonek, and the kingdom becomes historical Britain. The second is a poetic presentation of the Achievement of the Grail. Malory wrote of Galahad, Percivale and Bors's Achievement, but not of King Arthur and his whole company of the Round Table, of King Pelles, Merlin, women and servants. In the last poem, 'Taliessin at Lancelot's Mass', there is a gathering up, a renewal and co-inherence of the kingdom and the world.

In these poems, 'The Last Voyage' and 'Taliessin at Lancelot's Mass', Charles Williams moves through man's choices of good or evil, to the outward breaking of the Round Table in murder and civil war, and the journeying of the true knights and servants of the King to Sarras and to the Achievement of the Grail. They voyage in a ship which is also the hollow of Jerusalem, an image of the womb, each man's future. The life and death of Christ for man makes substitution and co-inherence now possible between men.

The thought is intricate but clear. Williams had written in *Cranmer* that words must not be used

> to escape
> into the unformed shadow of mystery mere,
> but find a strong order, a diagram clear,
> a ladder runged and tongued.[30]

In the climax of his rendering of the myth of King Arthur and of man he obeys his own rule.

In 'The Last Voyage' two concepts open the final story imaged in paintings inside the ship. One was Solomon, as the master of intellect, myth and 'sublime necromancy', with Queen Balkis as the sensuous art. The other was Poetry, painted as Virgil stretching to Taliessin a shoot of hazel—the hexameter, the decasyllabic line which was transmitted to English verse and Shakespeare. Williams's poetry here unites the movement and direction of the ship through the waves of the sea with the working of poetry through words.

The voyage is to Sarras, to the Achievement of the Grail, the end of the myth. On board were Galahad, 'the alchemical Infant', since he was born of substitution (his mother Helayne being substituted, when Lancelot was drugged, for Guinevere in his bed) to work the great return to Love, Percivale and Bors. They were still in their personifications, Galahad as man's capacity for Christ, Percivale as dedicated devotion, Bors as love in the work and life of the world. The people of Logres and the Empire were in the infinite flight of doves that weight the helm and so steer the ship. On the deck lay the dead body of Blanchefleur covered with a saffron yellow pall, perhaps the color of the sun. She died through giving a blood transfusion to cure a friend, and is here the human figure of exchange. As the ship drove on, the kingdom of Logres was being broken, the knights and King Arthur killed. The effort of Logres was withdrawn to Carbonek; the island became Britain. But man was saved.

In the birth of Galahad, child of substitution, man's capacity for co-inherence in Christ has been restored. In the triangle of fact, intelligence and flesh, such as Palomides sees in his experience of love, the necessity of being which is God has been communicated to Galahad. As he healed the wound of Pelles, Keeper of the Hallows, King Arthur and Pelles have become one 'by exchange of death and healing'.[31]

The victory of love is celebrated in the last poem of the book 'Taliessin at Lancelot's Mass'. Lancelot, who loved and suffered humanly above all people, began the service. Taliessin came when dew was bright on the grass, dew of early morning and of early youth. All the dead lords of the Table and all the people of the story gather to the old stone altar, standing between Nimue from Broceliande, mother of making, and Helayne from Carbonek, mother of the Achievement. Only Guinevere was alone in Blanchefleur's nunnery. As the service began, Guinevere came to reconciliation with the past, accepting substitution with Helayne mother of Galahad by Guinevere's lover. The world of the Grail became open to the world of Arthur, unseen powers became friends, not terrors. All the figures of the story, all their attributed virtues, were recalled; as at Pentecost, their glory fell as flames from new welcoming sky to new capable earth.

Using the Byzantine ritual which invokes the Holy Spirit in the Epiclesis, the mass went on, exalting the Unity of God, and of His creation; the Empire was known in unity and order from Caucasia to Carbonek. The transmutation of the Table and its company begins. Galahad was seen above the altar, as it were in the fire of love; the knights of the Table rose into the fire, together with all the figures of the myth and of these poems. Taliessin saw joy come to ways where no joy had been. Glories no longer contested, but intertwined. All could now find joy, among Taliessin's and Charles Williams's company, through the web of co-inherence in love:

> manacled by the web, in the web made free;
> there was no capable song for the joy in me.[32]

The last line of the poem, 'in the dispersed homes of the household, let the Company pray for it still', concerns Charles Williams's Order of the Coinherence (See pp. 173–74).

10

Romantic Theology and War

In the last year or two Phyllis Somervaille's marriage had broken down, and early in 1938 she returned from Java with her daughter Penelope Celia. She lived in London, and did occasional editorial work for the O.U.P. This sometimes brought her in to the Production office or the Library. She and Charles resumed very intermittent relations. He did not look for any renewal of the vision nor did he deny the past. He disliked her coloured finger nails and smartness but he did not say 'What a fool I was!' He pressed on with a very busy life.

He and C. S. Lewis had become acquainted in 1936 by exchanged letters, Charles admiring *The Allegory of Love* and Lewis *The Place of the Lion.*

In August 1937, while writing and rewriting the last section of *Seed of Adam* for the Chelmsford actors, Charles had on the 6th said to Phyllis Potter, 'I am pushing through a little book for Ellis Roberts. I hope to complete that within the next fortnight and then to devote my attention to finishing off the *Seed*'. Proofs of *Seed of Adam* were finally cleared on 17 August, so he probably finished the 'little book' in ten days. In was published in 1938 as *He Came Down From Heaven,* by William Heinemann Ltd.

On the flyleaf of C. S. Lewis's copy of *He Came Down From Heaven,*[1] in Charles's hand, is written 'At Shirreffs, 2.10, 4th July 1938'. He must have been spending a lunch-hour with Lewis at his favourite restaurant-bar, Shirreffs, at the bottom of Ludgate Hill, under the railway bridge across the road from the King Lud pub, and have given him a copy of this new book to read in the train home. At the end of his copy Lewis wrote 'July 26 1938', probably the date when he finished his reading and making notes. Sadly, Shirreffs has gone, and the site no longer holds a restaurant.

He Came Down From Heaven was commissioned under the title, 'I Believe: A Series of Personal Statements'. The first four titles of the series were listed as *What I Believe,* by J. D. Beresford; *Problems of Religion,* by Gerald Bullett; *Pan, Caesar and God,* by Renée Haynes; *And He Shall Come Again* by Kenneth Ingram. Charles's was the fifth. It is dedicated 'To Michal by whom I began to study the doctrine of glory'. His first book of theology, it is a model in 35,000 words of clear, concise writing. His gift was to be able to start at the beginning without being elementary.

The book has two parts. The first four chapters are concerned with the discovery of God's relations with man. The last three carry this on to man's life with man, in three degrees; personal romantic love, which contains the core of his unpublished *Outlines of Romantic Theology;* relationship to others with whom he comes in contact; and building a community or City.

He goes straight into the theme of the book's title and begins with heaven. 'Heaven . . . is beatitude and the eternal fulfilment of the Will, the contemporaneous of perfection. . . . There emerges and returns from that state of eternal beatitude something or someone charged with a particular intention towards men. . . . Religion is the definition of that relationship',[2] its records contained in the Bible and the rituals of the Church, the former mostly telling what happened, the latter what is happening. 'It is true that all that did happen is a presentation of what is happening; all the historical events . . . are a pageant of the events of the human soul. . . . Christendom has always held that the two are indissolubly connected; that the events in the human soul could not exist unless the historical events had existed'.[3] The coming of the kingdom of heaven 'was historic in order that it might always be contemporary; it is contemporary because it was certainly historic. It is the Bible which describes and defines for us the coming of the kingdom'.[4] In it, 'Individuals and companies, and mankind itself, are all finally set in relation to that non-human cause and centre which is called God. . . . The whole Canon signifies a particular thing—the original nature of man, the entrance of contradiction into his nature, and the manner of his restoration'.[5]

Though he dislikes the contemporary vogue for the Bible as literature, yet, he says, for most of us, 'it is precisely good literary criticism which is needed. . . . Bible-reading and meditation must be based on words; they are meant to extract the utmost possible meaning out of words'. Yet these 'are taken with meanings borrowed from the commonplace of everyday; comparatively few readers set to work to find out what the Bible means by them. The word "love" has suffered. . . . "God is love", it is generally assumed, means that God is like our immediate emotional indulgence, and not that our meaning of love ought to have something of the "otherness" and terror of God'.[6]

So the foundations of Charles's theology are established from the beginning, because he could not write or speak about God and man on any other basis—that man is not being asked by God what would make him happy, but he is being made aware of 'the nature of God, and to his existence alone all bliss is related'.[7] No one asks man what he would like. He can only like something that exists, in reality or in imagination, and only God creates and sustains both. 'Man's choice', he wrote to Phyllis, 'is not so much action as the acceptance and understanding of action. I have said it 100 times'.[8]

Williams had been thinking for a long time of the nature of man's original sin, the source of his obvious tendency to fail, be unhappy, earthbound in mind and body. In the poem, 'The Vision of the Empire' in *Taliessin Through Logres* he shows the two in Paradise wondering about God's commandment that they should know good and joy, but that the knowledge of evil was reserved for Himself. Adam mused on this:

> am I not too long meanly retired
> in the poor space of joy's single dimension?
> Does not God vision the principles at war?
> Let us grow to the height of God and the Emperor:
> Let us gaze, son of man, on the Acts in contention.

Leaves withered; Adam saw contention, conflict, venom as no longer secluded in God's knowledge of contingency, but at man's choice become real in earth and man.

This idea is developed in Chapter II of *He Came Down From Heaven*, with the support of St. Thomas Aquinas. Once man has chosen to know good also as evil, contradiction springs everywhere, good against good, truth against truth. Only in true romantic moments in love or poetry or what else, can this be known as pure fact. 'This also is Thou; neither is this Thou'.

The book goes on, in Chapter III, 'The Mystery of Pardon', to consider Job. St. Paul, rashly, did not allow the pot to ask questions of the potter. Job did, and Williams agrees with him. 'A great curiosity ought to exist concerning divine things. Man was intended to argue with God'.[9] Ecclesiastes had said it was no use to do so, but at the end of a coruscating chapter Job 'refused to put up with what came, until in the end the Lord himself came, compelled out of the air into the whirlwind of reply by the challenging voice of his creature'.[10] Ecclesiastes represents the wise man's view, 'there is nothing to do but to put up with what comes'. But 'The mystics and the saints desire and demand and promise; the storm of divine anger and divine peace rages from the heavens; an infinite riddle of substitution is sung to the heart of the devout'[11]—and among them was Williams.

Chapter IV is the Gospel story of the coming of the Godhead in created human flesh in common conditions. 'He works miracles of healing; he controls spirits; he teaches with authority'. 'Yes, but what gospel'? . . . 'It is a state of being, but not a state of being without which one can get along very well. To lose it is to lose everything else. It is intensely dangerous, and yet easily neglected'. 'It is the denial of the self and the lifting of the cross'. It was said, and is denied by our faithful friends the scientists, that at the Crucifixion there was darkness over the whole earth. 'But that the life of the whole of mankind began to fail in that hour is not incredible; that the sun and all light, without as within, darkened before men's eyes, that the swoon of something more than death touched them. . . . The Thing that was, and had always been, and must always be; the fundamental humanity of all men; the Thing that was man rather than a man . . . the Thing that was Christ Jesus, knew all things in the deprivation of all goodness'.[12] This was the choice of Adam in the myth of original sin, to know evil as well as good, when all things were good.

Secondly, mankind could not by itself endure the results of its choice to know the deprivation of good, nor could mankind recover the joy it had before its choice. But 'What mankind could not do, manhood did, and a manhood which was at the disposal of all men and women. It was therefore possible now for mankind itself to know evil as an occasion of heavenly love'.[13] The condition is repentance, which is an intention to know things after the mode of love, followed by pardon as a re-identification with love.

The last three chapters of the book describe human experience and practice of the knowledge of the first four, working outwards from the particular to the general. 'The Theology of Romantic Love' gave him his first opportunity to publish what had been an early and continuing meditation. Some emphases have changed: he is less religious, though equally theological; more Dantean as his studies thus have taken him, more humanly and poetically experienced in married love. He can speak now with authority of the endurance of romantic love, of moments of the glory in *caritas,* and of the need for 'a mind disposed to examine the pattern of the glory'.[14]

'The pre-eminent moment of romantic love', he says, 'is not, of course, confined to the moment of romantic sex love. There are other moments of intense experience combined with potentiality of further experience. Great art has it and politics and nature and (it is said) maturity'.[15] The supreme expression in English is Milton's Adam speaking of Eve:

> when I approach
> Her loveliness, so absolute she seems
> And in herself complete, so well to know
> Her own, that what she wills to do or say
> Seems wisest, virtuousest, discreetest, best.
> All higher knowledge in her presence falls
> Degraded.[16]

He goes on: 'There has been and is, now as always, only one question about this state of things: is it serious? is it capable of intellectual treatment? is it capable of belief, labour, fruition? is it (in some sense or other) *true?* ... Can this state of things be treated as the first matter of a great experiment? and if so, what exactly is the material? and what exactly are the best conditions of the experiment? The end, of course, is known by definition of the kingdom: it is the establishment of a state of *caritas,* of pure love, the mode of expansion of one moment into eternity'.[17]

The greatest European master of this romantic theology is Dante the thirteenth-century Italian. Williams says in this chapter that the range of his 'whole work provides a complete account of the making of the experiment and of its success'.[18] What we have here in this chapter about Dante Alighieri's love for Beatrice Portinari is an introduction—but a necessary introduction—to Williams's later full-length book, *The Figure of Beatrice,* where his doctrine of romantic love is fully worked out in Dantean terms.

In terms of his own experience of love, he sees how the personal consciousness of the beloved can lessen as 'full immingled zones of beatitude open'.[19] He even understands the loss of one's beatitude and the agony which can be 'now the very pulse of the final exaltation'.[20] 'My covenant shall be in your flesh' is a daily knowledge to him. The death of Beatrice, the disappearance of light and beatitude are realities to him. 'The City is widowed'[21]—Charles had lived, still lives in the widowed City, and knows that though Dante in Paradise imagined the sight of Beatrice 'more clearly and more strongly, he had not known anything different, in essence or in principle, when the face of the Florentine girl flashed her "good morning" at him along the street of their City'.[22] The St. Albans girl, the London girl, was as potent as the Florentine.

It is possible, he says, to follow the Way of Romantic Love 'without introducing the name of God. But is is hardly possible to follow it without proposing and involving as an end a state of *caritas* of the utmost possible height and breadth, nor without allowing to matter a significance and power which (of all the religions and philosophies) only Christianity has affirmed'.[23] The proposition doubtfully attributed to St. Bonaventura (roughly contemporary with Dante) that God is a circle whose centre is everywhere and circumference nowhere, gave the diagram of process that Charles was seeking. 'If . . . we retain the name and idea of God, and if there is any common agreement about the state of exalted experience known as the state of "falling in love", then it is possible to go further and relate that experience to the Incarnation of the kingdom. . . . The beloved (male or female) is seen in the light of a Paradisal knowledge and experience of good. Christ exists in the soul, in joy, in terror, in the miracle of newness. *Ecce, omnia nova facio* (Behold, I make all things new.).'[24]

Finally, he holds that 'Hell has made three principal attacks on the Way of Romantic Love. The dangerous assumptions produced are: (1) the assumption that it will naturally be everlasting; (2) the assumption that it is personal; (3) the assumption that it is sufficient'.[25]

As for the first assumption, the Beatrician state 'is eternal but is not everlastingly visible, any more than the earthly life of Christ'.[26] But there must be an accepted authority in it—'certainly some kind of pledged fidelity would seem to be a condition'.[27] And so 'The appearance of the glory is temporary: the authority of the glory towards pure love is everlasting; the quality of the glory is eternal, such as the heavens have in Christ'.[28]

Upon Hell's second assumption, the lover must not regard the state of love as a personal possession, nor the beloved as a personal adornment. 'Once the emotions have yielded to that falsity, the intellect too often is either thwarted or even betrayed into supporting them . . . love does not belong to lovers, but they to it. It is their job, as it is their direction, and salvation'.[29] For this reason, all sins of envy and jealousy, mental and sexual, are mortal, against the way to *caritas*. They are idolatry, the desire to retain the glory for oneself.

Third, the lover must not stop in the early stages of love. 'To be in love must be followed by the will to *be* love; to be love to the beloved, to be love to all, to be in fact (as the Divine Thing said) perfect'.[30] But lest we become unbearable, 'Shakespeare gave us the the healthy opposite and limit in that as in so much (he, the everlasting corrector of the follies of the disciples of Dante); in our consciousness of such things as regards ourselves we had better not go further than the point at which "with a pure blush we may come off withal'".[31]

And so 'The kingdom came down from heaven and was incarnate; . . . The beloved—person or thing—becomes the Mother of Love; Love is born in the soul; it may have its passion there; it may have its resurrection. It has its own divine nature united with our undivine nature'.[32]

The next chapter moves on to consider 'The Practice of Substituted Love' within the concepts of co-inherence, exchange and substitution which he had long been considering.

'"It is no more I that live, but Christ that liveth in me" is the definition of the pure life which is substituted for both', for self-sacrifice without love, or self-gratification also without love. But the taunt flung at Christ on the cross, "He saved others; himself he cannot save", 'was an exact definition of the kingdom of heaven in operation, and of the great discovery of substitution which was then made by earth'.[33]

Long before, the law of man's responsibility for man had been shaped when murder was first condemned in Cain, 'At the hand of every man's brother will I require the life of man'. The prophets of Israel recognized the law when they clamoured for social justice. In taking responsibility, one puts oneself in the other's situation, there is an acknowledgement of substitution. But such earthly moral law was not 'enough unless the burden of the law, of the law kept or the law unkept, could be known to be borne by heaven in the form of the Holy Thing that came down from heaven. Earth had to find also that the new law of the kingdom made that substitution a principle of universal exchange'.[34] We ourselves can be, slowly or quickly, changed and exchanged, and his life at moments of effort or vision substituted in us for our selves.

Christ left behind him the Church, 'not an organization of sinless men but of sinful, not a union of adepts but of less than neophytes, not of *illuminati* but of those that sat in darkness. Nevertheless, it carried within it an energy not its own, and it knew what it believed about that energy'.[35] If offered 'a new way, the way of return to blissful knowledge of all things', and also 'a new self to go on the new way'.[36] In practice, men's efforts divide into degrees of (1) the old self on the old way; (2) the old self on the new way; and (3) the new self on the new way—the second group being the largest—and not least in romantic love. 'It aims honestly at better behaviour, but it does not usually aim at change'.[37]

The need is for change in oneself. When young people told Charles of their loves, he looked in them for change in their conceit, bossiness or bad temper; so in considering the soul he knew that many people transfer their uncured vices to other motives. The old self 'uses its angers on behalf of its religion or its morals, and its greed, and its fear, and its pride. It operates on behalf of its notion of God as it originally operated on behalf of itself'.[38]

Because 'the mystery of the Atonement . . . had brought all things into the Atonement', Christ could say 'herein is that saying true, one soweth and another reapeth'. Williams goes on: 'The harvest is of others, as the beginning was in others, and the process was by others. This man's patience shall adorn that man, and that man's celerity this; and magnificence and thrift exchanged; and chastity and generosity; and tenderness and truth, and so on through the kingdom'.[39] Charles's poem, 'Apologue on the Parable of the Wedding Garment', enlarges the idea delightfully. At the Fancy Dress Ball given by the Prince Immanuel

> This guest his brother's courage wore;
> that, his wife's zeal, while, just before,
> she in his steady patience shone.
>
> . . .
>
>   magnificence
> a father borrowed of his son,
> who was not there ashamed to don
> his father's wise economy.[40]

This sense of a substituted life opens on to the book's last chapter, 'The City'. The phrase reflects the heavenly City of St. John's vision in *Revelation* as it does also the title of St. Augustine's book *The City of God*, and the City of London where man works. Within every willing person's life can be a web linking each to all, and to the love of God, in *caritas*—joyous goodwill. Which does not mean forced cheerfulness, that 'We are to be bright; we are to smile at strangers; we are (last horror of daily life!) to get into conversation with strangers'.[41] Instead, 'The word that runs through the Bible, the word that defines the yonder side of the demanded *caritas*, is glory', and 'The pattern of the glory is a pattern of acts'.[42]

The idea of the City as a web of exchange offers, 'the two modes of knowledge, knowledge being the chief art of love, as love is the chief art of knowledge: earth a directness, heaven a substitution'.[43] The City holds both. All the cruelty and misery of mankind and beyond them of the animals is created and sustained by God, as the First Cause. God has recognized the responsibility. He has become what he has made, in the condition to which it had, by his consent, brought itself. No fate compelled Him, as in all the sun myths, sacrificed deities and fertility rites. 'At the hand of God himself God has required the life of man'.[44] So comes the City, the web linking all men to all, and all to God. 'There is only one reason why anything should be loved on this earth—because God loves it'.[45] Having nothing, in the web of exchange we possess all things. The Lord's own prayer outlines it. Glorious moments of love can be a pattern, an order and an instinct in the manner of knowledge which already exists in heaven.

The book ends with a reminder, to himself as to the reader, that 'To think of the pattern is not to be part of the pattern; talk of exchange is not to exchange'.[46] The old self must by choice, deeper than words, move to grow into the new. It is simple, but there is a hint of threat: 'Blessed is he whosoever shall not be offended at me'.[47]

Poetry, office work and evening lectures went steadily on. Spare time was overloaded with *Judgement at Chelmsford* and answering Phyllis Potter's letters. A letter accepting an appointment which needed an hour's train journey says: 'the gratification with which one contemplates an hour of complete loneliness can hardly be exaggerated'.[48]

Americans were beginning to call on him at his office and talk about his books. In a latter to Thelma Shuttleworth he wrote: 'let us leave that to the Americans of the future when they write studies of me. I hope I shall read some of them one day: but probably other things, less pleasant, will occupy me'.[49] The letter goes on to a need for attention to words, especially to familiar words, such as the seven ages of man speech. 'It is almost impossible to hear at all—as you say, justly, about the Bible. But you must remember, it is not only admiration that does it; 'tis the refusal of the maturer mind to trouble. It is a lack of real critical love in us. On how many subjects do you really allow you may be wrong—serious subjects? On Christianity? on pacifism? There must be, don't you think? something of that intellectual willingness to be wrong in order that words may be heard? Thus people can never read the Bible for either they believe it or they do not believe it, but either way, they do not notice what the words are'.

During 1938, Phyllis Somervaille had made the acquaintance of Dougal, then a naval reservist, who first came into the Library in connection with his speciality of naval history. Phyllis often came down to the Library to check some matter of her work, and we would all talk. After a while I noticed that Phyllis and Dougal were becoming interested in each other.

In January 1938, Charles and Michal went to Paris for his only visit to the Continent, where he had been invited by the British Institute to lecture 'On Byron and Byronism' at the Sorbonne. He wrote to me on the 15th, 'All being well, I go to Paris on Saturday. The papers are full of pictures of the French military with stacked rifles waiting for trouble'.

Throughout the year, the threat of war tightened all our nerves. In the spring, Germany made the first move to absorb Sudetenland from Czechoslovakia, and by October had accomplished it. Charles wrote a long letter which was published in the *Sunday Times* in June, on liberty, and the risk at the current time of destroying it by too ardent organisation to defend it. He referred to the danger of words—liberty, intellectual honesty, freedom of speech—losing their meaning, a process familiar in time of crises. He asked for attention to language, to style 'in the spreading panic', as help towards order and peace. It is 'the best and most certain organisation of liberty' and intellectual freedom.[50] On 27 September he wrote to Phyllis Potter, who had connections with the Home Office, asking her to get his name put forward 'if there was any literary work that they wanted done as they did in the last War'.[51] Remarks on the likelihood of living longer— or not—passed through his letters.

I had married Peter Miller in 1935, and during 1938 I left the O.U.P., as I was going to have a baby. Living in London, I kept in close touch with friends at Amen House. *The Oxford Dictionary of Quotations* was in proof, and I had made a 150,000 word index. 1939 came in. Charles was still working on *Judgement at Chelmsford* and now writing *The Descent of the Dove,* while the country was turning to building Hurricanes and Spitfires. On 31 March, Britain promised help to Poland should it be attacked. In April, the military occupation of Czechoslavakia by Germany and of Albania by Italy made it likely that Poland would be next. Conscription (as we called it then; it became National Service later) was introduced in the United Kingdom, while it became clear that Eire would remain neutral.

Charles began to agree to his friends' pressure to form an Order concerned with his ideas of co-inherence, substitution and exchange—a step he had refused for three years. His letter to *The Sunday Times* probably links with the change. He wrote to a friend of both himself and his wife, Ursula Grundy, 'I am all but quite seriously proposing to make this small motion towards the Order. I have gone as far as making up six short statements as a beginning, and I am disposed at least to promulgate them among the household. It is a curiously mixed business, but I have a slight feeling that it is desirable from every point of view. I will try and have a set of the sentences for you by Friday and you can turn them over in your mind'.[52] He regarded it as established by September:[53] and *The Descent of the Dove* is dedicated as 'For the Companions of the Co-inherence'.

The sentences, ultimately seven, follow as Charles Williams wrote them.

1. The Order has no constitution except in its members. As it was said: *Others he saved, himself he cannot save.*

2. It recommends nevertheless that its members shall make a formal act of union with it and of recognition of their own nature. As it was said: *Am I my brother's keeper?*

3. Its concern is the practice of the apprehension of the Co-inherence both as a natural and a supernatural principle. As it was said: *Let us make man in Our image.*

4. It is therefore, *per necessitatem,* Christian. As it was said: *And who ever says there was when this was not, let him be anathema.*

5. It recommends therefore the study, on the contemplative side, of the Co-inherence of the Holy and Blessed Trinity, of the Two Natures in the Single Person, of the Mother and Son, of the communicated Eucharist, and of the whole Catholic Church. As it was said: *figlia del tuo figlio.* And on the active side, of methods of exchange, in the State, in all forms of love, and in all natural things, such as childbirth. As it was said: *Bear ye one another's burdens.*

6. It concludes in the Divine Substitution of Messias* all forms of exchange and substitution, and it invokes this Act as the root of all. As it was said: *He must become, as it were, a double man.*

7. The Order will associate itself primarily with four feasts: the Feast of the Annunciation, the Feast of the Blessed Trinity, the Feast of the Transfiguration, and the Commemoration of All Souls.† As it was said: *Another will be in me and I in him.*

By the middle of May, Charles had finished *The Descent of the Dove* (it was then being called *A History of Christendom*), which the distinguished firm of Longmans‡ were to publish in 1939. Probably Tom Burns, a young member of its staff, advised the firm to invite Charles to write it. Charles later commented that Tom said the effect of the manuscript on him was that it seemed like 'an unsatisfactory but pleasant and desirable love affair between the Manhood and the God-head'.[54]

The country continued to prepare for war, but sherry parties still went on, and Charles, still doing some book reviewing, went to Lady Rhondda's: 'purely official: I loathe Lady Rhondda's politics,§ but I like getting a few books out of *Time & Tide*'.

Meanwhile, business firms with offices in London had been making their plans. The Oxford University Press had investigated possible build-

---

*Christ

†Those of us, whether members of the Charles Williams Society or not, who count ourselves members of the Order, arrange meetings as near as possible to the dates of these festivals.

‡It was published in New York, also in 1939, by Oxford University Press.

§They were Liberal.

ings for the evacuation of Amen House to Oxford, chose Southfield House in Hilltop Road, and planned necessary alterations. It made contingency lists of lodgings or billets for the necessary staff who were over call-up age or exempt, and made tactful moves toward congruity.

Martin Shaw was concerned with the music for *Judgement at Chelmsford*, and booking of tickets began. A rare glimpse of Charles's general health comes in a reply to Phyllis Potter's offer of a week's visit for a holiday, as she was worried about the tremor of his hands. He refused, thanking her. 'I have had to put up with it all my life, and a damn nuisance it has been. It is a little worse since the operation, but it does not get any worse through a little work'.[55]

Rehearsals of *Chelmsford* went on. Charles considered the soul, and the need for it to acknowledge a hierarchy in its life, not fixed but essential. On 23 August he wrote to me of his wife's bad week of pain in her back, of the British Ambassador flying to Hitler and Ribbentrop to Moscow, of Amen House. He had been talking to Lynton Lamb and they had agreed that the Amen House irony did not cover all, though Lamb said he had been impressed by it at first. There was a world beyond the laughter, and that world kept the laughter sweet. On 25 August (ten days before our Declaration of War) came the first doubt about putting on *Judgement at Chelmsford*, or where the O.U.P. might be next week. By 28 August, Phyllis Potter was making blackout curtains instead of costumes and referred to Charles being moved to Oxford. On the 29th he replied that they had not moved to Oxford. 'We vibrate in continual expectation, but nothing has happened so far. The Spaldings have offered to put us up and I am considering the possibility of dispatching my people there this week. But there seems to remain a faint possibility of quiet'.[56] On 28 August he had written to Ursula Grundy that 'Miss Spalding has sent to invite us all three, says her parents whom I haven't met, would be delighted: she offers room for two or three others from the Press. . . . it is a noble gesture'.[57]

Poland was attacked by Germany at dawn on 1 September. The British ultimatum to Germany was delivered at 9.30 P.M. on the same day, and a second and final ultimatum on 3 September at 9 A.M. At 11.15 A.M. the Prime Minister broadcast that we were at war.

11

Oxford and The Inklings

Amen House emptied, fifty of the staff being transferred to Oxford. Younger people, including the invaluable Ralph Binfield, Charles Hadfield and Lynton Lamb vanished—to reappear in uniform on flying visits. Charles had to go through his desk drawers and cupboard, taking down brick by brick the house of his life and of his poetry. The Auxiliary Fire Service moved into the lower part of Amen House, and on 13 September, Charles wrote: 'if anyone tries to sleep in my room, they will have to curl themselves up in a very complicated way'.[1]

At the war's outbreak, in the shocked stillness that fell on us all, he held to the friends in his Order of the Co-inherence. He wrote to several. Now was the time for it, and to know co-inherence, including the enemy, including Hitler and he with us, and all in Christ. Now if ever we must think it. Its dark point is deeper than causes or principles. Even when we had to fight 'There, there, we are in one'.[2] In the pressure, Sir Humphrey came out of his solitude and talked to Charles. He who had believed so deeply in intelligence, in sane development, was 'driven' Charles wrote 'to admit at last that culture is not the soul. Nor—it is my chief fear—is talking about the soul'.[3] On 7 September, Charles wrote a letter to Dr. Walter Lowrie, a fair example of one from a literary-religious editor at the onset of war. It begins, 'My letter of 24 August was too, too accurate! You will see from the above heading that we have moved from London, and you will have gathered how, like the men of Nehemiah the Tirshatha, we work between gas-masks and sirens. And so—what?' There follow five clear points on publishing five new titles of Kierkegaard and forecasts of probable paper shortages. Phyllis Potter had written to a contact in the Home Office, and in a few days Charles thanked her: 'I shall be only too glad to do something intelligent'. He hopes to get on 'with my next three books, but I am not doing so at present'.[4] Nothing came of the approach to the Home Office, and Williams was to stay where he was, at Southfield House, throughout the war.

He had been young in one war, and his two greatest men friends had been killed. Now his young colleagues at the Press, his students or students' husbands were at risk again—his 1940 letters are full of them. The gift he brought to Oxford in wartime was affirmation. Belief must have experience, and experience must admit affirmation. In work, love, religion, business, politics, he recognised and could experience validity, and the need to explore the experience and maintain the validity in good times as in loss and defeat.

By 7 September, Charles and Gerry Hopkins had become members of an Oxford University household, Professor Spalding's, at 9 South Parks Road. The road leads off Parks Road, which starts in Broad Street opposite the Sheldonian Theatre, so the house was close in to Oxford's centre. It was a big, comfortable Victorian house, where the Spaldings had regular domestic help living in. Both men were lucky, for Oxford was crowded with evacuees, the staffs of business firms and sections of government offices.

Michal and Gerry's wife, however, both stayed in London. Michal had come down to see Charles's new surroundings but felt that if she had to pay the rent of a London flat, she might as well live in it. Also, with young Michael living at home awaiting his call-up, it would have been almost impossible for all three to lodge in 9 South Parks Road. Charles declared that Michal bloomed in crises and had been 'astonishingly and persistently good'.[5] The absence of their wives probably drew him and Gerry together, for they remained good friends for the five and a half years of the war.

H. N. Spalding, founder of the Spalding Chair of Eastern Religion and Ethics, and his wife were in the United States when Charles arrived. Ruth Spalding, the younger daughter, had worked before the war as a travelling producer for the Religious Drama Society, and in June had produced *Seed of Adam* in St. Mary's Church. On that occasion Charles and Michal had come to Oxford to see it and had lunched at 9 South Parks Road. When the war began, E. Martin Browne had formed The Pilgrim Players at Canterbury to take religious plays to the people, whereupon Ruth formed a second independent company, the Oxford Pilgrim Players, to do the same.

Management of the house therefore fell mainly to the elder sister Anne because Ruth was often away with her work. The job was a demanding one, with food rationing, strangers lodging, meals needed at different times and, once fire-watching (watching in the buildings normally unoccupied at night for the fall from enemy aircraft of incendiary bombs and then putting them out) had begun, members of the household up regularly at odd hours of the night.

Anne told me that she had been disinclined to manage people. When she surveyed the lodgers, among them Charles and Gerry, her hasty desire to abdicate led her to consoling thoughts that the regime would work as a democracy. It was made and kept clear that it was a monarchy. Gerry and Charles, and no doubt others, listened to all the problems, supported her in crises, gave full attention to sifting evidence on hours and rations, outlined alternatives, and refused to decide for her. She said she was a queen with her ministers (strictly advisory) and that whatever she decided, they would follow to the death. They also praised and thanked her for doing her ordinary duties, and she began to wonder what the business was about the disgruntled housewife. Fortunately, the domestic staff had been with her family a long while.

Charles showed himself expert in domestic work. He was never late for meals, including breakfast. He cut the bread for everybody, in spite of his shaky hands, opened windows to air the room after meals, plumped up all the cushions every night before bed. He was a faithful drier-up, and would break up the most absorbing theological talk to dry the 9 P.M. cups of tea— unless, as Anne remembered, the conversation was of real moment to the visitor, a condition he sensed with accuracy. Making his bed was his boast. In this, he and T. S. Eliot held themselves to be outstanding. They both exclaimed on the stupidity of 'poetic' men being helpless about the house and both claimed to make a bed neatly in seven minutes or, Charles said, in the time he would take to write a sonnet.

On the first Sunday morning, Anne asked him if he wanted to be called for early church. He said no, thank you, he would leave it to the Holy Ghost whether he should go or not. As far as she could remember afterwards, It was always in favour of his going. He went to St. Cross Church at eight after knocking on Anne's door to make sure that she was awake. Sometimes he went to a later Eucharist, and sang vigorously as he had done in St. Albans Abbey, with rhythm but no knowledge of intonation. The Creed and the Gloria seemed to rouse his special enthusiasm, and he crossed himself with large swift gestures. After church, the rest of Sunday was given to writing, though after lunch he would read a detective novel. Weekday evenings were spent in lectures or writing.

He could write in his bedroom in the mild September weather, even in October; but as winter came on and bedrooms could not be heated in wartime, there was a severe loss of privacy, for he had to gather with others round the sitting room fire, among the general activity which regularly included a typewriter, and write on his little pad on a crossed knee. He had of course no private sitting room to which he could take anyone for a talk. Old friends down from London, had, like young courting couples, to make do in cafés and pubs.

Southfield House stood on a rise between the Cowley and Headington Roads in east Oxford, in a quiet area of playing fields and open land. Charles, almost alone of the staff, had an office to himself, sited in a bathroom. It was a large roomy bathroom, leading off the first-floor landing and overlooking the entrance. The covered bath made a good shelf for piles of manuscripts and books. On the opposite wall were bookshelves with Charles's desk between, looking out of the window over the drive and into a tall hedge. Leading off the same landing were Sir Humphrey's room and his secretary Budgen's, and the Juvenile Department's offices. The rest of the publishing was carried on in bedrooms and sitting rooms all over the house. Later, Sir Humphrey took over the ground floor room by the front entrance.

If one came to Southfield House by car, one approached from the Headington side and so up the main drive. Charles and Gerry must have walked from 9 South Parks Road down to the High (Street), then caught a No. 1 bus for a mile or so up the Cowley Road to the *Magdalen Arms,* then walked up a gravel path beside college playing fields to the garden gates of Southfield House and along the path which came out by the porch. Charles was surrounded by countrified peace and silence, and protected from co-inherence with the outer world by a carefully planned green belt. There is no reason to suppose he was grateful. He had been fifteen years in one room at Amen House and, like all the staff, he felt a snail without its shell. There was no Library and no privacy, as the unsettled life led to ways of popping in and out looking for people which reasonable men would not have tolerated in Amen House. However, he remained always exactly the same: punctual, rapid, undismayed, gloomily cheerful, efficient. Public changes did not impair his personal functioning. He was not alone in this. All the staff rallied admirably.

Oxford society expected men to wear tweed jackets and flannel trousers. Charles impressed everyone by wearing his blue suit and Homburg hat, and carrying an umbrella. Anne Spalding said it was like Sunday morning all the time. Other members of the Oxford Press staff changed to local costume sooner or later, but Charles did no more than abandon the hat.

Phyllis Somervaille soon arrived in Southfield House, seeking work, and the sudden sight of her in unfamiliar surroundings shook Charles. Gerry told him that her divorce had been made absolute and that she would be married to Dougal as soon as he got leave from his ship, now stationed at Grimsby. Meantime, she would work in Miss Peacock's office as before. 'In God and the Order', Charles exclaimed for support.

He wrote to me in October: 'I ran into her on Friday for five minutes. The image and the loss of the image—yes: I maintain it. But heavens, when the image is there . . . She has gone off for another week at Grimsby. . . . O, I wish I were free'.[6] It was not freedom from his marriage he longed for, but from the thirteen-year-old passionate vision through Phyllis. More and more he realised the process of romantic love as committed to the taunt, 'He saved others, himself he cannot save'. 'There is no hope, none', he wrote to one in like trouble, 'but that Love is in that, and is that. But O the word means something very different from our young romantic visions, though it still means them. Themselves they cannot save'.[7] The darker side of his nature surfaced in scraps of bitter, almost sneering, verse on Phyllis. He recognized the impulse for what it was and said to me, 'I remark the other side of the way again!' 'The Other Side of the Way' is the poem in *Windows of Night,* on the town street, the way to heaven on one side and the way to hell on the other, with the road being repaired in between.

Home relations, however, began well. He had gone up for a weekend to Michal, who had heard by chance the news of Phyllis' return from Java and presence at Southfield House. Yet 'The weekend, in the marvellous ways of the Dove, was entirely admirable; my wife was infinitely full of affection and goodness. I (it is to be admitted) faintly sacrificed Sir Humphrey and Michal allowed herself one scratch. . . . I was secretly annoyed, but that is the kind of thing I never fight. But otherwise all was happy'.[8] And he was back in London. He was willing to agree that 'Oxford is beautiful, so long as you live in London'.

Isobel and Margaret Douglas settled into rooms in Oxford's Randolph Hotel. Isobel, well-off, widow of a Scottish minister, had been an accomplished pianist, and was accustomed to good literary and artistic society. She was tiny, elegant and white-haired. Margaret was partially-sighted, handicapped by her large size and slow walk. She had a heart of gold and true humility, with much observation and good sense. A trained typist, she had typed (unpaid) for the Children's Society for years. Quietly and efficiently she offered her one gift to Charles and saved armfuls of his verse by typing it and putting it in order as he showed her. Much that would have become illegible by age and bad treatment has been saved because she could ask him to decipher it. Also, the Douglas's accommodation had a small sitting room which they seldom used, and occasionally it was possible for Charles to talk to old friends there. Michal and Isobel detested each other, and were worthy antagonists. They made much discomfort for Charles when they met.

The upset to life and habits which dislocated the functioning of so many men of his age, caused no calculable impairment in Charles's work at his desk. But for a few weeks it affected his own writing. On 20 September he wrote, 'I haven't found it possible to do any work yet',[9] and was distressed that new Taliessin poems were 'irresponsive' in him. Early in October a letter to Anne Ridler said: 'There is no-one (NO-ONE) in Oxford to whom I can talk about Taliessin. This is a serious blow, and I only found it out yesterday. HSM is here, and Gerry and Page and Foss and Celia—and damn all a single one of them can be talked to about it, because they aren't interested in that way. I have been spoilt, I know'. He was working on 'The Prayers of the Pope', later to be included in *The Region of the Summer Stars,* and just then he wanted to talk about his idea of the young Pope having white hair—'The Pope (let us say) is time losing its beauties (by deprivation or will, not by mere passing change) but affirmatively. O I write it badly . . .'[10] What he eventually made of the idea can be found in lines 3-6 of the printed poem.

My husband was in the army, and I remained in our London house. On a visit to Oxford soon afterwards to see Charles, I arranged to do some Arthurian reference research that he needed. By then he had got himself re-started, doubly helped by the publication of *The Descent of the Dove* and by C. S. Lewis.

Copies of *The Descent of the Dove* arrived in the third week of October, 1939. Soon afterwards it was chosen by The Religious Book Club. The book has as frontispiece a black and white reproduction of Lodovico Brea's painting, 'Paradise'. A panel at the base shows the dead body of Christ, with the mourners. Above, the painting presents a concourse of all degrees of men and women, adoring the Holy Trinity depicted as crowning the Blessed Virgin in a nimbus of glory. The subtitle is 'A Short History of the Holy Spirit in the Church.' A chronological table of this history, at the end of the book, has for the first entry 'A.D. 30—Ascent of our Lord and Descent of the Holy Ghost', and for last '1939 European War: second period of military operations', and contains thirteen dates of official warfare. Charles had always declared that a state of war was part of man.

To change the title as he did from *A History of Christendom* was in itself a motion of the Holy Spirit, for this is not a book about a movement in the world's history like, say, the *Philosophes*. It is about history itself, in the book mostly European but looking also 'at the ends of the earth',[11] for Charles saw it all as the result of the Spirit's activity, the Church's role being that of revealing the divine purpose behind the history and reconciling humanity to it. *The Descent of the Dove* tracks some workings of the Holy Spirit in the Church and the spreading non-religious world, with the inspiration, courage, endurance and disasters that have resulted. *The Descent of the Dove* seems to be close to those prophetic books of the Bible in which the heroes of the story speak directly from God: 'Be it known unto thee, O king, that this day thou diest'—and he does.

Like *He Came Down From Heaven*, the book starts from a beginning removed from man, at a point outside time, at 'the meeting of two heavenward lines', one along the ascent of Christ and the other along the descent of the Paraclete or Holy Spirit at Pentecost. There is involved a process of the Spirit towards Christ in our humanity, with its beginning and end in heaven. The Church is seen as beginning in the life and words of Christ, his ascension, and the opening, in wind and tongued flames, of the secrets of the Paraclete to the little number of the church who were themselves one of the secrets. Just as in his reading of poetry Charles asked questions of the poet rather than saw patterns or gave answers, so in following the human records of the Holy Spirit, from the clear words of the first martyr, Stephen, at his death, to the fathomless depths of simple statements by St. Paul, he asked what the feeling intellect could find here, 'whose twilights were more clear, than our mid-day'.[12]

From the first century, when believers expected every day the return of Christ in glory, he moves to the reconciliation with time, and the finding of a different kind of return—rebirth in the soul. The civilized world of the Roman Empire became formally Christian. The Fathers wrestle with common sense and social custom to discover the Nicene Creed and to establish the glory of the body in the Athanasian Creed. They came also with dread to the writings of Dionysius the Areopagite: 'the climax of one great mode of speculation and of experience; they are hardly, yet they are, within the orthodoxy of Christendom. They provide the great negative definitions infinitely satisfying to a certain type of mind when it contemplates intellectually the Divine Principle'.[13]

In the martyrs and in the Eucharist Williams found the experience of substitution and co-inherence: 'another will be in me who will suffer for me',[14] 'My Eros is crucified'.[15] 'who ... took Bread; and, when he had given thanks, he brake it, and gave it to his disciples, saying, Take, eat, this is my Body which is given for you: Do this in remembrance of me'.[16] 'For as in Adam all die, even so in Christ shall all be made alive'.[17]

Six hundred years of discovery and experience were given, and then came the enemy. In 628 the Eastern Emperor, then in Jerusalem, chief defender of the faith, received a message 'signed Mohammed, Messenger of God', bidding him abandon his beliefs, and confess the Resignation.[18] Two years later 'the first Army of the Resignation and of the Unincarnate Alone, offered battle to the central City of the Co-inherent and Incarnate'.[19] Great cities and whole areas of eastern Christendom fell, North Africa, Spain, Asia Minor. Jew, Mohammedan and Christian were each an outrage to the others, the very nature of Christ in the union of manhood (matter) and Godhead (spirit) splitting the whole society of man. But far away in the western ocean, in Ireland and the islands farther north, a new growth of Christendom arose, solitary and peaceful, not yet affecting the main body, but safely separated.

The year 1000 approached, and once more Christendom expected the Second Coming. But 'the expectation of his coming had changed. Interior illuminations were discouraged. Exteriorly, the Second Coming had turned into something similar yet different; through all those converted masses it was presented now as the Day of Judgement'.[20] It did not come, and the second millenium 'opened with no greater terror than the ordinary robberies, murders, rapes, burnings, wars, massacres, and plagues, and the even less noticeable agonies of each man's ordinary life'.[21] Charles might have added, as he did in conversation on this theme, 'or of the life of Nature'.

Charles continues to examine the history of Christendom from the angle of ideas as causes and events as results. This keeps central the sense of the Holy Spirit. 'What is going on, if anything?'[22] gave us Abelard, Anselm, the Middle Ages; the dangerous belief in belief gave us the organization and the Orders of the Church and also the great doctors, St. Thomas Aquinas and Duns Scotus. Devotional ideas became more literary. The Grail and Arthurian romances produced Galahad, conceived in the dark night of the soul.[23] 'Poetry can do something that philosophy can not, for poetry is arbitrary and has already turned the formulae of belief into an operation of faith . . . poetry, like faith, can . . . survey reason all round'.[24] More and more in human society it was Man and not Man-in-God who absorbed attention. So we feel the impact of the Crusades, of Corpus Christi, of witchcraft, the Templars, the mystics, and schism in the Papacy.

The 'appalling and ambiguous' statement of Jesus, 'Behold, I am with you always',[25] is recalled at the opening of the Renascence and the Reformation. In the Renascence, Man became his own end and purpose.

' . . . he was left to take glory in, and to glorify, himself and his works'.[26] 'The cry of "Another is in me" had faded, and the Renascence glory was not attributed to the Acts of that Other'.[27] Acts, not faith, mattered. But 'The cry for Reform which is always heard in the Church was no less vocal then',[28] and 'two characteristics of Christendom—exchange and conversion'[29] projected the crisis of the Reformation.

Chapters VIII and IX, 'The Quality of Disbelief' and 'The Return of the Manhood', comprise the last third of the book. They cover the period from St. John of the Cross and Queen Elizabeth I of England to Pascal, Voltaire, Wesley, the advance of scholarship, the 'humanitarian Jesus', the movement of the dispossessed, the Russian Revolution and rejection of religion for Communism in 1917, the 1920 'Appeal to all Christian people' issued from Lambeth by the Bishops of the Church of England, and a mention of the fighting in Spain. This section is again one clear seeing of the whole from the operative ideas working in details. Charles defined that power he had felt since youth behind man's movements. Contrition, humility and doctrine are again energies following from the descent of the Dove. The last sentence of the book is true of every year of its two millennia of history: Christendom's 'only difficulty will be to know and endure him when he comes, and that, whether it likes or not, Messias has sworn that it shall certainly do'.[30]

A postscript follows on Charles's thoughts about co-inherence—natural in conception and pregnancy, acknowledged in baptism by godparents, and declared by the Christian faith 'to be the root and the pattern of the supernatural as of the natural world . . . it might indeed be worth the foundation of an Order within the Christian Church. . . . The Order of the Co-inherence'.*[31]

Charles saw very clearly why so many people did not like the Church, and feared any religious organisation. But he also saw that notwithstanding the Inquisition and witch-hunts and the regular practice of making God as undisturbing as possible, the Church had, with the assistance of the Holy Spirit, remained just on the good side in humanity's values rather than on the bad. It had never accomplished enough, but Charles was always tender to anyone who shrank from fearful effort. He regarded the compulsion of the Holy Spirit as so horrifyingly disturbing and the practice of giving up one's life to save it as so full of shock and agony that the less one was forced to deal with such things the happier one was. He did not limit his vision of the working of the Spirit to those lives ranged on the

---

*In fact, many have already chosen to be members of this Order. The sentences defining it can be found on p. 174.

side of religion or the Church. The great enemies of the Church, like Voltaire, Marxism and Leninism, were as much moved by the descent of the Dove as Wesley or Alphonsus Liguori. So with the intellectual enemies, rational or scientific. The life of the Church co-inhered with and lived from contention with them. 'The great arguments continued, and continue today; it is much to be hoped that they will not stop',[32] said Charles in the last chapter, and indeed he would have found any world trivial without the clash of dogma. Yeats wrote of 'the supreme theme of Art and Song',[33] but to Charles the supreme theme was poetry and men coinherent with God and each other.

He reaffirmed his sense of the validity of the Church of England. Of her new life independent of Rome he wrote: 'She was threatened with Calvinsim at one time and reconciled to Rome at another. But she was not overthrown by another Church, old or new. . . . She continued to operate formally, and she retained a continual spiritual awareness of herself. The idea that there was at any time any break in the steady outward hierarchical succession or the use of the Rites or the repetition of the Creeds . . . is abandoned. . . . Between the "slight column" of Calvin counterweighing the ocean-mass of Trent, the Church of England pursued her odd (but not, for that, necessarily less sacred) way, still aware of herself as related to all the past, and to the ceremonial presences of Christ'.[34] Of the nineteenth century he wrote: 'In England the Oxford Movement was already in action; Newman's Tract 90 had appeared in 1840, and Newman himself was received into the Roman Church in 1848. It was supposed he would be followed by his followers, but they were not his followers as much as they were followers of religion, and religion did not lead them with him. Neither of these two great schismatics, Wesley nor Newman, shook the centre of the Church of England, nor could; what they did was to direct attention to some sin, some negligence, some chill. Fervour awoke again, and doctrine, or perhaps not so much doctrine as the assertion of doctrine. And as in England, so elsewhere'.[35] As Charles's mind deepened he cherished ever more dearly the distinctive characteristics of the Church of England in her decision not to define more closely than within a range of choices of belief, certain vital operations of God in the Church and in the soul; and secondly her teaching that the whole Church is more than any single part, however hallowed. In his Introduction to Evelyn Underhill's letters, published in 1943,[36] he makes the point that she never left the Church of England, but 'thought it her proper place'.

Dr. Glen Cavaliero has well written of *The Descent of the Dove*: 'It is an outline of Church history in terms of the Church's developing awareness and understanding of the co-inherence of men and women in God, and Man in God, and Man in men and women, and men and women in each other. Learned, witty, radiant, profound, it is a revolutionary book whose significance has still to be appreciated'.[37]

Oxford has, of course, its own history of religious development and was not, perhaps, an easy place for an author of a history of Christendom to be. However, *The Descent of the Dove* was well received there as well as in London. Reviews came in. Charles did not think that all were intelligent. The crackle of epigrams grew tiresome, and some admirers did not know the history of the Church and so were considering only the intensity of the writing. The subject was what mattered, and what the subject showed for men in every age.

It was, Humphrey Carpenter tells us,[38] the first theological work that W. H. Auden had studied, and it led him on to Kierkegaard. Auden wrote to Charles, who told his wife that 'he just wanted to tell me how moved he was by the Dove (and he no Christian)', and he had said 'though I've only met you twice, in times of difficulty and doubt recalling you has been of great help to me'. Later he wrote again to Charles that 'one day the *Dove* will be honoured for the great book it is'.

While he was reading Williams and Kierkegaard, Auden began to attend church 'in a tentative and experimental sort of way' and early in 1940 began writing 'New Year Letter', saying that the *Dove* was 'the source of many ideas in the poem'. He rejoined the (Anglican) Episcopal Church in the U.S.A. 'New Year Letter' was now expanded to a book, *The Double Man.** In the *Dublin Review* Charles wrote of the book that 'It is, after its own manner, a pattern of the Way'.

Meanwhile, C. S. Lewis had moved quickly. He had been a fellow of Magdalen College and tutor in English Language and Literature for fourteen years, and had become a leader in the development of the English School at the University. He invited Charles, as soon as he was settled in Oxford, to join an informal literary group, the Inklings. There Charles met J. R. R. Tolkien, then Professor of Anglo-Saxon, Gervase Mathew, Roman Catholic priest and University lecturer, Owen Barfield, Hugo Dyson, Lewis's brother W. H. ('Warnie') Lewis and other literary men, and so senior University life was opened to him.

When Williams had been in Oxford for about two months, Lewis suggested that he should 'do something at Magdalen'—presumably lecture—probably after he had heard him read a paper at one of the women's colleges, and judged his lecturing technique. That autumn term Lewis had himself lectured on Milton, with Charles, who got time off from work in

*Its American title.

exchange for permission to work through the lunch hour, in the audience. They talked much about Milton. Humphrey Carpenter, in *The Inklings*, quotes Lewis as determined 'to smuggle him into the Oxford lecture list, so that we might have some advantage from the great man's accidental presence in Oxford'. And so he did, Williams's lack of a degree notwithstanding.

The lecture course was to be on Milton, who was at the time under considerable modern attack. Charles had been invited by Sir Humphrey to write an introduction to the 1940 reprint of *The English Poems of John Milton* in the Oxford University Press Series, 'The World's Classics', (CLXXXII) where he began: 'We have been fortunate enough to live at a time when the reputation of John Milton has been seriously attacked'. Notable among the attackers was T. S. Eliot, who declared Milton's style damaging and, says Carpenter, found the theology of *Paradise Lost* 'repellent'. This of course was known to Williams and Lewis. On 29 January 1940 Lewis and Tolkien escorted Charles to the University's Divinity School to give the first lecture. Gerry Hopkins had come to enlarge the audience. It went well, and the four of them celebrated afterwards in the Mitre Hotel bar.

It was the second lecture the next week that made a stir and impressed Lewis seriously. This was on Milton's masque, *Comus*. In mythology, Comus is son of Bacchus, the first grower of vines, who fell to the charm of the witch Circe, and fathered Comus. He has power to assume a simple exterior and then to tempt man or woman with drink or deceits and turn them into beasts, as his mother did. All this is known in English literature. Milton's masque opens with a lady who has lost her way in a wood and been parted from her brothers, a fate most incident to ladies in verse. Her brothers search for her, and almost run a sweepstake on the chances of her virginity surviving the night. Charles went to the heart of Milton's poem, which was love of virtue and in this lady's case, chastity. Lewis wrote and spoke of the lecture afterwards: 'Simply as criticism it was superb because here was a man who really started from the same point of view as Milton and really cared with every fibre of his being about "the sage and serious doctrine of virginity" which it would never occur to the ordinary modern critic to take seriously. But it was more important still as a sermon. It was a beautiful sight to see a whole room full of modern young men and women sitting in that absolute silence which can *not* be faked, very puzzled but spell-bound'. He recognized the power of the lecturer. 'That beautiful carved room had probably not witnessed anything so important since some of the great mediaeval or Reformation lectures. I have at last, if only for once, seen a university doing what it was founded to do: teaching wisdom'.[39] What intellectual virtue and generosity there was in Lewis. Warm-hearted and highly intelligent, he was to give immense help to Charles in wartime Oxford.

We can only dimly imagine what the Milton lectures meant to Williams. Hitherto, though within the great world of London, his life had been lived in a comparatively narrow realm of home, evening institute lecturing, and editorial work within the stimulating but enclosed world of Amen House. Oxford was the origin and base of his own employers, who traced their first printed book to 1478, and the home of Britain's premier university, some three hundred years older still. Within five months of his arrival, here he was, a self-made literary man with no university degree, lecturing, not to gatherings of mainly middle-aged or elderly students collected for him by the London County Council, but to educated undergraduates of a great university, under the sponsorship of men of academic reputation such as Lewis and Tolkien. At last, he must have thought, he was moving in a society of intellectual equals, and moreover one of men. No wonder he coruscated to his wife: 'Am I only to be followed by the feminine? No; you will be attended—you—by the masculine minds: great minds, strong males, brothers of our energy—those who know our work—Lewis—and Tolkien. . . .'[40]

Two lines of development now opened. Within the University he began to lecture regularly and to tutor at St. Hilda's College. Slowly the pace of his academic involvement built up, until in 1943, apart from a heavy programme of tutoring, he was giving eight University lectures on Wordsworth and eight on Shakespeare at the Taylorian, as well as 'The Arthurian Tradition in English Literature' at Lady Margaret Hall, 'After Falstaff' to the Oxford Graduates Society and at Lady Margaret Hall, 'Is there a Christian Literature?' in a series at Pusey House, and 'Religion and Drama' to the Student Christian Movement in the Old Library of St. Mary's the University Church. In 1944 he gave thirteen lectures on Shakespeare and eight on eighteenth-century poetry; in 1945 eight on Milton.

He had long been lecturing and tutoring by invitation. Now the Dante Society wanted him as a member, for which a university qualification was needed. It was felt by his University friends that he ought to be invited to join the English faculty, if not at once, then when he retired from the Oxford University Press in 1951. For this also he would need to have a degree. So, in the degree-giving of 18 February 1943, the honorary degree of Master of Arts was conferred on him, the outer world thus catching up with the inner just in time. With him were five others, including Mr. L. S. Amery (Secretary of State for India) and Mr. Percy Scholes.

Charles sent Michal details of the coming ceremony—she and, he hoped, Michael, would be there. The Douglases were to give a lunch for friends and Ursula Grundy and Gerry Hopkins. Gerry Hopkins would take the party 'under his academic wing'. At the official lunch Charles and his wife sat between the Vice-Chancellor and Mr. Amery; the Public Orator, Mr. Barrington Ward, said (in Latin) that Charles was 'a penetrating literary critic and at the same time a talented poet' who refuted the saying that critics were those who had failed in literature and art; that he had achieved noteworthy success in the Pindaric style of verse;[41] that he was a reader to the Oxford University Press; and gave lectures on the poets—'with what acuteness of mind did he interpret them, with what fervour and spirit did he deliver them'. He was an 'accomplished and literary man'. A fulfilling moment for Walter and Mary, a noble and happy part of those Hertfordshire walks forty years ago.

The citation referred to *Taliessin Through Logres* and the new style of poetry which Charles had first developed in *Thomas Cranmer of Canterbury*. Probably Lewis had been consulted upon it. Sir Humphrey had said he would pay any fees involved in the degree, which half-pleased, half-irritated Charles. He did not want to feel under any obligation to the O.U.P. in this matter. He wrote to Michal: 'I hope the conclusion of Underhill* and the coming of the degree are favourable omens. I give it—this morning in church—to the Holy Spirit; we will be in him and for him all through'.

Reaction after the day's ceremony was severe. He told Michal: 'This exhaustion catches me every now and then. I want to be nice and good, but I'm not feeling so a bit. You will have to keep me faced in the right direction, as you have done so often. There are wells of hate in one which are terrifying—wells of suspicion and even malice. This is nice talk isn't it? And a fine start for new things . . . forgive me'.[42]

There were, however, those who considered that his friends in the English School had been unduly carried away by his brilliance, and that he was never the figure that some thought him. But whether London or Oxford were the better judge, Oxford gave him undoubted acceptance.

The second line of development came through his involvement with the Inklings, about whom Humphrey Carpenter has written an excellent book, in which he gives special attention to Tolkien, Williams and Lewis.[43] It seems fair to say that the group, and those who joined it, were linked year by year by an addiction to life-long interests, literature and ideas, rather than by the novelties or fashions of a time. They were likely to be,

---

*He had been writing an introduction to her letters, published by Longmans, Green & Co. in 1943.

in turn, old-fashioned and advanced. They found no special value in opinions for being young, or liberal, or established, or destructive. They preferred those which were to them lively, valid, and with intellectual ancestry. T. S. Eliot and John Betjeman were rejected among poets, and F. R. Leavis among critics and teachers. Charles's own view was put in a letter of early 1941 to Anne Ridler. He was not interested, he says, in 'culture, contemporary writing and so on. We waste energy in resenting what is a matter of indifference, and it isn't for us to waste our energy. I think that is what I do feel very strongly; it is perhaps a little snobbish—in fact it is undoubtedly snobbish—but I am sure that is our real superiority—*not* to be disturbed. "The lesser breeds without the law" grow feverish with their culture (so to call it). But our culture is—culture, and a part of us, and we afford all they can't".[44]

Charles went regularly to the Inklings meetings at Magdalen and joined the others of the group for weekly lunches at the Eagle and Child or the White Horse pubs. The talk was good, and the criticism of his work (which, like the others, he sometimes read aloud) interesting. He was quick to respond to criticism of exact words and meanings, on which the students of language and derivations were experts. On the whole the group liked the things he read to them and were interested in his ideas, but nothing could make Charles an academic. He was an original, and had all his life been different from the groups he worked with. In the mixed world of Amen House, he had been valuable in any group, but in Oxford each man had his own speciality as Charles had his. His method and style were often criticised, and Charles attended to the criticism.

If we should ask ourselves how important the Inklings were to Charles, the answer might be that in one sense he did not need the Oxford life it represented, however useful were the opportunities that came to him through it, and especially through Lewis. He was glad, naturally, that Lewis appreciated his Arthurian poetry, liked his plays, and attended to his verse. He had a real personal affection for Lewis. He never gave any sign of noticing the jealousy that Tolkien is said to have felt for him because of Lewis, or his Roman Catholic dislike of Charles's religious thinking.

Yet Charles attended regularly. Why? One answer could be that never, since the days of his relationship with Lee and Nicholson, had he been on terms of equal friendship with a group of men who were not part of the organisation for which he worked, demanded nothing from him, but instead were busy with conversation on politics, the war, religion, poetry, based on knowledge, experience and facts. And so, with a glass and a cigarette, one leg dangling over the arm of a sofa, and the other stretched out,

he could listen, interrupt, talk, be interrupted, until it was time to go—
back to the world of personal employment and literary demands. So in
another sense the Inklings meant a great deal. Deep down, he did not need
them, but on another, easier level, he enjoyed them.

Charles and Michal had both wanted young Michael to get a job and
some independent life in the two years before his call-up age. Charles
found him a niche in Blackwell's bookshop in Oxford from 1 April 1940.
He therefore moved from London to 9 South Parks Road. His presence
agitated his father with fears of a quarrel or a storm of nerves or misery.
Charles was conscious of being the kind of father of whom a growing lad
is ashamed, a literary creature ignorant of all the young world knew, films,
music and theatre. He sent me his new daily reading anthology, *The New
Christian Year* (1941), with this note: 'Such compilations do at least prevent one being proud of one's own stuff—as, for some obscure reason, does
the fact that I have just rung up the New Theatre to try and book two
seats for my son to see Bebe Daniels. . . . It is, it seems—this adolescence—
a very important period; character is forming; and they need Security and
Interest. Labouring at supplying at least the second—the first is beyond
me—I try and distinguish between film stars; not I fear very much or very
satisfactorily. Strangers in Blackwell's, not knowing him, ask him for, and
even buy my books. I am not sure whether this sends my stock up or down.
I think up a little'.[45] In C. W.'s own adolescence, in the Methodist Book
Room, security and interest had been notably lacking. But there had been
Walter, his father, and now the strength of that relationship emerged
again. For eighteen months, father and son lived together in Oxford, going
home to London for most weekends. Sometimes Michal joined them at
Oxford instead, at weekends or when a play of Charles's was being acted,
as in May 1940, when Ruth Spalding's company put on *Terror of Light*
in the first version. Michal wrote to Phyllis Potter about it, saying she had
thought poorly of it and said so, and that on the Sunday Charles worked
again on it until she had said it really was good. The Douglases were
annoyed with her, and told her so over a lunch. 'I fled from Oxford at the
earliest moment. I knew it would be a mistake to go. But they* have entire
possession of Charles again and that should make them happy'.[46]

Hitler's springtime came in April 1940. I was in London, my husband,
Peter Miller, with the British army in France. Hitler attacked the coastline
of Norway by air and sea. The German land forces then invaded Belgium
and Holland, and pressed on into France, making for the Channel ports.
'England, thou sleep'st, awake!' sounded in every heart across the narrow

*The Douglases.

sea. The French line of resistance melted. The last strength was in the British forces, in north east France and Belgium. It became urgent to withdraw them to defend the last free country at war, Great Britain and Northern Ireland. Through May the effort went on, with the Germans pressing in huge strength towards the north French and Belgian coasts. As the world crumbled hour by hour, Charles, remembering 1914-18, wrote: 'I have seen all Europe on the edge of absorption twice, and each time saved by—by a miracle? at least by five minutes or five yards. I see no reason why it should happen again, of course. I hope for nothing but more retreats and then, in God, the last turn at the last moment. It may not be, but it may'.[47] Every day in London, we expected to be bombed. Charles wrote of the possibility of Oxford being bombed and himself killed. 'Am I not to leave my reputation in your care? Do I not depend on you to prevent me being called a thousand things, sentimentalist, philanderer, and the rest?'

Each hour the country's effort grew. 'You are right about the volunteers; it is the nearest to a levy-en-masse. The backbone goes down to Caucasia; we fight the last battles there'.[48] For many the last battle was fought in that late spring. The English troops in France south of the German breakthrough were cut off from the evacuation of Dunkirk. On 20 May, German planes and tanks reached Amiens and most of my husband's Cinque Ports battalion of the Royal Sussex Regiment was killed or captured. I read on a London newspaper placard that the Germans had reached the Channel coast near Boulogne, north of Amiens. News of casualties did not come through for three weeks or more. The enormous effort to evacuate our forces from France, through Dunkirk, was absorbing everyone's effort, and the to-and-fro across the Channel of every craft that would float, while our air force held the strip of sky above, until nearly 340,000 men had been rescued. The City gathered itself into our island and stood in complete co-inherence under King George VI and Winston Churchill his prime minister.

News of my husband Peter's death at Amiens came through in mid-June, as casualty telegrams poured in. Charles wrote to me about him. 'He did not find a bad fortune—to die at the height of his imagination. It was he working in his imagination "If it were now to die 'twere now to be most happy"'.[49] In all deaths the mind is occupied with more than the present instance and losses return again. The young men of 1915 and 1917, Harold Eyers and Ernest Nottingham, returned to Charles in the deaths of 1940. He wrote again to me: 'He dies for my life, and I live his actual death; in a way perhaps he lived through—if not my death at least my pain. And both of us mysteriously live and die through you. O there is no end to it, or to our despair. But in you it is a living despair; it is knowledge, princess—a living death. The past is our food: what you had, you have. No damned nostalgia. The phrases of communion at the Eucharist hold it. "The body . . . which was given for thee, preserve . . . unto everlasting life. Take and eat this. . . ." Eat it: Peter and me'. 'Pain, pain, everywhere, for ever, pain. I do not presume to be sorry for you'.[50] And a month later: 'Let us deride the First Cause together! It is proper to our honesty—only the fatal answer defeats us: "see if there be any sorrow like mine". When he wept for Lazarus or for Jerusalem, what moved those tears? "Lord by this time he stinketh—" profound maxim of love! "Said I not unto you that if ye believe ye should see the Glory . . . ?" believe for me . . . I know but can I believe? Yes, if I choose, but you do it then. The Eucharist holds the dead—dead men and dead facts and the living of them again in the Mystical Body.—"Those good works thou hast prepared for us to walk in"'.[51]

For Charles, it was more than a question of sympathy. He was widely expected to be a pacifist, or to admit the essential ground of pacifism that to take human life is wrong and that evil can never be overcome by that which is wrong. Knowing his fundamental position, centred on the co-inherence of all love, many people expected it to lead to the conclusion that in all circumstances it is wrong to fight and kill any other part of the co-inherence. Charles did not see it so. He had an accurate knowledge of history. Chesterton's *G. K.'s Weekly* had said that pacifism implied that war was destroying freedom. Charles said firmly that this might be so, but no one in English society had resisted the step-by-step destruction of freedom in Germany and Italy before the war. He refused to support its destruction now. Truth lay in aeroplanes. Life and death were for man's decision in war and the world's activities. To him the important thing was to maintain everywhere the co-inherence, to despise and reject no one even while you killed him or he killed you. Below life and death lay a profounder union in a more significant bloodshed on Calvary. It might be necessary, with whatever pain, to take the risk of being killed or of killing in the establishment of some decision, but a greater necessity lay on everyone to acknowledge a sin and a life shared and exchanged with the enemy.

The Germans held or controlled most of Europe and turned to face England. With us were our oldest partners, Wales and Scotland with her vulnerable islands, and Northern Ireland with her many family links with North England and Scotland. Behind our back stood neutral Southern Ireland (Eire), the unblacked-out lights of Dublin soon to show bombers the way to Liverpool and Belfast, her denied ports adding greatly to the sinkings of ships crossing the Atlantic and the total of lives lost. Our navy, most of our army and our small expert air force remained, with as many able comrades as had escaped or been rescued from Europe. With other civilians I spent many hours in London reception centres, receiving refugees in their distress and taking down what details were necessary to have each one guided to some point of practical human hope. Our civil defence and fire services, police, medical and hospital services were ready prepared, even if much equipment was still being hurried through the factories. The Local Defence Volunteers, both men and women, was growing fast.

I had a daughter one year old. My brother in the Royal Navy on the West Indies station wanted us to come to Bermuda and join his wife; he could get me work in Admiralty House. Charles wrote often. 'Do not forget me, whatever happens. More than I depend on that—Bermuda or wherever . . . I have seen life grow in you and the living death of part of it'.[52] About my leaving England he said: 'I find myself rather in favour of your going. This both surprises and annoys me, but there it is. . . . I find myself envisaging the faint possibility of a temporary German occupation. I do not think it really likely, and yet . . . like the P(rime) M(inister) I just look at it and away again. And anything could be preferable than to have a growing child in *that* atmosphere. . . . I do not think you would be less involved in the struggle for the City in Bermuda, and I do rather feel that I should like to know that, if the worst happened in England, the City would rally the reserves. . . . Your mind would be the Order and your heart, the Church'.[53] He wrote me a reference for a job and added in his letter to me, 'I cannot well say "she drank to *Taliessin* with me"'.*[54] He wished me 'a safe passage through all the impersonalities'.[55] And so, with Charles remaining in England, the child and I went off to Bermuda where we stayed until the end of 1943 and then came home.

---

*On the publication day of *Taliessin through Logres,* C. W. and I had gone out to Shirreff's and had drunk, standing up, to the book and to Taliessin.

12

The Figure of Beatrice

Williams's first years at Oxford continued that concern with religion and theology—including romantic theology—which had begun with *Thomas Cranmer of Canterbury* and *Seed of Adam,* and came into full development with *He Came Down From Heaven* and *The Descent of the Dove.* Watchful, a little detached, he regarded God, like earthly love, as being as dangerous as it was necessary, and also irrevocably involved in time and the events of man's life.

While still at Amen House, Charles had compiled a small book of Lenten readings, *The Passion of Christ.* Published in 1939, it was described by him as 'the gospel and narrative of the Passion, with short comments taken from the saints and doctors of the Church'. It contained quotations from the early Fathers through the mediaevals to Donne, Bunyan, Fox, Kierkegaard, Coleridge, Patmore and the Report of the Archbishops' Commission on 'Doctrine in the Church of England'. In his Preface, Charles wrote, 'These comments are meant for meditation; they are sources of power, as their speakers and writers were' and goes on to his theme that words should be allowed to speak for themselves: 'Nothing (outside the spirit) can be more desirable than that we should receive a knowledge of the great tradition of Christian comment; the riches of it are too little known. It is to this that we should return; the sayings are there'.

In October and November 1939 he wrote two more verse plays, *The House by the Stable* and *The Death of Good Fortune,* for Ruth Spalding's

Oxford branch of the Pilgrim Players. Later, as Anne Ridler tells us, 'the same company gave performances of *The House by the Stable* in halls, air-raid shelters, garages, churches, schools and theatres in many parts of the country; *The Death of Good Fortune* was also performed a good many times, in an expanded version'.[1] The former play was taken to the Forces in northwest Europe in May 1945 by E. Martin Browne and was broadcast.

The year 1940 saw articles by Charles on 'The Image of the City in English Verse' *(Dublin Review)*, 'The Church Looks Forward'* *(St. Martin's Review)*, 'The Recovery of Spiritual Initiative' *(Christendom)*, and also an introduction to Kierkegaard's *The Present Age,* published by Oxford. The last sentences of that introduction read: 'Kierkegaard . . . claimed to recognize the unique. . . . The reader to whom Kierkegaard looked forward was the man who, in terror, in despair, in humility, in trust, was also able to recognize the unique. "It is God who waits. Leap, then into the arms of God"'.

During the earlier part of the year, too, he had been researching and writing *Witchcraft,* commissioned by Faber's, and published in March 1941. He called it a compilation and described it in the Preface as 'a brief account of the history in Christian times of that perverted way of the soul which we call magic, or (on a lower level) witchcraft, and with the reaction against it'. At the end of the book he uses the same word—the Way of the Perversion of Images. It is a book which shows how close to ordinary life he knows evil to be, how acceptable it is, the first step how easy, its slavery how complete. One has only to refuse to accept that one has been created and has need of redemption. One lives from and for oneself. The attitude is common enough. It has in myth its own Great Original, once that Prince of Light who refused to admit he existed from God and desired to exist only from himself. The myth says that he indeed has his desire and exists forever separated from God, feeding his torment to each man in whom he darkens the light he extinguished in himself.

Witchcraft is not 'exciting' or horrible. C. W. was not excited or horrified by evil—any more than he was by his neighbour—and the book's grip lies in that similarity. To him, evil was as ordinary and as real as people, and by its ordinariness and reality, the more to be utterly excluded. The idea that to be good is boring and to be bad is thrilling was simply silly to him, because he had real knowledge of what it is to be good, and what it is to be bad. The plain and slowly mounting sense of evil which

*Both reprinted in Anne Ridler's *The Image of the City.*

grows out of the pages of *Witchcraft* moves one sharply to lay hold on that which is good.

The reviewers of the *Times* group were perceptive. The *Educational Supplement* said: 'As gripping as any novel and far more instructive of the nature of man than many homilies', and the *Literary Supplement:* 'The belief in witchcraft, and the practice of witchcraft, and the treatment of the practitioners by the believers, are a grave matter needing to be gravely handled; and so they are handled by Mr. Williams. He deserves the gratitude of all who hold that the human mind and soul, even in their aberration and abasement, are entitled to the historian's respect'.

By now air-raids on London had begun. Charles saw from Hampstead hills the night sky burning in the huge docks fires in East London, and observed that there were advantages about living in Oxford. 'I have been up in London for five nights of the bombing', he wrote to me in October 1940, saying he had experienced 'plain panic, unbecoming and obscene'. He sent me the little World's Classics *Milton* with his Introduction, the substance of so many living hours of learning and experience, and wrote in it:

> Exile to exile—this is Rome
> and the strong towers of our home;
> your heart in mine, my heart in yours,
> derives, conceives, begets, endures.

Anywhere but London was exile, even if for safety. He wrote to me, 'I am a little sick at heart—Oxford, however nice, is still a kind of *parody* of London'.

But, apart from fire-watching at night, life in Oxford was peaceful. 'I sit here still alive', he wrote two months later; 'I have changed my bathroom certainly, and am now across the landing in a smaller bathroom. Thus, alone in Southfield House, retaining a room to myself—unworthily!' In fact, in these first two years in Oxford, with University lectures and tutorials concentrated into three short eight-week terms, his life was, for him, reasonably easy. He continued to look after his mother's and sister's insurance, Michal's finances, and details of the maintenance of the London flat. His wife came down fairly often and stayed with him at South Parks Road; he went almost every other week to the local repertory theatre, the Playhouse; he lunched and dined all over the city; and made a great number of friends. He talked to Eliot, who often came to Oxford, was most warm, and said that he was not to let anything stand in the way of the Taliessin poems. Charles was touched by Eliot's earnestness, but naturally remarked to himself that at the same time Faber's, Eliot's firm, was pressing him to write other books which took his time off the poetry. This was true, but the poems that were to be included in *The Region of the Summer Stars* grew steadily.

Both Lewis and Eliot urged him on to more and more writing. Lord David Cecil dropped in to talk, Redwood Anderson and Herbert Palmer chatted, Auden wrote frequently from America. The weekly or twice weekly meetings with Lewis, Tolkien, Mathew and the other Inklings were a pleasure, and so was the companionship of the learned men of the university. During his last two years, his interest flagged and it all grew a little burdensome, but in 1940, 1941 and 1942 it was very pleasant.

It was not the habit of university dons to 'make friends' with the undergraduates of each year. It would have been a burden upon their time and attention. Their job was to develop their own subjects and to encourage each student to reach the highest standard attainable. Personal relations with two or three would alter the balance. But Charles had never experienced college life at a university. He treated responsive undergraduates as he had treated his evening lecture students of any age. He took them seriously, included them in the channel of his own thinking, saw them as sharers in a common metaphysical life, sparking off now and then a flash from an image in Arthurian poetry. Many dons, not knowing him well, did not like him, often because of this attitude. But he regarded all as equal, undergraduates, graduates or those outside the university who came to talk with him about poetry or problems. Often he could ill spare the time to talk or write, and had to work later at night afterwards. But no awkward middle-aged man or woman was shaken off, or evening class students of the 1920's or 1930's who came to Oxford to see him, members of Amen House staff now in the forces or civil defence, or new acquaintances made at Oxford. Among them were Raymond Hunt, John Topliss and his wife, Joan Wallis, and Thelma Shuttleworth from London lecturing days, Anne Bradby, now married to Vivian Ridler in the Royal Air Force, Charles Hadfield and myself from Amen House, and new friends such as Lois Lang-Sims and Anne Renwick (now Anne Scott).

He was now being asked to speak to librarians, members of the Student Christian Movement, girls' and boys' schools, students of Reading, Birmingham and London Universities, medical students and nurses, army recruits in training, naval cadets at Oxford and WRNS* in a hostel, and to take part in radio discussion programmes and once broadcast to India.

*Women's Royal Naval Service.

Churchmen also came to him: he was invited to preach, to speak in convents and to address conferences of clergy, ordinands and laity.

Writing to his wife, he said he was 'not keen' on the increasing clergy-speaking, and not sure he was good at it. His mind turned much on the past. He mused on his wife and their long love together, now separated by the war. 'I always have loved us two tinkering about the flat, when you were feeling fit, *and* I had just enough silver to pay for oddments. It's always been the nearest thing to absolute *leisure* I have ever known. Perhaps of freedom. I say "perhaps" because great art can give a sense of freedom, but it doesn't give quite that sense of delightful *time*'.[2]

From many letters and many weekends spent in London, it seems that his marriage put out new life and found new warmth in these last three years of his life. Charles went up to Amen House on a day's business, and in some corner of a shelf found a copy of *The Silver Stair*. He was pleased to have it with him and wrote: 'It is a very long time since first, Madonna, we talked of it on Holywell Hill, and since you read the Ms. "Those were the days"? O no; I love you more now, both because I like to and because I ought to, and because I *do*. The third is the best cause—fortunate that it holds'.[3]

In January 1941, he had slipped on an icy road and from his fall had bruises and slight tooth damage. He was now included in fire parties as part of his fire-watching, for he learned to work a stirrup-pump,* and to use a long-handled shovel to carry sand to put out incendiary bombs. Michael, then living in 9 South Parks Road, also had to do fire-watching at night, and Charles had tea and a hot-water bottle ready for him when he came in, and brought him breakfast in bed next morning.

A grief came with the death in 1941 of Henry Lee, priest and friend, whom he had first met in the golden years of 1917–18, and with whom, and with Nicholson, he had shared so much talk. 'There are others I could have better spared!'[4] He was asked to write the notice of Henry for the diocesan chronicle. He had read that 'a bomb destroyed a shelter in the Essex Road near the Angel at the top of Pentonville Hill. It is absurd that one should remember one's childhood's wanderings there, but that is more part of me than (except for you) St. Albans, and much more than Oxford. I used to walk over to Leyton along there'.[5] He had 'a quite religious sensation!—the oddest thing. I felt suddenly "Well, but then I am eating only for Christ's work, and all is but to be that". It went in a moment, but there it was'.[6] Many of these letters are signed 'Serge'.

---

*A small hand pump incorporating its own water supply, used to attack incendiary bombs.

In a letter of March 1941 he remembered my coming to Amen House, 'a good day and a secret; fair secrets but very hidden when we first met on the stairs. Most admired, you little thought what was coming to you there. . . . You cannot lose the age you were when we published *Taliessin*. Others you may gain, but not lose that. No simultaneity; It is God's gift still to me to see it, which the world calls plain stupidity, but we know better'.[7]

Ever since its publication in 1938, his central joy lived in *Taliessin*. In an unpublished poem he wrote:

> The august Authority, holy Imagination,
> living in body and soul, the great single
> revealed Union (short of the final Union)—
> this is all I was saying in Taliessin.
>
>   . . .
>
>   O arms, arms!
> everything sensual and metaphysical there
> rides together: the central neural spasm
> blurs it, too much considered; the arms are space,
> the arms are in the hazel—I saw it so once. . . .

In October 1941, Michael's age group was called up and in November he joined the Royal Air Force at Penarth in South Wales. The parents, as always, were more agitated than the lad seemed to be. He went off well. On the other hand, Sir Humphrey's son Robin, whom Sir Humphrey had commended to Charles's help, was in Oxford before being released from the Army by the doctors. Charles talked with him. 'He looks pretty bad. It is a very odd thing—all these young geniuses seem to be even more distressed than we were when we were young. I feel sometimes it's a good thing I have always had to work or I should have done less—and less good—stuff than I have!'[8] Ralph Binfield came in, Second Lieutenant in the Royal Artillery, cheerful and cheering. Charles Hadfield came on a day off from London bombing. David Higham, the literary agent of Charles and of scores of other writers, was in the army, and news of him was passed round.

Then on 7 December 1941 the American naval base at Pearl Harbor was attacked without warning by the Japanese. The United States declared war on Japan and shortly afterwards on Germany and Italy. The result of the war could hardly now be in doubt, though it was not until the middle of 1944 that American forces in the field exceeded the British.

Charles Williams recognised how evil, always acting in mind or spirit, pined for possession of matter. A poem of this time contains the lines:

> everything is in the body—source and measurements:
> I am the most material poet that lived
> since Lucretius; almost as sensual indeed
> as the Lady Julian of Norwich, that recluse of sanctity—
> who said that where the soul and flesh met, God
> built his City. It is the City we explore—
> the hazel, Blanchefleur, Galahad; modes of the City.[9]

Affirmation or rejection was equally a mode of the City, and the same man might need to use both. One should hold, he wrote to me, the awareness of both ways in one's mind as a mode of courtesy, whichever way one chose. They were best understood so in the life of exchange, and (our minds in wartime turning much upon the subject) only so could anyone understand the nature of sacrifice. But our cities of bricks and architecture also held our hearts. Every street off Ludgate Hill, Newgate Street, Gray's Inn Road and his evening class suburbs beat with his heart.

In an article, 'The Church Looks Forward', he had written of the way of affirmation: 'It was once suggested . . . that among all the Orders of the Christian Church there lacked one to our Sacred Lord as "a gluttonous man and a wine-bibber". . . . Food and wine are here the definite symbols of the "creature". . . . It is the following of our Lord in this knowledge of the creature which has been a part of the work of Christendom and may well be a greater part in the future. The doctrine of our Lord as God with its corollaries took centuries to work out. . . . The other doctrine of His Manhood, with its corollaries, has still to be worked out and put into action'.[10]

He went on in 1941 to write two pamphlets, *The Way of Exchange* in the New Foundations series published by James Clarke & Co., and *Religion and Love in Dante*, from the Dacre Press. In the first he set out clearly and concisely the principles as he saw them of co-inherence, exchange and substitution, and in the second, those of the theology of romantic love.

In *The Way of Exchange* he sees the continuing family as an example of all three principles. 'The value of the sexual act itself is a kind of co-inherence; the two participators intend . . . a renewal of mutual vigour from the most extreme intimacy of physical relationships'. From that may follow 'one great natural fact . . . which involves a relation very much of the nature of exchange . . . the fact of childbirth. . . . New life (literally) exists. It exists by the common operation of the woman and the man, and that involves something of the nature of substitution. That substitution produces the new life. . . . With conception comes the physical inherence of the child. And this is renewed through all the generations; each generation has inhered in that before it; in that sense without any doubt at all, we carry, if not another's burdens, at least the burden of others. Such is the natural fact. At the root of the physical nature of man . . . lie exchange of liking, substitution, inherence. The nature of man which is so expressed in the physical world is expressed after the same manner, only more fully, in the mental and spiritual'. And later he says: 'From childbirth to the Divine Trinity Itself the single nature thrives; there is here no difference between that natural and that super-natural. Our chief temptation is to limit its action.'

Religion and Love in Dante is plainly sub-titled 'The Theology of Romantic Love'. That theology is set out in terms of the Beatrician experience; in the *Vita Nuova* of Dante's love for Beatrice, and in the *Commedia* of Beatrice's love for Dante. Here, too, we have an example of Charles's gift for presenting a beautifully clear outline of a difficult literary work. He had done it earlier for *The Aeneid*[11] and *The Ring and the Book*,[12] and now in twenty-five small pages we gain a lucid understanding of the essential story of the three books of the *Commedia*. Lastly, there is a suggestion—there are others elsewhere—of his experienced renewal in his own marriage.

'It is true the Dantean way is not confined to marriage, otherwise its principles could not apply to any known love—in marriage, in the family, in friendship, which they probably do. But it is also true that marriage is a unique opportunity of following that way. Marriage becomes a Way of the Soul. It is the elucidation of that kind of Way of the Soul with which Dante was concerned'.[13]

The Dante booklet was to be the precursor to *The Figure of Beatrice* (1943). But meanwhile, in August 1941, he wrote *Grab and Grace* for Ruth Spalding's company, though mischances prevented its production; August also saw the publication of *The New Christian Year*, which he had compiled in the autumn of 1940. War time demanded books with the maximum of pith and the minimum of paper. This book must therefore have been welcomed, for 1942 saw a second impression. Its continuing value, however, is shown by the extreme scarcity of second-hand copies.

The book is a selection of readings for every day of the Christian year, 'arranged, for convenience, according to the Sundays and chief Holy Days of the Book of Common Prayer of the Church of England. . . . An effort has been made to ensure that all passages chosen shall have in them some particular greatness of phrasing. The works of the teachers and saints of the Christian Church are full of such phrases. . . . A recovery of a greater knowledge of the greater men is much to be wished'. The astonishing breadth of Williams's reading is exhibited, within which he draws attention to the recurrence of four names: Kierkegaard, William Law, John Donne and 'that curious collection of goodness and of dreams, the account of the eastern hermits which is called *The Paradise of the Fathers'*.

The book stands upon the way of affirmation, which Charles continued to practise. He wrote to Margaret Douglas, shy and upset by her helplessness, 'Do not be angry, do not underrate yourself . . . you were meant to be *Margaret* after all, to be Margaret and no other; there is no other in all the masses of creation, who can be *that'*.

He acknowledged his own indebtedness to other people continually. But each person must have a central point which depends on intention, not indebtedness. A great deal of life is only the pursuit of that intention into deeper and deeper causes of consciousness. 'Somewhere it will turn to bay and we shall be united with it'. Till then, he would leave it alone, be content to be indebted, and press on with daily life.

He wrote to Anne Ridler about her verse play *Cain*, that she had done well in presenting Cain as thinking that he could begin all over again, and that God may take back the blame of human sins. 'I am sure we ought—dare we breathe it?—to see the Crucifixion as God standing by his nature in supernatural justice pursuing the sin to its Cause; but perhaps we can only do that in poetry, not in theology. Anyhow, let us keep as much of it as we can!'[14] This thought comes out strongly later on in *What the Cross Means to Me*.

He had been asked by the publisher Geoffrey Bles to write a short book on *The Forgiveness of Sins;* it was to be published in 1942 and dedicated to the Inklings. Experience of the literary and literate world told him how little this title would interest people. 'Yet if there is one thing which is obviously part of the universe or not—and on knowing whether it is or not our life depends—it is the forgiveness of sins'. Briskly he proceeds to curdle the reader's blood with an outline of the need for forgiveness and exchange, unnoticed in a greater concern for the war, or economics, or ideals.

He himself had been thinking about forgiveness for many years, contemplating, considering how it could be, entering into Shakespeare's concentration on it in Cleopatra's sense of some change linking her to forgiveness, 'My desolation doth begin to make/ A better life',[15] which moved deeper in *The Tempest* into Ariel's songs of change, and Prospero's realization that 'the rarer action is/ In virtue than in vengeance'.[16] Deeper than both is in *Cymbeline,* where the play gives glimpses of a changed way of life when the injured Postumus says to his enemy, 'The power that I have on you is to spare you'.[17]

In Chapter III, 'The Sin of Adam', one which has selections from Wordsworth, Aquinas, Augustine and St. Paul, he uses his own pages 16–19 from *He Came Down From Heaven* on the coming of sin in the Bible story of Adam and the fall of man. His feeling is for exchange moving into a state of simultaneity, in a free generation of love in the Incarnation, in which the future was present 'for himself and for his creation'.[18] Long ago Charles had known this in an instinct which worked through him to words in 'The Departure of Merlin' in *Taliessin Through Logres*.[19] Following 'The Coming of Galahad', a state is known where time (moons and suns)

> are come away from sequence . . .
> here all is cause and all effect;

time has distinction, but a greater order,

> grace ungrieved

sustains all

> in simultaneity to times variously veined,

a line looking towards an idea of forgiveness at the Crucifixion 'by which the sin was to be brought into perfect accord with the original good, the incoherence into the co-inherence, the opening hell into the opened heaven'.[20]

How deeply he honoured the body, saw every ability as in the flesh and bones and nerves as well as in the mind and spirit! His poetry is full of it. People have thought him influenced by the poet Blake, and Chapter VII, 'Forgiveness and Reconciliation', is probably their evidence. He looks closely at some of Blake's verse and visions, and deeply admires them. But the relationship seems to be more of a family nature, literally 'familiar', but not formative of a vision or main line of thinking. Flesh heals, but minds cling to ills, refuse to forgive or ensure forgiveness. The Atonement is carried out in the blood, as well as the soul. ' . . . the final seal of all things in this creation of our Lord God's is physical',[21] the foundation of the Way of Affirmation. 'The Lord God formed man of the dust of the ground, and breathed into his nostrils the breath of life',[22] says the old myth. Charles remembered 'In Adam I fell, in Adam I was cast out of Paradise, in Adam I died; how shall the Lord call me back, unless he find me in Adam. . . .'[23]

Williams the craftsman knew how to end a book strongly. 'The weight of glory is the weight of the carrying the cross, "customary life's exceeding injocundity". The labour towards our enemy . . . is a continual duty—all Christians say so . . . it is easier to write a book repeating that God is love than to think it; it is easier, that is, to say it publicly than to think it privately. Unfortunately, to be of any use, it has to be thought very privately, and thought very hard. . . . It is the thought of the world which matters, but thought, like charity, begins at home. It has indeed been held that thought and charity were one; certainly charity is not so much a colour of thought as a particular kind of thought . . . a change of mental habit; it is the restoration of accurate mental habit. This is everyone's business, for his friend's sake and his enemy's and his own. And if indeed we are all in danger of hell, then very much for his own'.[24]

In 1942 also, 'The Index of the Body' was published in the *Dublin Review* and reprinted in *The Image of the City*. Tightly packed with thought, it illustrates Williams's peculiar ability to draw significances together to make each one deeper and more piercing. He had made and used indexes. He knew the astrological attributions to man's eyes, arms, sexual organs, buttocks. Wordsworth had seen the human form among the hills, the solitary leech-gatherer, as an index to a volume written in a strange language. Patmore, Hopkins, Browning saw in the body glimpses, understandings and "replies to some like region of the spheres".[25] Williams saw in Celia's wrists and arms indexed entries to an understanding which he searched and found in verse.

The Three Temptations, C. W.'s only radio play, was broadcast in November 1942. He used a new technique well. John Heath-Stubbs writes of it: 'The events of the beginning and end of Christ's earthly ministry are brought together in a simultaneous relation, in a manner which would scarcely be possible in a stage play. Another new and striking—indeed appalling—conception is that of Judas Iscariot as Everyman. This gains at least part of its power from the fact that a radio play is addressed not to an audience in a theatre but to the individual listener by his own fireside'.[26]

Charles's Introduction to *The Letters of Evelyn Underhill* appeared in 1943. Evelyn (1875–1941) was a pupil and friend of Von Hügel, and a devout mystic, writer and lecturer. 'She had perhaps an especial grasp of the fact that a soul may so ask for a thing that it receives, in the end, that gift and no other—and then cannot bear it. It exclaims then, and the whole universe—we must not say the Creator—answers only: "Vous l'avez voulu, Georges Dandin!"'[27] Evelyn too had a fear of cant, of self deception in religious words. Of her book *Mysticism* he observed, 'It was a great book precisely not because of its originality, but because of its immediate sense of authenticity'.[28] The mind, the heart instantly realizes that what it needs is true and has always been known at some level until now not opened. He recognised in her 'The equal (or all but equal) swaying level of devotion and scepticism which is, for some souls, as much the Way as continuous simple faith is to others'.[29] It was distress to her, but a fact to him. He wrote: 'We are here talking . . . not only of intellectual belief and intellectual doubt, but rather of that felt in the blood and in the soul— "utter and intimate unbelief". She wanted to be *sure*'.[30] Charles saw this as temptation.

A priest, Father Benson, had written to her, 'I really do not think you have enough reverence for the stupid'. Charles suggests that both these temptations 'are only indications of her conflict with the final psychic egotism'.[31] This egotism he uses in Simon the Clerk in *All Hallows' Eve*, as it is an element in all of us. In Evelyn he saw in her conflict 'something more, some conjoining of sacrifice with sacrifice'.[32]

He mentions that he and Evelyn had met and talked, and that she had spoken of one of his novels which had a theme of substitution. 'He endured her sensitiveness, but not her sin; the substitution there, if indeed there is a substitution, is hidden in the central mystery of Christendom'.[33] He writes 'It was a well-meant sentence, but she charmingly corrected it. She said something to this effect: "Oh, but the saints do—they say they do. St. Catherine said: 'I will bear your sins'"'. She spoke from a very great knowledge of the records of sanctity, but I should be rather more than willing to believe that she spoke from a lofty practice of sanctity and from a great understanding of the laws that govern, and the labours that are given to, sanctity'.[34]

He sent a copy of the book to his sister Edith who, he once said, was the most mystical person he knew. Edith had gone a long way into the mystical life, while living efficiently in the world of her secretarial college. Later she was to be drawn to the Society of the Hidden Life (a group within the Anglican Church), both on the practical level as helping with secretarial work, and on the contemplative as seeking a devotional life at a continuous and deeper level.[35]

The year 1943 saw a great achievement, the publication about the end of June of *The Figure of Beatrice*, the title using a formal meaning of the word 'figure'—a mixing of idea and shape—as a blending of imagination and fact. Here is a full-length working out of the theology of romantic love in those Dantean terms that had been glanced at in Chapter V of *He Came Down From Heaven* and outlined in *Religion and Love in Dante.*

The book studies Dante's *Vita Nuova* (The New Life), *Convivio* (The Banquet), *De Monarchia* (Concerning Sovereignty) and *Divina Commedia* (The Divine Comedy). The first three are short works concerned with man's life and living. The last, in three books each containing some thirty cantos of *terza rima,* is Dante's long poem on the life of love in man. First is the *Inferno* (Hell), where the instinct of love shows first as self-preservation, then as turned towards one's own awarenesses, at first delicate, romantic, tragical, then increasingly deteriorating through greed, sullenness, pride, ambition, hate, to the rejection of every notion of good, every awareness of another person, in an icy stillness of treachery. Second is the *Purgatorio* (Purgatory or Freeing) where the being of man chooses to escape and to learn step by step what love is and to know how to love—to see an aim, a function, a person, other than oneself; and then to submit to learn how to love or serve it; and then to see love as the cause of all action; to learn its nature, step by step, to be eager, not self-pitiful; to douse that secret burning of self-esteem and will, and to be for the first time, free and able to love. The third book is the *Paradiso* (Paradise) of the state of love, and man's realization of its nature and consent to it, his discovery of its many levels, wonders and powers. He finds his own personality growing with his knowledge till he has an awareness of union with all life in earth and heaven.

All four works of Dante are treated by Charles as one poet treats another's writing, as all about one central nature, in different guises, and all relevant to the contemporary reader, English poets, Wordsworth, Coleridge, Keats, Patmore, Shakespeare, being brought to share in the illumination.

The New Life is the story, in prose and poetry, of Dante's first sight of Beatrice. She is eighteen when she first speaks to him. He is seized by his first experience of all that is to come, and like other young people, he feels a violent body shock—when the heart trembles, the sense-perceptions have a feeling of blessed absorption, and the body staggers under the notion that it will fully love nothing, no one, but Beatrice, this. Choices are settled. All to come is to attend and love.

Then in Chapter III Beatrice dies—either bodily or as the object of the lover's joy. The lover knows that the quality of his experience with Beatrice 'desires the total and voluntary conversion of the lover'[36] to become the life of love he has seen in her, and has, for a moment, lived.

She is dead, and Dante has to go on living. In Chapters IV to VI, Charles studies the common life which Dante has now to live, and live well, seeking to develop in it the life of love as discovered in his brief, clear contact with Beatrice; the life of citizen, poet and friend, of the company of women and men, of the business of political beliefs and activities, and of earning a living. He finds that each in his own life must nourish energy, valour with nobility, interior contemplation, loyalty in following and acting on the good he knows, courtesy to all good and wonderful things, and repugnance to foulness. There is nothing here of general good-will or hoping for the best.

He or she may love another later on, as Dante may have done: ' "The Lady of the Window" . . . gleams for a moment and disappears. Perhaps she too was disappointed; perhaps this intense intellectual passion was not at all that for which she had looked. Or perhaps she was not; perhaps it was more than all. . . . She had had at that moment a great vocation; she was then at the beginning of a movement in the mind of man, of which we do not yet know the end; happy those who have a part in it. Wish her well, and pass'.[37]

Certainly she may have been Philosophy, as is often argued, or the European Empire, the Papacy, or political and social theory. These were important. Their inclusion prevents Dante's Way of Affirmation being either a mere sentimentality or a disguised egotism. It was moral, because Dante perceived that images existed in their own right, and not merely for his. In the *De Monarchia* and the political points in the *Commedia* Williams saw the validity of these images for Dante as authority and responsibility in man's earthly and eternal life. Authority alone did not move Dante, but the right judgement behind it. When after exile, he was told he could return to Florence on payment of a fine, Dante refused. Should he pay money for injury, for injustice?

The *Vita Nuova* had been about Dante's love for Beatrice; the *Commedia,* to which Williams gives the remaining chapters of the book, was about Beatrice's love for Dante, and his response. Beatrice, through the eye of blessed love, sees Dante on the verge of going downhill into a state of hell, and asks the poet Virgil to help him. The two poets go through the experience of hell and its inevitabilities together. Virgil then leads Dante up to the light and air again in the *Purgatory,* encouraging him through great vexations with the certainty that he is learning how to love. Of the pain and suffering in this learning, Dante says, 'I say pain and should say solace'.[38] 'The words pain and pleasure are as much an unfair dichotomy as body and soul. We must use them, yet we betray ourselves in using them. We have indeed too much lost "il ben del intelletto"—the *good* of intellect; we lie helplessly, and we are bound to untruth. . . . The memory of the lesser solace might sometimes hearten us to the endurance of the uncomprehended greater'.[39] Poetry and learning can do no more for Dante, and Virgil stays behind as Beatrice comes to him again. The last third of the *Purgatory* is of the growth of Dante's understanding and vision until he is, with Beatrice, in the state of love called the *Paradise*. Simple at first as moonlight, it grows stronger in every experience until he catches the full light of heaven, which is 'the profound and shining being of the deep light' of the Trinity, in three circles 'of three colours and one magnitude'.[40] Desire and will are as one in Love as they were in Self at the depth of hell on the opposite stretch of the same journey.

The validity of the original 'falling in love' is continuously re-asserted. Charles's own experience with Celia wrote: 'The deepening beauty of Beatrice is a part of the poem; that is, it is (in the poem) known to us because Dante knew it. Her beauty is her own, but its publication is his; more— it is in his sight of it and worship of it that it grows deeper—so that all the infinite gratitude is not to be only on his side. In the exchange of their celestial love, she becomes more Beatrician by the measure of the Dantean knowledge'.[41]

'The image of Beatrice', he had written in his 'Introduction', 'existed in his thought; it remained there and was deliberately renewed. The word image is convenient for two reasons. First, the subjective recollection within him was of something objectively outside him; it was an image of an exterior fact and not of an interior desire. . . . Secondly, the outer exterior shape was understood to be an image of things beyond itself. . . . Beatrice was, in her degree, an image of nobility, of virtue, of the Redeemed Life, and in some sense of Almighty God himself. But she also remained Beatrice right to the end. . . .' The Beatrician figure, he goes on, 'is the greatest expression in European literature of the way of approach of the soul to its ordained end through the affirmation of . . . images, beginning with the image of a girl. It is this particular way of approach which these pages pretend to examine'.

The Figure of Beatrice has therefore three themes: the way of affirmation of images as man's way in to God, the way of romantic love as a particular mode of the same, and the involution of this love with images of the community or City, with poetry and human learning.

It is a book about Dante and Beatrice. It is also about Charles and all lovers.

It is about young love, loss, and continuing to make a good life in the world: about a vision given at a time when there seemed no hope and affirmation of that vision. But the way lies through the chapter on the *Inferno*, each sentence of which follows the last like a step onward in hell: 'We take advantage of the heresy in our blood; we encourage and petrify it: "much more than you think the tombs lie laden"—much more than we think the great deceptions multiply in us. Even to write such a sentence, even to read it, may be such a deception. The Popes whom Dante condemned most often, like Paolo, have indulged themselves in the *lussuria* of sermons, orations, discussions and theological works on the good. It is sometimes the office of Beatrice to point the deception in her lover out to him; little gratitude need she expect, and much danger to herself she runs, in doing it. ' . . . all these retributions, which are in some sense the sin itself, have about them the quality of infinity, in which quality there is but one change—the increased sense of it which must come when these souls are reunited to their bodies. This infinite quality equalizes the torments; degree vanishes in unending duration'.[42]

Yet the second half of the book leads the poet—and us with him—through his life in the growth of knowledge, of evil and of good, of pursuit of himself or of love as he originally understood it. The process of life brings goodness:

> O joy! that in our embers
> Is something that doth live,
> That nature yet remembers
> What was so fugitive!
> The thought of our past years in me doth breed
> Perpetual benediction.[43]

Charles himself recognised that benediction, not as a single awareness but as continually breeding afresh in himself, in committees, in friendships, marriage, in reading as in writing poetry. He delights in Beatrice gently laughing at Dante in the pageant in the opening of the *Paradiso*.[44] The learning of love by lovers goes on, and one way to the Way is attention: 'look', 'look well'. Do not pretend to yourself. So Beatrice said to Dante in their agony of meeting after separation.[45] They bring power to each other, to reject, to be able, to purify, to pray. Lives become rooted in each other, even the not very bright or very spiritual. Loving behaviour and thought grow as easy and natural as once they were new and revolutionary.

Charles returns at the end of the journey to his urge that we should attend to and examine our experience. We must not take thoughts and poetry as a film moving past us, but stop, think, look into the meaning, not just the technique. What is love or devotion or vocation about? Is our self willing to change towards it? 'Wherever any love is—and some kind of love in every man and woman there must be—there is either affirmation or rejection of the image, in one or other form. If there is rejection—of that

Way there are many records. Of the affirmation, for all its greater commonness, there are fewer records. "Riguarda qual son io"*—we have hardly yet begun to be looked at or to look'.[46]

The Figure of Beatrice is worthy of its subject. For many readers it is Charles's greatest work. In it his thought is gathered, searched and deepened, with an orientation peculiarly his own. The flashes we saw in novels, biographies, verse and *He Came Down From Heaven* are here sustained and steady. Here is the Incarnation, the eternal worth of the body, love, exchange and co-inherence true and false, mystery, intellect and psychology. 'Crowned and mitred over himself',[47] Charles moves with unswerving speed and sureness among the stars and gulfs of heaven, tracking out the path.

This greatest of his prose works is dedicated 'For Michael in redemption of a promise'.

The manuscript of *The Figure of Beatrice* had been sent to T. S. Eliot at Faber's on 28 July 1942, though minor work was done on it after that. The reaction after writing it left Charles in gloom and heaviness. He felt a sense of failure to cope with the *Commedia:* 'It has slid from being what it ought to be down to what I could make it. One's past rules one; a hundred immoralities that obscure the high things here. Any jealousy, any envy, any sullenness, any pride thrust one's poor capacity away from its end—I mean any of them in the past. Judgement, my Irene, is a fact of human life . . . I allow, of course, that not more than 7 people—one to a century—have been born since Dante who could have coped'.[48] *Beatrice* was well received and reprinted in 1944, though reviews came slowly.

Charles had known Dorothy Sayers for many years. James Brabazon[49] suggests that it began when Charles wrote to Victor Gollancz, who had published *The Nine Tailors* in 1933, 'Your Dorothy Sayers. . . .! Present her sometime with my profoundest compliments. It's a marvellous book; it is high imagination. . . . The end is unsurpassable.' They met not long after and subsequently he had suggested her as the author of the Canterbury Festival play next after *Cranmer*—the result was to be *The Zeal of Thy House* in 1937.

Thereafter they met and corresponded, till in 1943 he seems to have administered a sharp jolt. Brabazon suggests Dorothy Sayers 'had been expatiating on her two favourite arguments—the importance of the dogmatic pattern in Christianity; and the comparative values of the work and the worker, the writing and the writer'. Charles wrote in August: 'There is a point at which you and I will no longer be able to get away with an

*Open your eyes; see what I am.

explanation of how admirable we think the pattern is. . . . I know as well as you do of the byways of the literary mind, but I do not feel they are going to be much excuse. There are awful moments when I think that perhaps it is precisely people like us, who are enthralled by the idea and stop there, who are really responsible for a great deal of the incapacity and the harm'. He followed it up in June 1944 with 'The temptation of thinking that the business of writing frees one from everything else is very profound. . . .'

Upon which James Brabazon comments: 'The byways of the literary mind were her life. She had defended them again and again under the twin banners of intellectual and artistic integrity. . . . The clear implication that she herself, the human person, mattered more than these great abstractions, and that when she thought she was upholding them she was in reality hiding behind them, must have been most frightening. Worse: Williams was saying the hiding had to stop'. And seemingly her attitude did indeed change.[50]

Dorothy read *The Figure of Beatrice,* after which, knowing no Italian, she set herself to read Dante for the first time in parallel texts. Next she set herself to learn Italian, to retranslate the *Commedia,* and to write new notes upon it, writing to Charles that 'I have embarked upon an arduous enterprise for which you are entirely responsible'.[51] Meanwhile she poured out a stream of excited letters about Dante to Charles, ' . . . What a writer! God's body and bones, what a writer!' and also took to visiting him for long conversations—as late as 2.30 A.M. Later Charles was to suggest that 'you will consider turning your letters into some sort of small pamphlet. I am convinced (and this seriously) that they might be of great use to a large and probably innocent public of whom a certain few might read (a) them and (b) Dante. And they might have their whole consciousness of Dante altered by reading you, and turned into a much happier and more truthful apprehension'.[52]

Charles went almost every Sunday to the Eucharist. It was the centre of his thought and so of his life. He never tired of meditating on it. He wrote in answer to a question from me: 'I think the Sacrament is more than images; how and after what mode is another matter. I think the elements are drawn into him at the moment of the flesh-death-resurrection. The method of the union is obscure enough, and I'm a little inclined to agree that if there is nothing but He there, there is hardly a sacrament. . . . I will genuflect and adore the Presence, because it seems to me consistent with the general movement that he should so have withdrawn creation into him. On the other hand, I am shy of the arguments; the Rite which culminates in an adorable Mystery of co-inherence will serve for me!' But he wrote too, in this year 1943, 'At bottom a darkness has always haunted me—as you know. I am a Christian (as far as I am) by compulsion of mind and sense; "I think, not natural"'. He was a Christian because in the whole world within him and without him there was nothing else which finally he could be. It was not for the joy it brought him, or for any consolation, but that he found it alone existing and operating in every extremity. He had known extremity when

> The void profound
> Of unessential light receives him next
> Wide gaping, and with utter loss of being
> Threatens him, plunged in that abortive gulf.[53]

It was the year when wartime endurance had been long and hope in many people was lowest. Charles was asked to contribute 'The Cross' to a collection titled *What the Cross Means to Me: A Theological Symposium*.[54]

This long essay shows clearly his rejection of comment, and concentration on searching out meaning. He wrote from the centre of that darkness which he recognised in himself. God's original act of creation can be believed to be good. The gift of free will can be believed to be for choosing as well as receiving joy in God and creation. If there is free will, man can choose the opposite of joy. 'But it is not credible that a finite choice ought to result in an infinite distress, or ... that the Creator should deliberately maintain and sustain His created universe in a state of infinite distress as a result of the choice. No doubt it is possible to Him.' By Charles's own knowledge of co-inherence he agreed we were Adam when he chose, and we choose. It is not the state of outward war which reveals the climax. '... the agonies of the present time ... are more spectacular and more destructive, but not more lasting, nor perhaps very much worse, than the agonies of a more peaceful time ... the very burden of ... existence too often seems a curse. The whole creation groaneth and travaileth together'. Charles's answer to the pain of his own life is that God submitted himself to man's choice. 'He became as helpless as we under the will which is He'. This belief of Christians is 'unique in the theistic religions of the world'. Christ was put to death by men doing their best in the duty presented to them—condemning a blasphemer, maintaining the peace.

Referring to the war, 'At the present time, for example, it is clear that one man must suffer for the people'—each single man in action. Crucifixion was obscene and slow, much slower than hanging or shooting. 'Again and again, we become aware of a sense of outrage in our physical natures'.

Blood is antagonistic to itself, as family life can show. What about Easter? Easter is inseparable from the cross. Is the idea of immortality attractive? Charles does not think so. But 'the idea of annihilation is more repellent'. God had sustained the wood of the cross, and the iron of the nails as they matured through the years, the shaping of the spear, as well as the body and nerves which they were to pierce. 'The Cross therefore is the express image of His will'. Christ's last words, 'It is finished', spoken 'while He is not yet as speechless as the wood', announced the culmination of the act which is the beginning of Easter. 'Life has known absolutely all its own contradiction. He survives; He perfectly survives'.

'There has indeed been much admiration, much gratitude, much love, that God should be made like us, but then there is at least equal satisfaction that it is an unlike us who is so made. It is an alien Power which is caught and suspended in our very midst. "Blessed be God", said John Donne, "that He is God only and divinely like Himself!"' Our experience of good need not, must not, be separated from our experience of evil—bombings, cancer, starvation. And planned cruelty. What of Christ's 'comment on Judas, "it were good for that man if he had not been born". And who caused him to be born? Who maintained his life up to and in that awful less than good? It is in the Gospels that the really terrifying attacks on the Gospel lie'. 'He accepted Job's challenge of long ago, talked with His enemy in the gate, and outside the gate suffered (as the men He made so often do) from both His friends and His enemies'. 'This then has seemed to me now for long perhaps the most flagrant significance of the Cross; it does enable us to use the word "justice" without shame—which otherwise we could not. God therefore becomes tolerable as well as credible. Our justice condemned the innocent, but the innocent it condemned was one who was fundamentally responsible for the existence of all injustice—its existence in the mere, but necessary, sense of time, which His will created and prolonged'.

That was the objective side of Charles Williams's contemplation, and yet it is the most existential utterance. As in his historical writing, his sense, as a modern theologian puts it, of sharing a common existence of which one fact in time can communicate meaning to the existence of another, produces a true understanding of the historical fact of the Crucifixion far beyond an assessment, however competent, of evidence and argument. Here also, unlike his approach in his nativity or religious plays, Charles Williams shows a strong awareness of the Jesus of history, the true, historical man who was crucified. The sorrow and the obscenity were 'examples of that dreadful contradiction in our experience of life which is flatly exhibited in the living of life by Life'. 'This is what Almighty God, as well as we, found human life to be. We willed it so, perhaps, but then certainly He willed that we should will'.

The Cross was the point at which it all happened. There the problem of suffering and disvalue finds an answer comparable to its stature. There Christ became 'the very profoundest Cross to Himself. . . . His will in His Father's will had maintained a state of affairs among men of which physical crucifixion was at once a part and a perfect symbol'. This He had always known and proposed to endure. He was both the endurance and the thing endured. Substitution is the crux of the justice of God. 'By that central substitution, which was the thing added by the Cross to the Incarnation, He became everywhere the centre of, and everywhere he energized and reaffirmed, all our substitutions and exchanges. He took what remained, after the Fall, of the torn web of humanity in all times and places, and not so much by a miracle of healing as by a growth within it made it whole'.

In this opening of light Charles ends his essay: 'It is the Christian religion that makes the Christian religion possible. Existence itself is Christian; Christianity itself is Christian. The two are one because He is, in every sense, life, and life is He. It is to that, in the Triune Unity, that there is ascribed, beyond all hope, to that only Omnipotence, as is most justly due, all might, majesty, dominion, and power'.

13

'Peace and the Perfect End'

Charles Williams in 1942 and 1943 completed *The Figure of Beatrice,*
The Cross, and the Arthurian poems that were to be published in 1944 as
The Region of the Summer Stars. Thereafter the pattern of his life
remained the same, but there was less thrust. A verse play, *The House of*
the Octopus, a novel, *All Hallows' Eve,* and a biography, *Flecker of Dean*
Close, were still to come, together with *The Figure of Arthur,* unfinished
at his death. He had hoped, also, that Sir Humphrey would publish his
lectures on Wordsworth, but, probably because paper supplies were so
very limited, nothing came of it.

His affirmation of the goodness of life in all its images was maintained,
and co-inherence with his many friends and with the life of poetry and
love was secure. It lived now, however, from its own root and not from
him, as he had wanted it to live when he wrote, 'They only can do it with
my lord who can do it without him'.[1]

Charles's mother and sister were still living in 15 Victoria Road, St.
Albans, and he went, sometimes with Michal, to see them. An uncle, probably Charles Wall who had helped Walter and Mary to buy the shop,
died in December 1943, at age 83. Charles went to the funeral—and wondered if he had twenty-five more years to live.

He kept up relations and correspondence with his friends, who often
broke wartime journeys at Oxford to see him. Writing to Anne Ridler,
now a poet herself, gave him a chance to talk poetry, or argue about his

vocabulary—'I like "shent"—the sound describes a purged triumph'. He linked the Orkneys (for Anne and her husband in the Royal Air Force) and Bermuda (for me) among the seas of Taliessin's Empire. He wrote much to his latest student, Anne Renwick.[2] After she went down from Oxford, and *Beatrice* was published, he referred in a letter to her to 'My own Lady of the Window, whom we met in the Mitre'.[3] Phyllis' husband, Dougal, became ill. She was in grief and told Charles about it. He tried to rally such prayers and meditations as he could and asked Anne Renwick to recollect it in her prayers and at the Eucharist 'in the general life of the church and of Our Companionship'. He asked Anne Ridler to do the same.

He used the Companions in their proper service of exchange, asking each one to help another when he or she heard of trouble, Margaret Douglas, Ursula Grundy, Phyllis Potter, Charles Hadfield, Thelma Shuttleworth and many others. To Joan Wallis, who had her own troubles, he wrote a great deal, and they met when possible.

He was worried about his wife's painful back, and went up to London whenever he could. One weekend in August 1943 he was there and sent his wife for a rest to her sister. Michael was back in the flat; he, like his mother, had refused Oxford and Charles was much involved in finding him work. Soon, Michael took a job in the famous bookshop, Bumpus of Oxford Street, where he did well.

Charles continued always to be tidy and clean, with no wife to see to him. Buttons were never off, shoelaces not broken, socks not wrinkled round his ankles. He never wore a ring, or tie-pin, nor any colour except blue, grey or dark-blue suits, and white or unnoticeable-coloured shirts such as he had always worn, with a handkerchief stuffed up his sleeve, gold-rimmed spectacles and black shoes. He never seemed to be ill, or developed sore throats, coughs or other minor ailments.

He went to Morning Prayer more often now—that service 'which is so despised by the moderns but has probably been responsible for a great deal of my own thought. . . . It is from that, largely, that our comments on Dante spring; (e.g., "we have followed too much the devices and desires of our own hearts" in the way down through the Inferno; "In knowledge of whom standeth our eternal life" stage by stage up the hill of Purgatory increasing our knowledge); it was there that We—O young, O foolish, O well-meaning, first saw something that the Great now take—I write like a fool'. That morning the psalm contained 'that thou mayst see thy children's children . . . and peace upon Israel'. Into his mind came Anne Ridler's two children, and Raymond Hunt's two, and the divine Celia's two, and others he remembered. These, and peace—the promise filled him.[4]

After much effort and travel, I moved back to England and arrived at Liverpool in January 1944. On a bitter February day I went over to Oxford and met Charles again. He was rather thinner and a little more withdrawn behind his face, and over the grey suit he wore a heel-length black M.A.'s gown, since he had come from a lecture to meet me. But he was still erect, swift, intent, the beautiful hands quick to mark and define, the forehead's line unmarred by falling hair, the blue eyes behind their thick glasses as full of amusement and gentleness as ever.

We went to lunch, and began to talk about Taliessin and the poems; I was immediately employed to do Arthurian reading for him. After lunch we went to pick up books for me to start work on and to see the people of the Press again. Gerard Hopkins looked certainly thinner but magnificent as ever, Helen Peacock, brisk and firm and practical over possible jobs for me, Fred Page, smaller and his grey curls white, but still quick, and learned of eye. Sir Humphrey, slim, stately and white-haired, was there with weariness and fastidiousness marked more strongly in his face.

My return brought another event. While in Bermuda, I had been writing to another Press friend, Charles Hadfield, now on the staff of the National Fire Service. Once I was back, he and I met when we could, and in October 1945 we married.

Charles's life was being burst open by the university and town contacts that were increasingly pressing in on him. In prewar days it had been circumscribed, his days mainly occupied with a handful of people he had known for years. Now he lived almost wholly in public, even in his lodging, where strangers came and went and ate and spent evenings together. 'It seems as if this new kind of almost "impersonal" life which I lead', he wrote to Thelma Shuttleworth, 'took up even more time than the old— and by "impersonal" I mean that, as my lectures and tutorials and things continue, I become more and more a figure, a name, an influence perhaps; less and less a person. It is very amusing and a little thrilling in a way; more and more people, it seems, read me; the young positively throng my lectures; and yet I know none of them—even my own pupils do but come for their hours and disappear. . . . What fascination there is in observing change! I always said age ought to be fascinating, and so it is. But one had never begun to imagine *how*—the manner in which it would be. To be a name—that is egotistically pleasing; to be nothing but a name—that is fantastically delightful. But it makes my private life fuller of public occupations—in a small way—than ever'.

He had always been used to personal contact and had talked over his vision in exchange with his friends. Now the method of working was different. The new generation of young was there, 'I allow they are, appar-

ently, there, but they are far off and stranger. If they hear "enchantment",
it is a remote impersonal noise'.

His second volume of Arthurian poems, *The Region of the Summer
Stars*, came out in 1944. He chose the title from a line in the poem of
Taliessin in the *Mabinogion*. [5] That region was the vault of heaven and
not Milton's 'abortive gulf'.[6] But the stars have grown to be lights from a
life which had known both waste and darkness, and the love which is their
life has lived in, and united to its own existence, the depth of the abortive
gulf. The book was published by the Sinhalese publisher Tambimuttu
under his imprint 'Poetry London'. Charles had naturally hoped that the
O.U.P. would publish it, but demands on paper were too great, especially
as most of the poems in it had already appeared in periodicals.

The poems are very different from those of *Taliessin Through Logres*,
though of the same blood and spirit. The intense vision has grown now to
concern the whole Empire, not Logres only. The end comes before the last
battle between King Arthur and Mordred, and the death of the King, as
if this battle in the poetry was felt to be the approaching conclusion of a
known world.

The background given in the 'Prelude' is of the first Christian Church
of young love and discovery of glory, with also the knowledge of vileness
still in man waiting for an opportunity to wreck the glory. The poems open
with 'The Calling of Taliessin', a deep delight in the nature of poetry and
its growth in a poet. Pure lyrical verse enchants in it, as not often in
Charles's work. 'Taliessin in the Rose-Garden' contains among many
developments a study of the body as an index to other creations. It now
uses the changed name of Dindrane for Taliessin's love Blanchefleur. 'The
Founding of the Company' and 'The Queen's Servant' concern the nature
of co-inherence and the Order which Charles promoted. The ideas and
motives of evil in 'The Meditations of Mordred' show the negative chill
which Charles knew in evil. 'The Prayers of the Pope' is a long poem on
the world of Charles's time, on the 1939–45 war, and on his affirmation
of images together with his last developed concept of superfluity.

The book opens with 'Prelude', a short poem on the themes of the story.
Immediately after the life of Christ in human flesh, His followers discovered by their love and faith that His life was substituted in them for their
own. 'The young Church breakfasted on glory; handfasted,/her elect func-
tioned in the light." They caught again a glow of His transfigured bodily
glory in their own flesh, particularly in young love and in the natural marvel of the earth from which, later, young Wordsworth drank 'visionary
power'. Matter had not been thought of in the ancient world as a peculiar

vessel of divinity. The discovery was dangerous, and arduous, but for a time it was known so, 'and the earth flourished, hazel, corn, and vine'.

The next theme in 'Prelude' is the coming of the Grail, the mystery of the blood of Christ given for all and to all, nourishing all and subdued to the need of all. Matter was again the chosen medium, communicated everywhere in the Eucharist and in the legend borne in the Grail. The fact of evil, the 'vile marshes of P'o-l'u' remained in the mind of man, but energy and concentration were concerned with blessedness. Experience of this came secretly from Sarras, the City which is not mapped, being for each man's finding. Every Eucharist returns to the shedding of Christ's blood. Every month in menstruation, 'little by themselves understood', women

'shared with that Sacrifice the victimization of blood'.

All is known through the poetic genius of Taliessin, which lies open, clear and serene, gazing on the depths beyond depths of the region of the summer stars.

The young poet in 'The Calling of Taliessin' grew up in our ordinary world, where there was myth, goodness and imagination, but all without Christ. There was power and knowledge, but everything came round to the same thing in the end, decay and death. He heard a rumour of a new life, the beautiful, unheard-of kind of love which made the soul free, and he set out to travel the world to Byzantium to find it. His own self, his country, Logres, was without order, 'a storm of violent kings at war', and nearby lay the wood of Broceliande, the unknown lair of the deep forces that make up man. He feared to venture in. Through the dark trunks sea inlets glowed red in the sunset, the sea he must cross and which could lead to Sarras or to P'o-l'u. He was afraid, but held his purpose. He encountered Merlin (Time) and Brisen (Space). Night came on, the poet slept.

> Done was the day; the antipodean sun
> cast earth's coned shadow into space;
> it exposed the summer stars; as they rose
> the light of Taliessin's native land
> shone in a visible glory over him sleeping
> Rarely through the wood rang a celestial cry,
> sometimes with a like reply, sometimes with none.
> The trees shook, in no breeze, to a passage of power.

In his sleep the young poet became conscious of the operation of the feeling intellect that had sustained Wordworth and of the operation of time (Mer-

lin) using accidents to bring on events. No more was genius and nobility
of nature fated to the old cycle of decay, but in the new life nothing was
lost, everything had glory, even 'the stones of the waste glimmered like
summer stars'.

He saw the coming of good; a new coming which was to be of some
immense import to himself; he heard Merlin speak of the life of love and
of Taliessin's future part in bringing many to it from suburb and waste.
If the establishment of a common glory should fail and the kingdom of
Arthur be broken down 'at the evil luck of a blow dolorously struck', then
the rule of the Kingdom must be kept in individual souls gathered by Taliessin. Even in a world of war, the way of Christ in each man, which was
shown in the life of Galahad son of Helayne, might yet be found in any
true lovers. The vision ended. In the morning Taliessin sets off for Byzantium, to study and declare the order of glory.

In 'Taliessin in the Rose-Garden' Taliessin considered love shown in
the body, suffering in the body, analysed in the body, setting its nature and
its operation there to be learned through the flesh as completely as it also
set itself to be learned in the spirit. He did not limit its exposition to sexual
love, or to the time of youth and beauty of the body, but showed the nature
of exchange in every bodily operation. 'My covenant shall be in your flesh'.
Taliessin saw three women in the rose garden; the Queen who is 'the con-
summate earth of Logres', and its life and administration; Dindrane who
is illumination; and the slave who is the natural undeveloped base of society and body. Gazing into the ruby of the Queen's ring he became aware
of a sense of blood, of coming war and bloodshed in the land of Logres, in
the nature of man, of bloodshedding in the body of the king Pelles who
bled for the sins of the land. Making his poem, Taliessin thought of the
design of love traced in the body, the qualities of love whose principles
were shown in the eyes, hands, or pelvis, all relating to each other and yet
having authority and meaning in themselves.

He saw the vision of the body and the City in glory, as they were
intended. But glory had not been enough, man wanted also to have not-
glory. So the body and the City were experienced, lived in, endured, not
in glory. Eyes, hands or genitals no longer had authority and joy but only
recalled them in broken flashes during an existence at the best laborious,
at the worst ruined. So with neighbours or work companions. The shedding of Christ's blood was not only a glory in the Eucharist, but also a
chronic trouble every month in women's flesh. There is staunching, with
age, as there is healing in the wound of the king at Carbonek, but to most
women age is not welcome, nor the change of life recognized as arrival at
Carbonek on the body's journey from Camelot to Sarras, the city of joy.

Truth indeed speeds from the taunt 'he saved others, himself he cannot save'.

Taliessin gazed on the Queen, and on Dindrane. They saw him. He mused on his vision of love. The Queen too thought of love, of Arthur and of Lancelot. Just so in London, in Amen House, had Charles talked with his friends; just so had there been that little raillery from the effective and the great. 'Has my lord dallied with poetry among the roses?'

The next poem, 'The Departure of Dindrane', is concerned with the learning of love through all circumstances and not insisting upon being free to express oneself, to live one's own life, have one's own way, or any of the cries which come so readily to us. The princess Dindrane was choosing the life of an enclosed nun, choosing complete subjection to a rule, and the rejection of all images of love in order to approach more nearly to freedom and the love behind all images. The slave girl had done her time of service and would soon be free to choose any life she liked. As she considered the princess, she realised that love was everywhere to be learned, and a fancied freedom or her own narrow routine could equally well be the medium of learning it. A frame of life was kin to all form and measurement. Poetry is submitted to the metre of a line. Love has submitted to be known in acts, words, and bodies. The point of life is to know and to learn love and its laws of working, which make demand for special circumstances irrelevant. The consenting, even the presence, of the beloved is not essential to learning love.

> They only can do it with my lord who can do it without him'.

The decision to do it is the step that counts.

The next poem, 'The Founding of the Company' sees decision as the mark of the soul—personal decision to assent to this and not to that, to achievement and not to frustration. *Quicunque vult*—'Whosoever wills'— is the opening of the Athanasian Creed—the way of faith can only open from a man's narrow choice.

In the Company the life of exchange is lived by those friends of Taliessin who chose to assent to the principle they felt to be a law of their own being—based on the perichoresis, as understood to be the mutual indwelling of the Three Persons of the Trinity. The Incarnation brought the co-inherence of God with man, and a new life exchanged. Now Taliessin's glimpse of the End of the way to which it led is no lightning flash or ethereal vision, but something of infinite strength, weight and solidity:

> a deep, strange island of granite growth,
> thrice charged with massive light in change,

clear and golden-cream and rose tinctured,
each in turn the Holder and the Held—as the eyes
of the watcher altered and faltered and again saw
the primal Nature revealed as a law to the creature;

'The Founding of the Company' is a very lovely and warming presentation, among many other things, of the Companions of the Co-inherence. If
that is what we think we are, that is what we must answer to. Well for us
perhaps that the Household was dissolved by Taliessin, before the breaking of the world in 'The Prayers of the Pope'; well perhaps for Logres that
the Grail withdrew from the blunders of its lovers; and for all of us that
love is known through the images of life and spares us the sharpness of its
full light. Since the Household was dissolved and Taliessin withdrew into
a farther co-inherence, there has existed the Order, spread now into the
New World, unorganized except by individual choice, keeping all these
things in its heart, and turning the stones of the waste into the summer
stars,

by love, by increase of peace,
by the shyness of saving and being saved in others:

There is then freedom and power and joy, whatever the terrors of our time,
the teaching of rational observers, or the failures of ourselves.

In 'The Queen's Servant' the life of exchange is shown working. A
young household slave about to be promoted found she was able 'to gather
freedom as once she gathered servitude'. A girl from a suburb, a clerk in
an office, yet she was free to be in herself as Dindrane, princess, lover and
worker of exchange.

It had been, at some moment, her own choice. There were other choices
she could have made, and they all lead the way of the next poem, 'The
Meditation of Mordred'—to be beholden to no one, to be your own salvation and make your own terms, to turn morals and sense and judgement
away from co-inherence and use them only for yourself, to hold the spiritual world as so much fairy mechanism to make your wish come true—
and in all this to be respected and liked by your fellows, even adored with
a certain acceptable dread by your nearest. On one way or the other we
all go.

Christ is not attractive. How bitterly both Kierkegaard and Charles
knew and declared that. He is only not, finally, an illusion, and everything
else is. 'Not that the Way is narrow but that narrowness is the Way',[7]
cried Kierkegaard; and both he and Charles knew that it was so narrow

that to get through squeezed the blood from the heart. In the last poem, 'The Prayers of the Pope', Charles saw man's life, even Christian life, as

> a thing unrequited,
> plighted in presence to no recompense, no
> purchase of paradise; eyes see no future:
> when the Son of Man comes, he brings no faith in a future.

When Christ comes, there can be war and destruction, love turned against love, hope against hope, joy against joy. So the Pope saw it, and we also when we are serious. The abolition of war and the establishment of world-wide peace has never yet appeared to be God's way. Certainly it is now man's will and man's urgent need, but that is not quite the same. When the way of co-inherence really becomes an issue with us, when the admission of the existence of another, say a rival in love or money, strikes at our life we find

> savage growths, moods infinitely multiplied
> across the bleak plains, under rains and snows
> of myths bitter to bondage, where in race
> by sullen marshes separated from race
> virtue is monopolized and grace prized in schism.

Do we not know it? How many marriages, how many families, show the ruins of this war!

> their wrath grew
> with vengeance and victory; they looked to no returning.

There is none. There can only be a new life and a new beginning. Everything else has failed or is known to be illusory. In the new life, reality sustains the loves and desires which we take for images, and they are no more only themselves but truly images of reality which holds and fills us even while it breaks us. We cannot even commit suicide, for that gives no escape from a reality in which we, body and mind and spirit, for ever co-inhere. In that knowledge, he wrote to a friend, 'A love renounced, we feel, *must* continue somehow in the City—yes, but it will be, O princess, the other side of Lear's 'Never, never, never, never, never'.[8]

In that state, the Household was dissolved and the outer forms of bonds and compacts abolished. The Pope saw that Christ's substitution had saved

man. Each man was capable outwardly as inwardly of the direct relationship with the unimaged Love,

> whether in body or soul they drink deadly,
> or handle malice and slander as they handle serpents,

> . . .

>   what recovers
> lovers in lovers is love; let them then
> go into every den of magic and mutiny,
> touch the sick and the sick be healed, take
> the trick of the weak devils with peace, and speak
> at last on the coast of the land of the Trinity the tongue
> of the Holy Ghost.

But 'The Company is for all the Companions to extend, as and how seems
wise to them. . . . "Fast to the Byzantine harbour gather the salvaged
sails"'.[9]

In this world the most hidden power of illusion, in the subconscious
mind or in the objective world, is rendered harmless if we choose so. Since
even hell is sustained by Love, as Love brings to fruition the will of every
creature even if the will be to separate itself finally from Love, then there
is love if we will see it even there, in the abortive gulf. And in the triple-
toned light the stones which have bruised us, in that gulf glimmer like
summer stars.

If all this is true, and so much wealth of love is poured out through us,
it were well for us that one should pray 'Send not, send not, the rich empty
away'.[10]

The Region of the Summer Stars was the last book of Charles's published poetry, though a verse play was to follow. He was happy that 800
copies were sold in five weeks, and the whole first edition by mid-
December.

At this farthest point, how sensibly and accurately do his early poems
read. In *The Silver Stair* he had heard a rumour of the end of love, the
grey monotony of some marriages, of dull pain and desolation and an inescapable togetherness.

> Is there none other end? yea, one there is.
>   Before Love's mazed, stricken, and hallowed eyes,
>   In earth, in heaven gleam bright virginities.[11]

He looked in vain for ease and consolation:

> But on our lips the words fail, and our eyes
> Look not to one another: a man dies
> In dusk of noon upon a barren tree.[12]

All love was only and could only be the living and dying within us of that man, and without His total loss on Calvary all our moments would hasten to a like loss which had no recovery and no exchange in itself with love. At the end of Charles's poetic life he maintained the same belief, in the prayer of the Pope:

> O Blessed, confirm
> not thee in thine images only but thine images in thee.

He had passed through the evil when opposites failed to inhere in his mind, and his life was darkened by gaps of solitary terror and struggle.[13] *Taliessin Through Logres* and *He Came Down From Heaven* are shaken with it, *The Figure of Beatrice* trembles, and the concluding of it is the agony in *What the Cross Means to Me*. The pure world after the resolution of that long pain shines out in *The Region of the Summer Stars*, and in his last novel *All Hallows' Eve*. He wrote to Robin Milford from Oxford, 'My own muddles are written over the earth and heaven, but I take refuge in God and the Order, and hope, under the Mercy, to smile at them all in the end'.

Charles Hadfield and he talked about 'after the war' in London. Sir Humphrey would still be there, and who else? Then he realised that younger staff would be there, and he could get a better flat, and take up again his City Literary Institute lectures. Of such a moment of realisation that a happy future was possible, C. W. wrote to me that 'something might *be,* a new being, both the old and the new. This very highly moved me, and made me happier for an evening than I usually am in Oxford'.

Oxford life also held its own advantages. He wrote to Michal on 5 February 1944, 'I found myself thinking how admirable it would be if I could get a Readership here when I retire. I know it may be only a dream; on the other hand, C. S. L. and Tolkien are only human, and are likely to take more trouble over a project which would enable them to see a good deal more of me than over anything which didn't. And I think, in the future, they *may* take steps. Let me know your reactions; you shall not live anywhere you do not wish'.[14]

In 1944 he completed the novel *All Hallows' Eve,* continued work on *The House of the Octopus,* thought and worked on *The Figure of Arthur* 'as a pendant to *Beatrice*' and began a short biography of Dr. *Flecker of Dean Close* School at the request of Flecker's widow. He was also involved all the year with Dorothy Sayers's study of Dante, with her activity in writing and promoting better religious plays for the current revival in religion, and working on committees with her. He had his own part to play also in giving talks, writing articles and polishing up plays like *Seed of Adam* and *The Death of Good Fortune* which were then only in acting versions.

In 1943, Williams began a new novel with the title, *The Noises That Weren't There*, but abandoned it after three chapters and used some of the material—notably Jonathan Drayton and his paintings—in *All Hallows' Eve*. The unfinished work has the war as background with night-raids on London and wartime conditions for the city and people, but there is hardly scope to develop a story, and much of the three chapters is an exposition of the working of magic, whereby the noises were not noises but 'a pressure felt in her body and changed by her body into the noise'.

Two points recall Charles's own past: the warm half paragraph at the beginning of Chapter II about a brother and sister relationship, and the reference to a glass of water being brought in the night—an incident he recalled deeply in his poem 'A Cup of Water' in *Windows of Night*. The writing is powerful. In the third chapter, it is a pleasure to find 'This also is Thou; neither is this Thou' in Charles's Latin: *'Et hic Tu autem; neque hic Tu'*.

Charles has come out of the world of Broceliande, the world of making, of looming powers and forms, in which he had written *Descent Into Hell*. His writing now is from a Christian world, though it has an understanding of Christianity more compelling than we have reason to think is common. *All Hallows' Eve* was published three months before his death. In the book he presents his imagination of goodness in the language and setting of plain fact, without defence, and without comment. In *Many Dimensions* Chloe Burnett had offered her will, and accepted the physical blasting. In *All Hallows' Eve* Betty Wallingford and Lester Furnival escaped the blasting and lived, one in the visible and one in the invisible world, in the life and power of good—with very curious results. In the climax of the last chapter neither Christ nor a Church is named, but there is the Ascension, the blood, grace, and the Hallows. There is also the world without Christ, without co-inherence. An adept in magic, Simon the Clerk is engaged in an attempt to seize spiritual power over this world and the world of spirits, and is—almost by accident—defeated by two girls. The scene is London, after the war, but it is also in the London as seen and understood by the souls of the dead, whether they are in process of redemption or obstinately preferring the opposite of redemption. Among the magical operations runs the relationship of an ordinary husband and wife growing more perceiving and more loving, the strength of friendship and the supernatural lucidity of infant baptism. Charles said the book was essentially the tale of one soul, and that of anyone. Faber's published it and Charles assured Eliot that it went on from the point at which *Descent Into Hell* left off. This was his aim for every work, to move forward from each point of awareness— exchange, patience, delight—because there was always more to discover. Discovery is a kind of pain, in the fact that our joys and loves do not and cannot survive without some life other than their own desire. Themselves they cannot save.

The House of the Octopus was published in 1945. As long ago as 1937 the United Council for Missionary Education had asked him for a play. He had refused then, but now consented. It concerns a Christian island in the Outer Seas, which is invaded by forces under an Imperial Marshal who plans to conquer the island by undermining its Christianity. The character of the Flame is the last in that line of commentators on the action which began with Satan in *The Rite of the Passion*. C. W. describes it in his Preface as 'that energy which went to the creation and was at Pentecost (as it were) re-delivered in the manner of its own august covenant to the Christian Church'.

Last of Charles's books, *Flecker of Dean Close* was written in 1944– 45 at the request of Flecker's widow and published in 1946, after his death. There are too many quotations from 'original sources', too many letters from pupils and admirers of Flecker. But it is remarkable for its appreciation of the Victorian Age and of the Anglican Church in that age, and for its grasp of the peculiar greatness of a far from famous man. More personally, it is also remarkable for its valuation of marriage and domestic life and the difficulties of dealing with Flecker's rather crudely adolescent son, the poet James Elroy. In doing so, it gives penetrating glimpses of Charles on married life, and on being a father: 'Few married men have not been astonished at the extreme accuracy of judgment and the extreme generosity of temper displayed by their wives'.[15] 'This is to trail one's coat before one's father, in order that one may be equally annoyed whether he does or does not jump on it. . . . There is generally a point at which the parent cannot any more bring himself to jump on the trailed coat'.[16]

When Flecker started his studies to be ordained, he was newly married and painfully poor. He rose at 5.30, worked until 7.30, had breakfast, taught all day in a school, then worked again in the evening, he and his young wife having agreed to be silent during his studying hours to allow him to concentrate. Later, writing of Flecker's very exacting routine of life at Durham University, Charles recalls the young students of the Middle

Ages, twelve years old, reading theology, 'that lordliest of all contemplations in the candle-lit cold of morning at the Universities'. Flecker and they were alike driven by 'the passionate desire of the serious heart to understand, define, and proclaim "the ways of God and man"'.[17]

Such a way of living, Charles wrote, seemed to Flecker, 'a rigour . . . imposed on him by the whole scheme of things; he was not, he knew, free to neglect or avoid opportunities; he was, on the contrary, bound to make them. The whole of creation was an opportunity which had to be, at all times and in all places, localized. If we accuse those great and ardent souls of being over-serious, they answer simply that about the Crucifixion of our Lord and the possible damnation of our souls, it is quite impossible to be over-serious'.[18] They are driven by their rational nature. They see that men's finer faculties, spiritual and moral, are not as keen as they would be if used constantly, while other perceptions are always in full working order. How often had Charles told himself this. 'Our ideas of God are not vivid enough', Flecker wrote, 'we think of him in a sort of dream, just as we do of Charlemagne'.[19] The book has a lucidity and calm that make principles visible in facts.

Williams also wrote five chapters of *The Figure of Arthur,* (already mentioned in Chapter 9), with the titles 'The Beginnings', 'The Grail', 'The Coming of the King', 'The Coming of Love' and 'The Coming of the Grail'. The first two he had read to Lewis and Tolkien in the former's rooms at Magdalen, and after Williams's death all five were published as part of C. S. Lewis's *Arthurian Torso* (1948).

Many of Charles's letters of 1944 and 1945 refer to events of the war—the heavy bombing of Berlin, the advance of Russia. His political sense was as sound as ever. 'The Russian insistence on a "friendly" Poland makes all but nonsense of talk of an "independent" Poland . . . . I distrust the whole Russian movement, *but* I do not see what our unfortunate government is to do except try and check and moderate it'.[20]

The living of life was becoming laborious. He wrote to Thelma Shuttleworth on 20 December 1944, 'I could say, daring to borrow from W'worth, that all action lies on me

> with a weight
> heavy as frost and deep almost as life.

This is definition, and not complaint, even if it is (a little) cause. . . . The immediate instinct, the immediate impulse, the immediate action, "the elasticity and fire", changes. Just as verse now has to be thought and planned, and considered and re-considered; just as prose needs writing two or three times where once was formerly enough; just as one can no more lecture on what one knows, but has to re-read what one *did* know . . . one must know something else, one must do something *else;* and not only something other but something almost of another kind. O I allow no one observes much difference in the result; at least no one sees anything better or greater. Like the Red Queen one has to run so very fast even to remain in the same place. I cannot make it too clear that I am not *grumbling* at this; I only say, it happens—and so, no doubt, it should. At 60 one ought not to be "a boy at heart", and I'm very glad I'm not'. Separation from home had much to do with it. 'More than one ever dreamed or thought . . . I depended on my wife . . . and flying visits, however frequent, are not the mutual exchange of unseen life. And one's distinguished friend at ————, however good and useful, is *not* that steady, unnoticeable nourishment and repose. . . . All I mean is that—shall I say—I have almost to begin again every time. One would think that past things—not meaning Your Excellency more than Shakespeare—would continue? They do, but their continuity is in their new beginning each time to be achieved. Excluding my wife, I can find nothing of which this does not seem to be true. This is not, I think, dryness, but the order of human things'.

As the impulse to write and speak slackened, he felt more and more deeply the value of living the life of which the poets and theologians wrote. More than *what* goodness is he felt the impact of the existence of goodness, that it *is*. To be good, to hold one's will open, to nourish in one's daily moments the child Love born there because He was once born in Bethlehem, became the validity whereby the grand art of poetry was measured. In marriage this was the life which must be attempted, and nothing less. He had always spoken of goodness so, but now still more. He declared that it was more to be desired than the life of poetry. 'Do not you over-envy the "creative life!" It's not all that fun, largely because one is never quite sure if one has "done it"; largely because one is always trying to avoid the sin of Egotism. But to live it in the other sense—yes. To be, ever new, the thing expressed; to live, in fact, the life of glory. It is, however, to the liver, also largely dull . . . but I have no doubt that it exists everywhere and at all times'.

He moved toward a little curiosity about what would come after. Immortality had always been as much of a threat as a hope. But merely to cease? Co-inherence, love? There must, he thought, be more to know about God who had exhibited these in his own fifty-odd years of life. So much was clearly unresolved. He wrote to Thelma, 'I am convinced that there must be a Redemption of Sin. It is not enough to leave either personal or public sins behind; your very selfishness, my angers, must be redeemed, and Poland, and the Germans. And us. This, all this, must be known in the good'. 'As far as "something after death" goes I believe in two things.

I believe that every soul experiences and understands fully the entire and living Justice of the universe. I believe that Justice to be a living, responsive and intelligent Existence—and one with Almighty Love. And I believe It makes Itself clear to every soul in the way that that soul chooses. I believe that that Being—that some thing consciously and deliberately existing— is, of Its own adorable Nature, non-temporal. But it is aware of, and present at, all points of time. Now I myself, as you know, have no passion for everlasting life. But I do not conceive that my personal wishes govern the universe; and—because of all the above—because Justice-in-Love exists, I believe in a Judgement, an Accounting. Or, to put it another way, I believe that we shall see our thoughts, words, and actions in that lucid Justice— that the past lives there, and we shall jolly well know it, where we have sinned and where not, and so on. And this means—if we are to know (what I should prefer to call) God and ourselves, some state in which we shall do it—"the Communion of Saints, The Forgiveness of Sins, the Resurrection of the Body, and the Life Everlasting"; four aspects of one state, four walls of one City, four realisations of one Fact. And I believe those who know those great Mysteries rightly enter into the joy of the Lord'.

In the meantime he got on with his crowded daily life. He reminded one about to get married that Christ said to St. Peter 'You girded yourself, and went your way; now I will gird you'. What was once a delight may have to be known in love as a burden. 'I have talked to and lunched with people I didn't want for no real reason except that I once did it with Celia, and (if there is anything beyond our personal pleasures in it) one must *not* pick and choose. Endure the—expiation? in a way. Enlarge fidelity. Believe in God'.

He had less time and energy for relaxation now. Lecturing, or listening to lectures by his friends, preparing and writing his own books, meeting with the Inklings, discussing Dante and the Grail and theology with Dorothy Sayers, doing his daily work, all now took up his time. Art and music continued to mean very little to Charles. He was polite about Oxford College architecture, but it was not important. As for nature, he was very little conscious of details like flowers or weather, but much aware of the spread of the sky and the distance-points of the stars. His only relaxations were detective fiction and halma. He played a good game of halma. His chief opponent in 9 South Parks Road was Anne Spalding. They would lie on the floor in the evening with the board near the fire and their feet in and out of chairs and table legs. The game, Anne Saplding said, also served as a torture to keep them awake during whole nights of fire-watching.

The reception of *The Region of the Summer Stars* was disappointingly quiet. Only five papers reviewed it. 'The T.L.S.—was the T.L.S.!; *Time and Tide* was (inevitably!) good; the *Birmingham Post* didn't like it; Mr Richard Church of *John O'London* said he wouldn't say anything because he didn't understand it; and the *Tribune* says it marks a new high level of tedium in last year's verse'. 'But then', Charles added to me, 'the *Tribune* alludes to the Grail Quest as "this simple subject"—which gives me a soft and continued joy'. He was indignant with a writer who put in a footnote saying that Charles seemed 'to be under the sway of an erotic spiritualism', and linked him with Berdyaev and the Gnostics. 'It sounds horrid and I think I resent it. Am I erotically spiritual?'

The growth of the Order continually amazed him. 'It is the secret and unknown balance of the wars: so small, so laborious, so incomprehensibly certain. The certainty is in others, and not in me; I believe in them from experience, in it by deduction'. He had trouble, naturally, with over-zealous adherents who wished strongly to make the Order fulfil the idea of their needs instead of attending to the idea of the Order. He had expected it and was firm. One woman felt that co-inherence meant being friends with everybody and every belief, and that it was non-co-inherent to be Christian about it. Charles wrote briskly: 'She must not be allowed to forget that the Order is, in its universality, Christian: by which I mean only that she must not have it as something she *likes*—"the old man on the new way". And at the least she must not attack—she must regard the *Idea*. . . . I don't want to deny the workings everywhere, but we cannot have the Centre of Co-inherence talked sillily about'. Old friends could fail too and wander in fields of illusion. I expressed some very striking and beautiful thoughts to him, combined with my discontents. He replied by mentioning ways in which I could be better spending my time. 'Your most revolutionary Excellency . . . must . . . be doing something towards the establishment—even on earth—of our desired and hierarchical Republic by ordering the desire and establishing a hierarchy within you. *Act,* blast you! Aesthetics here, aesthetics there; gospels and revolutions in great thrills of aerial wonder: *act.* Is thy servant a dog? Is the City a kennel that we get hold of to sneak into for our aesthetic orgasms?'

In this last maturity of his power, he was absorbed by the idea of superfluity, of being happily superfluous as Taliessin knew himself in 'The Founding of the Company'. An image was at the same time chosen, clung to, and totally superfluous. 'Everything turns on the fact that the Word in the beginning determined to take flesh, and might have done so merely in Himself without creating, but in order that we might be joyous He determined to have a Mother and the world: also He determined to owe His flesh to His Mother's will instead of merely creating it'. The double image of an idea, say, the beloved woman, being at once the sole medium of the revelation of love and totally superfluous except as love chose to do it that way, delighted his ambivalent mind. It was a union by nature of the ways of affirmation and of rejection. He had meditated on images of love all his life. In his last years he began through his work and through the Order to be to others that experience which he had so long studied. He began to be an image, and at that point he declared the superfluity of images of love. It was his own last comment on himself. *The Region of the Summer Stars* is full of superfluity. It made bearable, and of the nature of freedom, a necessary superiority or distinction. Taliessin was never named as lieutenant of the Company until it was settled that lieutenants were superfluous. Then it could be done and enjoyed for what it was worth, since it was worth nothing but the enjoyment. All claiming of grace, or authority, or exoneration, or knowledge *because* one was the beloved or the image was thereby impossible. He had often said it before—the vision was more than the prince through whom one sees it, the loving and learning of love more than the immediate will of the beloved—but now he found backing for it in the working of creation itself, in the Incarnation and every moment thereafter.

It was the last of his creative ideas. Almost it was in itself a relaxation of pressure, a kind of exclamation mark and finis. He was finding less and less energy for his work. 'I muddle on, everything sticks damnably. . . . I wish I did not feel so steadily, as if my work was done. Laziness? partly'. He was reading *The Faerie Queene* in January 1945, his mind heavy with approaching lectures, 'approaching Britomart in readiness for Comus. But I do not seem to be filled with new ideas about Milton. I keep on tending to lose myself in fancies and fantasies, and have less and less inclination to do a thing other. . . . All my present literary efforts seem to be made up of bits and pieces from my past. Re-shuffled, but recognizable to the lucid mind'.[21] 'I labour indefatigably here in extinguishing in the minds of the young the heresy that good is only known by contrast with evil'.[22]

A change was moving in his life. The shell of the past had been forcibly broken away from him, and he had emerged and shone upon a new horizon. But the broken pieces of the past were gathering again. 'Nobody will understand my relations with my wife who has not given the full place to that early verse'.[23] Sir Humphrey had withdrawn into himself, but still, sauntering down Southfield House stairs, it was possible to come upon him and on Gerard Hopkins, Fred Page, Helen Peacock, Hubert Foss—faces and voices from twenty years ago. His mother was still alive, still in St. Albans with his sister. The daily war news doubled itself into the echo of 1918, and in the streets the uniforms brought back the shapes of Harold Eyers and Ernest Nottingham. Old friends came to Oxford to see him whenever they could make time. I was often there. Charles Hadfield appeared for lunches when possible. Charles's mind dwelt on the images of the past.

He was now much supported by his wife, and the discovery of her reading *Taliessin* was a moment of joy. He wrote to Thelma Shuttleworth: 'In all our present dangers, I admit to a singular good fortune; many things I have lost, and many thrown away, and many were forbidden. But almost everywhere a *something* has—I hardly dare even say lasted, but *been*. There has been everywhere a point of good; it is astonishing and in a way terrifying—that lucid, often vanishing, often repudiated, point of— beauty? say, of fact. I should like to believe I should never emotionally deny it again'. 'There is to me an insane sense of reliving one's earlier life; the chief difference is that now I have no friends to be killed. . . . The people who lived through Napoleon must have had it . . . one might say, absurdly, that where I once preferred companions with a touch of the Images, I now begin to think that I prefer Images with a touch of the companion!'[24]

When I went over to Oxford to meet him we did nothing but loaf. We sat about in bars, chiefly in *The King's Arms,* and ate and drank a little, and talked. He recommended, or gave me, many books he had found valuable to read on theology, poetry or Kierkegaard. We walked up and down on sunny afternoons, savouring the time. There was a basking feel about it. Charles was secluding himself, or being secluded, and I felt it. In my company he need make no effort to maintain the present, nor to explain the past. He could follow his own processes, with the knowledge that I wanted nothing else. We talked endlessly, and when I had gone home he would continue the talk by letter. It was talk about poetry, or Taliessin and the Grail, or my coming marriage with Charles Hadfield and the nature of love. On his side, the personal talk was never much about his present victories, though he always mentioned any new trophy as soon as we met to keep me up to date, but about the past and its reappearance in or influence on the present.

The denizens of the O.U.P. loved him, though few other than Sir Humphrey entered into his ideas. Yet, however much they eluded him, he loved them. In that last year his mind dwelt continuously on the past, while handling the present with love and accuracy. In Amen House he had first heard, in those years from 1920 to 1929, the rumour of co-inherence and exchange; there he had first seen the inescapable vision. Other ways and other pleasures had been offered and delighted in, but he loved the gates of Zion more than all the dwellings of Jacob.

In March 1945 he went to St. Albans to see his mother and sister. Edith silently observed how tired and ill he looked. It was the last time she saw him. He was not specifically ill but he had worn his thread almost through. He was coming in to 'peace and the perfect end'.[25] The European war drew to its conclusion. On 8 May, the news of peace was expected the next day. A holiday was promised and most of the staff of Southfield House were arranging to go to London. Charles said to Miss Peacock, 'Well, you and I, Dorinda, will be there as usual at our desks,' and went on exactly the same. He met Gervase Mathew, and in the course of conversation asked him if he would say a Mass 'for anyone I have ever loved in any way'. Although nothing was specific, Father Mathew felt very strongly that Charles had a sense that he was going to die. The Mass was said.

The ninth of May brought the end of the war. Miss Peacock and Charles were indeed at their desks, almost alone in Southfield House. It was his last day at work, and perhaps there, with one of his oldest friends, to know peace restored was a not inadequate leave-taking. That night he went out with Anne Spalding and walked about the streets to see the bonfires lit for victory.

Next day he was seized with pain. He cancelled his arrangements and stayed in his room. Gerry Hopkins was much with him. A day or two went by with no improvement, but with nothing to cause alarm except that he grew very weak. By Friday, the danger was suddenly clear. His wife came from London, he was taken to the Radcliffe Hospital, and operated on for a recurrence of the internal trouble of eleven years before. He never fully recovered consciousness and died on the following day, Tuesday 15 May. He lies in St. Cross churchyard, Holywell, Oxford.

In his last letter to me, of 4 May, written in his late, unclear hand he said: 'It's a good thing, most noble lady, that whatever was done was done when it was done'.

Notes

Chapter 1

1. Edith Williams, MS 'Memories of Early Days at Home'.
2. Now Caedmon Road, London N7.
3. 'The Calling of Taliessin', *The Region of the Summer Stars*, 1944.
4. 'Memories'.
5. Ibid. Talbot & Co. in 1919 published *Christian Symbolism* by Michal Williams, Charles Williams's wife (for the name Michal see p. 33). Passages in the book are thought to have been written by Charles.
6. Ibid.
7. Ibid.
8. 'The Calling of Taliessin', *Summer Stars*.
9. 'To a Publisher', *Windows of Night*, 1925.
10. Adapted from 'Domesticity', *Windows of Night*.
11. Now demolished.
12. *An Urbanity,* 1926.
13. 'Memorics'.
14. Ibid.
15. A. M. Hadfield, *An Introduction to Charles Williams,* Robert Hale, 1959, p. 19, quoting George Robinson.
16. C. W. to Dorothy L. Sayers, 7 September 1944.
17. 'Memories'.
18. Marion E. Wade Collection, Wheaton College, Illinois, U.S.A.
19. *Flecker of Dean Close,* 1946, p. 70.
20. Charles Williams told me this while walking in Broad Street, Oxford, in 1944–45.
21. 'Memories'. On the other hand, Charles's mother told me that the tremor in his

hands developed after measles. He himself said, 'I have had to put up with it all my life'. In 1933 he had an operation, after which, he said, it was 'a little worse'. See p. 175. Certainly there was a change in his handwriting after 1933.

22. Ibid.
23. *Summer Stars*.

Chapter 2

1. Kindly made available to me by Mrs. Anne Ridler.
2. For a straightforward re-telling of the Arthurian stories, see Alice M. Hadfield, *King Arthur and the Round Table*, Dent (Dutton), 1953 and reprints.
3. 'Taliessin's Return to Logres', *Taliessin through Logres*, 1938.
4. Ibid.
5. 'The Witch', *Three Plays*, 1931, pp. 39–40.
6. 'In the Land of Juda', *Poems of Conformity*, 1917.
7. Anne Ridler, *The Image of the City and Other Essays*, Oxford University Press, 1958, introduction p. xvii, quoting 'As I Remember', an article in the American *Episcopal Churchnews*, 12 April 1953.
8. Ibid.
9. *The Silver Stair*, 1912, VIII.
10. Ibid., X.
11. For example, XVI, XXVII, LX, LXXVI.
12. *The Bible*, Eccles. 12:6.
13. C. W. to Alice Meynell, 25 June 1911.
14. C. W. to Alice Meynell, 9 July 1911.
15. C. W. to Alice Meynell, 27 July 1911.
16. C. W. to Alice Meynell, 12 January 1911 (more likely 1912) (Humanities Research Center, The University of Texas at Austin).
17. Quoted by C. W. in his letter to Alice Meynell, 27 November 1912.
18. 'Conformity', *Conformity*.
19. In *Divorce*, 1920.
20. C. W. to Alice Meynell, February 1915.
21. Both in *Conformity*.
22. C. W. to Alice Meynell, 14 July 1916.
23. C. W. to Alice Meynell, 9 November 1916.
24. *Image of the City*, xxvi.
25. C. W. to Alice Meynell, 14 July 1916.
26. Information from Mr. Robert A. Gilbert.
27. C. W. to Alice Meynell, 9 November 1916.
28. Alice Meynell, 'The Two Shakespeare Tercentenaries', *A Father of Women, and Other Poems*, 1917. Included in *The Poems of Alice Meynell* in Oxford Standard Authors series 1940.
29. 'A Song of Opposites', *Conformity*.
30. C. W. to Wilfrid Meynell, 21 February 1917.
31. In *Conformity*.
32. C. W. to Wilfrid Meynell, 13 April 1917.
33. C. W. to Alice Meynell, 3 July 1917.
34. Ibid.

35. C.W. to Alice Meynell, 30 July 1918.
36. A. E. Waite to C. W., 6 September 1917 (Marion E. Wade Collection).
37. C. W. to Phyllis Jones, No. 269 (Bodleian Library, restricted).
38. In *Taliessin*.
39. On C. W. and the Order of the Golden Dawn, see also *Image of the City*, pp. xxiii–xxvi.
40. C. W. to Anne Ridler, 18 May 1937.
41. *All Hallows' Eve*, 1945, pp. 200–1.
42. *The Collected Poems of W. B. Yeats*, Macmillan, 1939, pp. 113.
43. Marion E. Wade Collection.
44. A district of London west of Kensington Gardens.
45. Bonaventura, *The Oxford Dictionary of Quotations*, 3rd ed., Oxford University Press, 1979.
46. C. W. to Alice Meynell, 30 July 1918.
47. C. W. to John Pellow, 5 October 1923.
48. 'In Time of War—IV', *Divorce*.
49. 'Ghosts', *Divorce*.
50. *The Bible*, II Samuel VI, 14–23.
51. C. W. to Joan Wallis, 11 November 1940.
52. T. S. Eliot, 'Burnt Norton'.
53. 'House-hunting', *Divorce*.
54. Ibid.
55. Ibid.
56. 'Three Friends', *Divorce*.
57. C. W. to Phyllis Potter,14 February 1945 (Bodleian Library).
58. 'Chant Royal of Feet', *Divorce*.
59. 'Office Hymn for the Feast of St. Thomas Didymus, Apostle and Sceptic', *Divorce*.

Chapter 3

1. C. W. to John Pellow, 16 July 1920.
2. C. W. to Alice Meynell, 8 February 1921.
3. C. W. to John Pellow, ND (probably 1921).
4. Ibid.
5. C. W. to John Pellow, ND, 'In the Epiphany', probably early 1922. The colleague referred to was V. H. Collins, and the book *Poems of Home and Overseas*, Clarendon Press, 1921. It was re-issued in 1930.
6. 'To Michal: Sonnets after Marriage, IV, On her singing the Gloria', *Windows of Night*, ND (1925).
7. C. W. to John Pellow, ND, 'In the Epiphany', probably early 1922.
8. C. W. to John Pellow, 6 July 1922.
9. C. W. to John Pellow, ND, 'St Thomas' (21 December, probably 1922).
10. John Pellow gave me eight pages of extracts which he had made from *The Chapel of the Thorn*. He said that the work was early and pseudo-Miltonic in style. 'Re-reading it for the first time after many years I experience some of the admiration which prompted me to go to the trouble of copying patches of it.' These pages in my possession are all that seem to remain of the work.

11. C. W. to John Pellow, 16 June 1925.
12. C. W. to Alice M. Miller (Hadfield), 9 January 1940.
13. A book influenced by Charles Williams, William P. Wylie's *The Pattern of Love*, Longmans, 1958, well summarises these reasons.
14. 'Outlines of Romantic Theology', ch. 4.
15. In *Conformity*.
16. 'Romantic Theology', ch. 2.
17. Ibid., ch. 3.
18. Ibid.
19. Ibid., ch. 4.
20. *The Bible*, Acts 5:2.
21. 'Romantic Theology', ch. 5.
22. Ibid., ch. 4.
23. *The Bible*, John 14:9.
24. I think Humphrey Milford mixed two well-known quotations about an Indian:

(i) 'Lo, the poor Indian! whose untutored mind
Sees God in clouds, or hears him in the wind'.

(Pope, *An Essay on Man*, Epistle i, 1.99)

(ii) 'one whose hand
Like the base Indian, threw a pearl away
Richer than all his tribe'

(Shakespeare, *Othello*, V, ii.45)

25. C. W. to John Pellow, 6 September 1924.
26. The General Strike began on 3 May 1926 and ended ten days later.
27. C. W. to John Pellow, 13 September 1923.
28. C. W. to John Pellow, 2 December (1926).
29. C. W. to John Pellow, 19 December 1923.
30. See Peter Sutcliffe, 'The Music Department', *The Oxford University Press*, Oxford University Press, 1978, part VI, S.4.
31. Shakespeare, *The Winter's Tale*, IV, iv, 114.
32. C. W. to John Pellow, 14 April 1924.
33. C. W. to John Pellow, 5 September 1924.
34. In *Taliessin*, 1938.
35. The book is undated. Some bibliographies give 1924. But a letter to J. Pellow, probably of December 1924, says "*Noctis Specularia* won't be published till the eighth of January" (the title is a Latinizing of *Windows of Night*). A letter to Wilfred Meynell of 7 January 1925 accompanies a copy of "a new book" on publication.
36. 'In Time of Danger, III', *Windows of Night*, 1925.
37. 'Night Poems, I', *Windows of Night*.
38. 'Judgement', *Windows of Night*.
39. 'To a Poet going to Rome, I, II', *Windows of Night*.
40. 'On Meeting Shakespeare', *Windows of Night*.
41. 'The English Tradition', *Windows of Night*.
42. 'On the Sanctissimum, III, At Communion', *Windows of Night*.
43. Peter Jolliffe's (Oxford bookseller) *Catalogue* No 19, pp. 31–32.

Chapter 4

1. This and all other personal information has been given me by the former Phyllis Jones, personally and in letters.
2. For the background, see Peter Sutcliffe, *Oxford University Press*, 1978.
3. Shelley, 'Hellas'.
4. C. W. to Phyllis Jones, No. 222 (Bodleian Library, restricted; for all letters in rest of chapter).
5. C. W. to Phyllis Jones, No. 220.
6. 1927. The imprint on this and its successor reads: 'One hundred copies have been printed in England, for private circulation only', by Henderson & Spalding Ltd., London.
7. Cantos xxix, xxx.
8. Mrs. Thelma Shuttleworth to author.
9. C. W. to Phyllis Jones, No. 294.
10. C. W. to Phyllis Jones, No. 092.
11. There were two exhibitions for the Tolstoy centenary, at both of which the Oxford University Press had exhibits.
12. C. W. to Phyllis Jones, No. 293.
13. C. W. to Phyllis Jones, No. 231.
14. *The Rite of the Passion*, p. 164, in *Three Plays*, 1931.
15. See note 11. At the first Tolstoy exhibition, he and Phyllis had arranged the O.U.P. exhibit and spent some time looking after it.
16. The Dianeme series of poems is unpublished. The word derives from the Greek διανέμω (dianemo), to distribute, and C. W. used it as representing distributive justice, that being one aspect of Celia.
17. C. W. to Phyllis Jones, No. 211.
18. 'Notes' from Phyllis Jones to author.
19. Edith Sitwell, 'Lo, this is she that was the world's delight', *The Penguin Poets*, 1952.
20. *Thomas Cranmer of Canterbury*, Oxford University Press, 1936, p. 53.
21. C. W. to Phyllis Jones, No. 336.

Chapter 5

1. C. W. to A. E. Housman, 18 September 1929 (O.U.P. file No. 5545).
2. O.U.P. internal memorandum to O.U.P. New York Branch, 15 February 1929 (O.U.P. file 6531).
3. *Poems of Gerard Manley Hopkins*, ed. Robert Bridges, 2nd. ed. with 'a Critical Introduction by Charles Williams', Oxford University Press, 1930, pp. xii, xiii.
4. O.U.P. internal memoranda, VHC (V. H. Collins) to SCTY (Secretary to the Delegates), 16 October 1925, and KS (Kenneth Sisam) to VHC, 19 October 1925.
5. Sir Edmund Chambers, *William Shakespeare: a Study of Facts and Problems*, 2 vols. Clarendon Press, 1930.
6. *A Short Life of Shakespeare with the Sources*, abridged from Sir Edmund Chambers book by Charles Williams, 1933.
7. C. W. to T. S. Eliot, 17 May 1930.
8. C. W. to T. S. Eliot, 28 March, 11 May, and 26 September 1929.
9. G. W. S. Hopkins to W. Bridges Adam, 5 January 1929 (O.U.P. file 6531).
10. C. W. to Kenneth Sisam, 20 March 1930.

11. Ibid.
12. H. S. Milford to Kenneth Sisam, 11 March 1930.
13. Ibid.
14. C. W. to Kenneth Sisam, 20 June 1935.
15. In the prefatory note to *Three Plays*.
16. C. W. to Phyllis Jones, No. 11 (Bodleian Library, restricted; for all letters in rest of chapter).
17. C. W. to Phyllis Jones, No. 180.
18. Charles Williams Society *Newsletter,* 19, Autumn 1980, pp. 5–6.
19. C. W. to Phyllis Jones, No. 151.
20. Ibid.
21. C. W. to Phyllis Jones, No. 180.
22. C. W. to Phyllis Jones, No. 178. The book would have been *Heroes and Kings,* with its scarlet binding.
23. Unpublished.
24. C. W. to Phyllis Jones, No. 147.
25. C. W. to Phyllis Jones, No. 188.
26. C. W. to Phyllis Jones, No. 171. One reading of this undated letter could date Page's information to Mrs. Williams as after Charles's illness in 1933. But much would have to be altered to support this view.
27. C. W. to Phyllis Jones, No. 269.
28. Dante, 'Inferno', *Commedia,* Temple Classics ed., 1937, canto V, 16.
29. Ibid., 28–30.
30. Ibid., 31.
31. Ibid., 44–45.
32. The 'Century', VII (unpublished).
33. Ibid., XI.
34. C. W. to Phyllis Jones, No. 354.
35. The 'Century', XII.
36. C. W. to Anne Bradby (Ridler), 24 August 1934.
37. C. W. to A. M. Miller (Hadfield), 9 January 1940.
38. The *Myth of Francis Bacon* has been published in the *Newsletter* of the Charles Williams Society, nos. 11 (Autumn 1978), 12 (Winter 1978) and 14 (Summer 1979).
39. C. W. to Phyllis Jones, No. 171.
40. H. S. Milford to Kenneth Sisam, 22 September 1933.

Chapter 6

1. C. W. to Victor Gollancz, 18 June 1930 (Victor Gollancz Ltd.; for all letters in rest of chapter).
2. C. W. to Victor Gollancz, 24 July 1930.
3. C. W. to Victor Gollancz, 28 July 1932.
4. C. W. to Victor Gollancz, ND.
5. T. S. Eliot, 'The Writings of Charles Williams', *Literary Digest,* Spring, 1948.
6. C. W. to Victor Gollancz, 19 February 1932.

7. *The New Christian Year,* 1941, p. 28, quoting William Law, *An Appeal to all that Doubt,* 1740.
8. C. W. to Phyllis Jones, No. 89 (Bodleian Library, restricted; for all letters in rest of chapter).
9. *Many Dimensions,* 1931, p. 308.
10. *The Place of the Lion,* 1931, p. 70.
11. Ibid., pp. 71–72.
12. Ibid., p. 247.
13. *The Bible,* Genesis 2:19–20.
14. *The Place of the Lion,* p. 253.
15. Victor Gollancz to C. W., 5 March 1932 (Victor Gollancz Ltd.).
16. *The Greater Trumps,* 1932, p. 107.
17. Ibid., p. 109.
18. Ibid., p. 237.
19. *War in Heaven,* 1930, p. 283.
20. Ibid., p. 285.
21. *The Place of the Lion,* pp. 283–84.
22. Marion E. Wade Collection.
23. *Shadows of Ecstasy,* 1932, p. 285.
24. C. W. to Phyllis Jones, No. 354.
25. C.W. to Phyllis Jones, No. 292.
26. *The English Poetic Mind,* 1932, pp. 20–21.
27. C. W. to Phyllis Jones, No. 292.

Chapter 7

1. Later, some of Curtis Brown's staff left to start a new firm, Pearn, Pollinger & Higham, and Charles went with them. Nancy Pearn was Charles's contact.
2. That is, books published by the Oxford University Press or Victor Gollancz Ltd.
3. C. W. to John Pellow, 11 November 1933.
4. Unpublished.
5. Shakespeare, *The Winter's Tale,* IV, iv, 43–45.
6. *English Poetic Mind,* 1932, p. 3.
7. Ibid., p. 4.
8. Ibid., p. 165.
9. Ibid., p. 23.
10. Ibid., pp. 24–25.
11. Ibid., pp. 59–60.
12. Lewis Thorpe, *The 'Lancelot' in the Arthurian Prose Vulgate,* 1980, p. 19 (Wheaton College).
13. C. W. to Phyllis Jones, No. 3 (Bodleian Library, restricted; for all letters in rest of chapter).
14. Ibid.
15. C. W. to Phyllis Jones, No. 296.
16. Ibid.
17. C. W. to Phyllis Jones, No. 269.
18. Ibid.

19. C. W. to Phyllis Jones, No. 338.
20. C. W. to Phyllis Jones, No. 123.
21. C. W. to Phyllis Jones, No. 211.
22. C. W. to Anne Ridler, '9 weeks before Christmas', 1934.
23. Unpublished.
24. C. W. to Victor Gollancz, 31 August 1932 (Victor Gollancz Ltd.).
25. C. W. to Anne Ridler, summer 1934.
26. *Rochester,* 1935, p. 118.
27. C. W. to Phyllis Jones, No. 168.
28. C. W. to Anne Ridler, late 1934.
29. C. W. to Anne Ridler, 1935.
30. C. W. to Anne Ridler, 29 December 1936.
31. C. W. to Anne Ridler, 18 May 1937.
32. C. W. to Phyllis Jones, No. 290.
33. C. W. to Phyllis Jones, 1935, No. 360.
34. C. W. to Anne Ridler, ND (probably 1935).
35. C. W. to Anne Ridler, 1936.
36. C. W. to Alexander Dru, 19 February 1935.
37. *The Journals of Søren Kierkegaard,* ed Alexander Dru, Oxford University Press, 1938, p. 238.
38. Ibid., p. 468.

Chapter 8

1. *The Book of Common Prayer,* psalm 139, vv. 6–7.
2. C. W. to Phyllis Jones (Somervaille), No. 092 (Bodleian Library restricted; for all letters in rest of chapter).
3. C. W. to Phyllis Jones (Somervaille), No. 0355. The quotation is from Tacitus' *Agricola.*
4. C. W. to T. S. Eliot, 21 November 1935.
5. Bishop of Chichester to C. W., 18 April 1935 (O.U.P. file 7470).
6. C. W. to Phyllis Jones (Somervaille), No. 092.
7. John Milton, *Lycidas,* l. 157.
8. J. S. Bach, Cantata 199, 'My heart swims in blood'.
9. C. W. to Phyllis Jones (Somervaille), No. 0355.
10. C. W. to Phyllis Potter, 21 May 1937 (Bodleian Library).
11. C. W. to Phyllis Jones (Somervaille), No. 366.
12. C. W. to Phyllis Jones (Somervaille), No. 260.
13. W. Wordsworth, *The Prelude,* xiv, ll.225–31
14. Ibid., ll. 161–62.
15. Unpublished.
16. C. W. to Phyllis Jones (Somervaille), No. 361. For Caucasia, sometimes Circassia, see p. 152.
17. C. W. to Phyllis Jones (Somervaille), No. 310.
18. C. W. to Phyllis Jones (Somervaille), No. 361.
19. C. W. to Phyllis Jones (Somervaille), No. 364.
20. C. W. to Phyllis Jones (Somervaille), No. 361.

21. Shakespeare, *The Tempest,* V, i.275-76.
22. *Taliessin,* p. 35.
23. Shakespeare, *A Midsummer Night's Dream,* V, i.26-27.
24. Shakespeare, *Antony and Cleopatra,* V, ii.1.
25. 1961, University of Pennsylvania Press.
26. E. Martin Browne, *Two in One,* Cambridge University Press, 1981, p. 72.
27. Ibid., p. 101.
28. O.U.P. file 5362.
29. *Thomas Cranmer,* p. 38.
30. Ibid., p. 69.
31. Ibid., p. 43.
32. Ibid., pp. 43-44.
33. Ibid., p. 73.
34. Ibid., p. 55.
35. Ibid., pp. 57-58, 60.
36. Ibid., p. 66.
37. Ibid., pp. 71-72.
38. Ibid., p. 74.
39. Browne, *Two in One,* p. 107.
40. Dr. Glen Cavaliero, 'Charles Williams and 20th Century Verse Drama', Charles Williams Society *Newsletter* No. 24, p. 7.
41. W. H. Auden, *Secondary Worlds,* Faber & Faber, 1968, p. 28.
42. Browne, *Two in One,* p. 219.
43. *Good Speech,* April 1938, reprinted in *Image of the City,* pp. 55-59.
44. Quoted from Humphrey Carpenter, *W. H. Auden,* George Allen & Unwin, 1981, pp. 223-34.
45. Ibid.
46. C. W. to Phyllis Jones (Somervaille), No. 79. (Bodleian Library restricted for letters in rest of chapter).
47. C. W. to Phyllis Potter, 27 September 1937 (Bodleian Library).
48. C. W. to Phyllis Potter, 11 October 1937.
49. C. W. to Anne Ridler, 28 March 1940.
50. *Descent into Hell,* 1937, pp. 254-55.
51. *Seed of Adam and Other Plays,* Oxford University Press, 1948.
52. Ibid., p. 23.
53. Gerald Weales, *Religion in Modern English Drama,* University of Pennsylvania Press, 1961, p. 143.
54. C. W. to Phyllis Jones(Somervaille), No. 129.
55. *Seed of Adam,* p. 23.
56. 'Sound and Variations', 'Notes on the Way', *Time and Tide,* 3 September 1938, reprinted in *Image of the City,* pp. 51-55.
57. C. W. to Phyllis Potter, 21 May 1937.
58. William V. Spanos, 'Charles Williams' "Judgement at Chelmsford": A Study in the Aesthetic of Sacramental Time', *The Christian Scholar* 14/2 (Summer 1962).
59. *Judgement at Chelmsford,* 1939, p. 4.
60. As note 40.
61. *Gerard Manley Hopkins,* pp. 57, 60.

Chapter 9

1. *Three Plays,* 1931, p. vi.
2. The five chapters written are printed in C. S. Lewis, *Arthurian Torso,* Oxford University Press, 1948.
3. C. W. to Anne Ridler, 24 August 1934.
4. *Arthurian Torso, The Figure of Arthur,* p. 79.
5. The *Newsletter* of the Charles Williams Society (c/o Williams and Glyn's Bank, Holt's Branch, Whitehall, London, SW1, England) has carried detailed commentaries, written by some who knew Charles Williams personally, upon the poems in *Taliessin Through Logres.* Readers might also like to consult Joe McClatchey, 'The Diagrammatised Glory of Charles Williams's *Taliessin Through Logres,* in *VII,* vol. 2, 1981, published by Wheaton College, Illinois, and distributed by Heffers Printers Ltd., Cambridge, England.
6. *Taliessin,* p. 36.
7. Ibid., p. 70.
8. Ibid., p. 9.
9. Ibid., p. 18.
10. Ibid., p. 19.
11. Ibid., p. 21.
12. Ibid., p. 45.
13. Ibid., p. 30.
14. Ibid., p. 39.
15. *English Poetic Mind,* Clarendon Press, 1932, p. 161.
16. *Taliessin,* p. 41.
17. W. Wordsworth, *Prelude,* V, pp. 103–5.
18. Quotations from *Taliessin,* pp. 34–36.
19. Ibid., p. 43.
20. Ibid., pp. 44–45.
21. Ibid., p. 45.
22. Ibid., p. 42.
23. Ibid., p. 47.
24. Ibid., p. 50.
25. Ibid., p. 79.
26. Ibid., pp. 71–72.
27. Ibid., p. 29.
28. C. W. to Anne Ridler.
29. *Taliessin,* p. 82.
30. *Thomas Cranmer,* p. 42.
31. *Taliessin,* p. 88.
32. Ibid., p. 91.

Chapter 10

1. By courtesy of Mr. George Sayer.
2. *He Came Down,* 1938, pp. 4–6.
3. Ibid., p. 6.
4. Ibid., p. 7.
5. Ibid., p. 9.

6. Ibid., pp. 9–11.
7. Ibid., p. 2.
8. C. W. to Phyllis Jones, No. 274 (Bodleian Library, restricted).
9. *He Came Down*, p. 33.
10. Ibid., p. 56.
11. Ibid., p. 57.
12. Ibid., p. 77.
13. Ibid., p. 79.
14. Ibid., p. 95.
15. Ibid., pp. 87–88.
16. John Milton, *Paradise Lost*, viii, 546–52.
17. *He Came Down*, pp. 89–90.
18. Ibid., p. 90.
19. Ibid., p. 100.
20. Ibid.
21. Ibid., p. 102.
22. Ibid., pp. 104–5.
23. Ibid., p. 106.
24. Ibid., pp. 106–7.
25. Ibid., pp. 108–9.
26. Ibid., p. 109.
27. Ibid.
28. Ibid., p. 110.
29. Ibid., pp. 110–11.
30. Ibid., p. 112.
31. Ibid.
32. Ibid., p. 113.
33. Ibid., p. 115.
34. Ibid., pp. 115–16.
35. Ibid., p. 118.
36. Ibid., pp. 118–19.
37. Ibid., p. 119.
38. Ibid., p. 119.
39. Ibid., p. 132.
40. *Time and Tide*, 7 December 1940, p. 1186, reprinted in *Image of the City*, pp. 166–68.
41. *He Came Down*, p. 135.
42. Ibid., pp. 136–37.
43. Ibid., p. 138.
44. Ibid., p. 141.
45. Ibid.
46. Ibid., p. 146.
47. Ibid., p. 147.
48. C. W. to Phyllis Potter, 25 March 1938 (Bodleian Library) .
49. C. W. to Thelma Shuttleworth, ND (early 1938 ?) (Bodleian Library).
50. *Sunday (London) Times*, 12 June 1938.
51. Bodleian Library.

52. C. W. to Ursula Grundy, 19 April 1939 (Bodleian Library; for letters in rest of chapter).
53. C. W. to Ursula Grundy, 20 September 1939.
54. C. W. to Phyllis Potter, 11 May 1939.
55. C. W. to Phyllis Potter, 14 June 1939.
56. C. W. to Phyllis Potter, 29 August 1939.
57. Bodleian Library.

Chapter 11

1. C. W. to Phyllis Potter, 13 September 1939 (Bodleian Library).
2. C. W. to Anne Ridler, 'Outbreak of War', 1939.
3. C. W. to Ursula Grundy, 20 September 1939 (Bodleian Library).
4. C. W. to Phyllis Potter, 13 September 1939 (Bodleian Library).
5. C. W. to Anne Ridler, 'Outbreak of War', 1939.
6. C. W. To A. M. Miller (Hadfield), 23 October 1939.
7. C. W. to Thelma Shuttleworth, October 1939 (Bodleian Library).
8. C. W. to A. M. Miller (Hadfield), 23 October 1939.
9. C. W. to Ursula Grundy, 20 September 1939 (Bodleian Library).
10. C. W. to Anne Ridler, 6 October 1939.
11. *The Descent of the Dove,* 1939, p. 207.
12. John Donne, 'Of the Progress of the Soul, The Second Anniversary', l. 463.
13. *Descent,* p. 61.
14. Ibid., p. 28.
15. Ibid., p. 46.
16. *The Bible,* Luke 22:19, AV.
17. *The Bible,* 1 Cor. 15:22.
18. *Descent,* p. 92.
19. Ibid.
20. Ibid., p. 101.
21. Ibid., p. 102.
22. Ibid., p. 109.
23. Ibid., see pp. 115–17.
24. Ibid., p. 123.
25. Ibid., p. 155.
26. Ibid., p. 159.
27. Ibid., p. 161.
28. Ibid.
29. Ibid., p. 162.
30. Ibid., p. 233.
31. Ibid., pp. 235–36.
32. Ibid., p. 221.
33. 'After Long Silence', Macmillan, 1939, *The Collected Poems of W. B. Yeats,* p. 301.
34. *Descent,* pp. 184–85.
35. Ibid., pp. 214–15.
36. *The Letters of Evelyn Underhill,* ed. with an Introduction by Charles Williams, Longmans, 1943, p. 42.

37. In his Introduction to the edition of Charles Williams's *Witchcraft,* published in 1980 by the Aquarian Press.
38. See Carpenter, *W. H. Auden,* pp. 283ff., 300–1, 310.
39. Quoted from Humphrey Carpenter, *The Inklings,* George Allen & Unwin, 1978, p. 119.
40. Ibid.
41. Harvey's *Companion to English Literature* implies that the Pindaric style is 'characterised by the irregularity in the number of feet in the different lines and the arbitrary disposition of the rhymes'.
42. C. W. to Mrs. C. Williams, 17 [*sic*] February 1943 (Marion E. Wade Collection).
43. Carpenter, *The Inklings: C. S. Lewis, J. R. R. Tolkien, Charles Williams and their friends,* George Allen & Unwin, 1978.
44. C. W. to Anne Ridler, 27 February 1941.
45. C. W. to A. M. Miller (Hadfield), 3 March 1941.
46. Mrs. Williams to Phyllis Potter, 16 May 1940 (Bodleian Library).
47. C. W. to A. M. Miller (Hadfield), 16 May 1940.
48. C. W. to A. M. Miller (Hadfield), 5 June 1940.
49. Shakespeare, *Othello,* II, i.129.
50. C. W. to A. M. Miller (Hadfield), 25 June 1940.
51. C. W. to A. M. Miller (Hadfield), 17 July 1940.
52. C. W. to A. M. Miller (Hadfield), 25 June 1940.
53. C. W. to A. M. Miller (Hadfield), 5 June 1940.
54. C. W. to A. M. Miller (Hadfield), 30 July 1940.
55. 'The Departure of Dindrane', quoted in C. W. to A. M. Miller (Hadfield), 4 September 1940.

Chapter 12

1. *Seed of Adam,* Introduction pp. ix–x.
2. C. W. to Mrs. C. Williams, 28 January 1941 (Marion E. Wade Collection); for letters in rest of chapter).
3. C. W. to Mrs C. Williams, 18 August 1941.
4. C. W. to Mrs. C. Williams, 13 February 1941.
5. C. W. to Mrs. C. Williams, 11 March 1941.
6. C. W. to Mrs. C. Williams, 17 March 1941.
7. C. W. to A. M. Miller (Hadfield), 3 March 1941.
8. C. W. to Mrs. C. Williams, ND (probably early September 1941).
9. Unpublished.
10. 'The Church Looks Forward', *St. Martin's Review,* July 1940, reprinted in *Image of the City,* pp. 154–58, as 'The Way of Affirmation'.
11. *The Story of the Aeneid.* Retold by Charles Williams, Oxford University Press, 1936.
12. *The Ring and the Book* by Robert Browning. Retold by Charles Williams, Oxford University Press, 1934.
13. *Religion and Love in Dante,* ND (1941), p. 4.
14. C. W. to Anne Ridler, 5 January 1940.
15. Shakespeare, *Antony and Cleopatra,* V, ii.1.
16. Shakespeare, *The Tempest,* V, i.27.
17. Shakespeare, *Cymbeline,* V, v.419.

18. *The Forgiveness of Sins*, 1942, p. 17.
19. *Taliessin*, 1938, p. 76.
20. *Forgiveness*, pp. 33–34.
21. Ibid., p. 104.
22. *The Bible*, Gen. 2:7.
23. St. Ambrose, *On the Death of Satyrus*, quoted by Charles Williams, *New Christian Year*, p. 38.
24. *Forgiveness*, pp. 122–23.
25. *Image of the City*, p. 82.
26. *Collected Plays by Charles Williams*, with an Introduction by John Heath-Stubbs, 1963, p. xii.
27. *Underhill*, p. 34.
28. Ibid., p. 17.
29. Ibid., p. 36.
30. Ibid.
31. Ibid.
32. Ibid.
33. *Descent into Hell*, 1937, p. 137.
34. *Underhill*, p. 21.
35. This society is for people living in the world who seek a deeper commitment to a fulfilment of their membership of the Body of Christ, keeping a daily memorial or order of prayer and silence as a means of perfection in the aim of the life of the Christian 'hidden with Christ in God'.
36. *The Figure of Beatrice*, 1943, p. 37.
37. Ibid., pp. 55–56.
38. Dante, *Commedia, Purgatorio*, xxiii, 72.
39. *Beatrice*, p. 170.
40. Dante, *Commedia, Paradiso*, xxxiii, 115–17. Dent, Temple Classics, 1899.
41. *Beatrice*, p. 205.
42. Ibid., pp. 127–28.
43. W. Wordsworth, 'Ode: Intimations of Immortality'.
44. *Beatrice*, p. 192.
45. Ibid., p. 180.
46. Ibid., p. 232.
47. Paraphrased from Dante, *Commedia, Purgatorio*, xxvii, 142.
48. C. W. to Anne Renwick (Scott), 30 July 1942 (Bodleian Library).
49. James Brabazon, *Dorothy L. Sayers*, Victor Gollancz, 1981, p. 225.
50. Ibid., p. 226.
51. Ibid., p. 227.
52. C. W. to Dorothy Sayers, 13 September 1944.
53. John Milton, *Paradise Lost*, II, 438.
54. What the Cross Means to Me: *A Theological Symposium*, James Clarke & Co, 1943. Williams's essay has been reprinted in *Image of the City*, pp. 131–39.

Chapter 13

1. 'The Departure of Dindrane', penultimate line. *Summer Stars*, 1944.
2. Later Mrs. Scott.
3. C. W. to Anne Renwick, 6 July 1943 (Bodleian Library). The *Mitre* was a popular Oxford hotel in the High Street.

4. C. W. to Joan Wallis, 27 May 1943.
5. He uses the phrase in 'The Calling of Taliessin'.
6. John Milton, *Paradise Lost*, II, 441.
7. S. Kierkegaard, *Gospel of Sufferings*, James Clarke, 1955, p. 97.
8. C. W. to Lois Lang-Sims, 5 January 1944.
9. C. W. to Joan Wallis, 15 February, 1944. The quotation is from the last verse of 'Taliessin at Lancelot's Mass' in *Taliessin Through Logres*.
10. 'The Prayers of the Pope', *Summer Stars*.
11. *Silver Stair*, LII.
12. Ibid., XXXIII.
13. 'The Prayers of the Pope', *Summer Stars*.
14. C. W. to Mrs. C. Williams, 5 February 1944 (Marion E. Wade Collection).
15. *Flecker of Dean Close*, 1946, p. 31.
16. Ibid., pp. 65–66.
17. Ibid., p. 33.
18. Ibid., p. 21.
19. Ibid., p. 22.
20. C. W. to Joan Wallis, 26 March 1945.
21. C. W. to A. M. Miller (Hadfield), 5 January 1945.
22. C. W. to Phyllis Potter, 1 February 1945 (Bodleian Library).
23. C. W. to Joan Wallis, 26 March 1945.
24. C. W. to Thelma Shuttleworth, 7 July 1944.
25. *The Masque of the Manuscript*, 1927, p. 6.

Bibliography

The following list includes books and booklets written, edited, compiled or introduced by Charles Williams. Dates are of first publication in the United Kingdom, but not necessarily in order of publication within each year. For fuller bibliographies, the reader should consult Anne Ridler's *The Image of the City*, Oxford University Press, 1958 and Lois Glenn, *Charles W. S. Williams: A Checklist*, The Kent State University Press, 1975.

1912   *The Silver Stair*. Herbert & Daniel. (poetry)

1917   *Poems of Conformity*. Oxford University Press.

1920   *Divorce*. Oxford University Press. (poetry)

1921   *Poems of Home and Overseas*. Compiled by C. W. and V. H. Collins. Clarendon Press.

1924   '*Outlines of Romantic Theology*'. Unpublished manuscript. (theology)

1925   *Windows of Night*. Oxford University Press. (poetry)

1926   *An Urbanity*. Privately printed. (poetry)

1926   *A Book of Longer Modern Verse*. Compiled by E. A. Parker, prefatory note by C. W. Clarendon Press.

1927   *The Carol of Amen House*. Privately printed. Words by C. W., music by Hubert Foss.

1927   *The Masque of the Manuscript*. Privately printed. (verse play)

1927   *A Book of Victorian Narrative Verse*. Chosen and introduced by C. W. Clarendon Press.

1928   *The Oxford Book of Regency Verse*. Edited by H. S. Milford in collaboration with C. W. and F. Page. Clarendon Press.

1929   *A Myth of Shakespeare.* Oxford University Press. (verse play)
1929   *The Masque of Perusal.* Privately printed. (verse play)
1930   *Poetry at Present.* Clarendon Press. (literary criticism, with interspersed verses by C. W.)
1930   *Heroes and Kings.* Sylvan Press. (poetry)
1930   *War in Heaven.* Victor Gollancz. (novel)
1930   'The Masque of the Termination of Copyright'. Unpublished. (verse play)
1930   *Poems of Gerard Manley Hopkins.* Edited by R. Bridges, 2nd ed., critical introduction by C. W. Oxford University Press.
1931   *Many Dimensions.* Victor Gollancz (novel)
1931   *Three Plays (The Witch, The Rite of the Passion, The Chaste Wanton).* Oxford University Press. (verse plays with interspersed poetry)
1931   *The Place of the Lion.* Mundanus (Victor Gollancz). (novel)
1932   *The English Poetic Mind.* Clarendon Press. (literary criticism)
1932   *A Myth of Francis Bacon.* Privately printed. (verse play)
1932   *The Greater Trumps.* Victor Gollancz. (novel)
1933   *Shadows of Ecstasy.* Victor Gollancz. (novel)
1933   *Reason and Beauty in the Poetic Mind.* Clarendon Press. (literary criticism)
1933   *Bacon.* Arthur Barker. (historical biography)
1933   *A Short Life of Shakespeare with the Sources.* Abridged by C. W. from Chambers's *William Shakespeare.* Oxford University Press. (literary biography)
1934   *The Ring and the Book.* Robert Browning, retold by C. W. Oxford University Press. (prose re-telling for young readers)
1934   *James I.* Arthur Barker. (historical biography)
1934   *Imaginary Conversations.* W. S. Landor. Edited by F. A. Cavenagh, A. C. Ward, and T. E. Welby, introduction by C. W. Oxford University Press.
1935   *Rochester.* Arthur Barker. (historical biography)
1935   *The New Book of English Verse.* Edited by and Introduction by C. W. Victor Gollancz.
1936   *The Story of the Aeneid.* Retold by C. W. Oxford University Press. (prose re-telling for young readers)
1936   *Queen Elizabeth.* Duckworth. (historical biography)
1936   *Thomas Cranmer of Canterbury.* Oxford University Press. (verse play)
1937   *Henry VII.* Arthur Barker. (historical biography)
1937   *Stories of Great Names.* Oxford University Press. (short historical and literary biographies)
1937   *Descent into Hell.* Faber & Faber. (novel)
1938   *Taliessin through Logres.* Oxford University Press. (poetry)
1938   *He Came Down From Heaven.* Heinemann. (theology)
1939   *Judgement at Chelmsford.* Oxford University Press. (verse play)
1939   *The Passion of Christ.* Anthology made by C. W. Oxford University Press.
1939   *The Descent of the Dove.* Longmans. (religious history)
1940   *The Present Age.* S. Kierkegaard. Introduction by C. W. Oxford University Press.
1940   *The English Poems of John Milton.* Introduction by C. W. Oxford University Press (World's Classics).
1941   *Religion and Love in Dante.* Dacre Press. (romantic theology)
1941   *The Way of Exchange.* James Clarke. (theology)

1941   *Witchcraft*. Faber & Faber. (religious history)

1941   *The New Christian Year*. Anthology made by C. W. Oxford University Press.

1942   *The Forgiveness of Sins*. Bles. (theology)

1943   'The Cross', in a symposium entitled *What the Cross Means to Me,* edited by J. Brierley. James Clarke. (theology)

1943   *The Letters of Evelyn Underhill*. Edited by and introduction by C. W. Longmans.

1943   *The Figure of Beatrice*. Faber & Faber. (theology and literary criticism)

1944   *The Region of the Summer Stars*. Poetry (London) Editions. (poetry)

1944   *To Michal: After Marriage*. The Grasshopper Broadsheets, third series, no. 10 (poetry)

1945   *The House of the Octopus*. Edinburgh House Press. (verse play)

1945   *All Hallows' Eve*. Faber & Faber. (novel)

1945   *The Duchess of Malfi*. John Webster, introductions by George Rylands and C. W. Sylvan Press.

1945   *Solway Ford and Other Poems*. Wilfred Gibson, selection by C. W. Faber & Faber.

1946   *Flecker of Dean Close*. Canterbury Press. (biography)

1948   *Arthurian Torso* (containing the first five chapters of the unfinished *The Figure of Arthur*). With commentary on the Arthurian poems by C. S. Lewis. Oxford University Press. (literary history)

1948   *Seed of Adam and Other Plays, (Seed of Adam, The Death of Good Fortune, The House by the Stable, Grab and Grace)*. Edited by Anne Ridler. Oxford University Press. (verse plays)

1958   *The Image of the City and Other Essays*. Edited by and introduction by Anne Ridler. Oxford University Press. (reprints of short pieces on many subjects)

1961   *Selected Writings*. Edited by Anne Ridler. Oxford University Press. (reprints of C. W.'s prose and poetry, includes *Seed of Adam*)

1963   *Collected Plays by Charles Williams*. Edited by John Heath-Stubbs. Oxford University Press. (verse plays previously published, and also *Terror of Light* in prose and the broadcast verse play *The Three Temptations*)

Index

For the reader's convenience the Index contains the following symbols:
* denotes a character in a play
† immediately follows a principal reference
‡ denotes a character or place in a novel
§ denotes a character or place name in the Arthurian poems

Inklings, 186; lectures at Oxford on *Comus* and English literature, 187; receives honorary Oxford M.A., 188; *The Figure of Beatrice* published, 206; contributes 'The Cross', 213; *The Region of the Summer Stars* published, 219; last novel, *All Hallows' Eve,* published, 227; death, 235

Williams, Charles Walter Stansby, concerns and interests: Affirmation, Way of, 41, 90, 136,† 177, 201, 203–4, 208–11, 219, 233; Allegory, 143, 216; Anthologies. *See* Books compiled by C. W.; Arthurian poems and stories, 4, 10, 12–15, 23–24, 27–28, 31, 44, 48–49, 56, 62, 66–68, 72, 79–80, 82, 85, 114, 128, 133–34, 136, 147–63, 166, 181, 183, 188, 197–98, 200, 216, 218–25, 229. *See also* Poetry, 'Advent of Galahad', *Divorce, Figure of Arthur,* Grail, The, *Heroes and Kings, Region of the Summer Stars, Silver Stair, Taliessin Through Logres, Three Plays;* Article writing, 57, 127, 196; Articulation, 132–33, 150, 153; Biographical writing, 118–21,† 123, 138. *See also* Bacon, *Flecker of Dean Close, Henry VII, James I, Queen Elizabeth, Rochester,* Bibliography; Books compiled. *See New Book of English Verse, New Christian Year, Passion of Christ, Poems of Home and Overseas,* Bibliography; Books edited wholly or with colleagues. *See Book of Victorian Narrative Verse, Letters of Evelyn Underhill, New Book of English Verse,* Bibliography; Books retold for young readers. *See Ring and the Book, Story of the Aeneid;* Co-inherence, 32,† 51, 101, 127, 141, 145, 158, 161–62, 170, 173–74, 176, 182, 184–85, 193, 201–2, 204, 211, 213, 216, 219, 222–24, 227, 230, 232, 234; Dante studies. *See Figure of Beatrice, He Came*

Down From Heaven, Religion and Love in Dante, Way of Exchange, Sayers, Dorothy; Exchange, 32,† 101, 127, 130, 141, 145, 154, 157, 159, 162, 170–74, 184, 200–4, 211, 217, 221–23, 234; Feeling intellect, 131–32, 182; Historical writing. *See* Biographical writing. Plays, Theology; Immortality, 214, 230–31; Judgement, Last, 231; Lecturing, London, Oxford and elsewhere, 40–1, 59, 68, 74, 90, 108, 131, 172, 179, 186–88, 197–99, 201, 218, 226, 231, 233; Liberty, freedom, 173, 193, 199; Literary criticism, 11, 40, 73, 80, 189. *See also* Lecturing, *English Poetic Mind, Figure of Arthur, Figure of Beatrice, Poetry at Present, Reason and Beauty in the Poetic Mind, Shakespeare Criticism 1919–35;* London, city of, 14, 21–22, 58, 171, 180, 197, 199; Love, marriage, sex. *See* Theology, romantic; Magic, 29–31, 103, 227–28. *See also* Novel writing; Mathematics and Euclidean love, 134, 136, 155–56, 200–1; Monarchy, 8, 21, 119; Novel writing, 9, 30, 45–47, 73, 92–104,† 118, 141–42.† *See also All Hallows' Eve, Descent into Hell, Greater Trumps, Many Dimensions, Noises That Weren't There, Place of the Lion, Shadows of Ecstasy, War in Heaven;* Pacifism, 193; Perversion of Images, Way of, 196–97; Play-writing, 8, 73, 80–81, 95, 135–40,† 142–45,† 190, 214. *See also Chapel of the Thorn, Chaste Wanton, Death of Good Fortune, Grab and Grace, House by the Stable, House of the Octopus, Judgement at Chelmsford, Masques, Myth of Bacon, Myth of Shakespeare, Rite of the Passion, Seed of Adam, Terror of Light, Thomas Cranmer of Canterbury, Three Plays, Three Temptations, Witch;* Poetry, nature of, 12, 14–16,